PENGUIN CELEBRAT

HEGEMONY OR SURVIVAL

LaB

HEGEMONY
OR SURVIVAL

AMERICA'S QUEST FOR GLOBAL DOMINANCE

NOAM
CHOMSKY

PENGUIN BOOKS

PENGUIN BOOKS

Published by the Penguin Group
Penguin Books Ltd, 80 Strand, London WC2R 0RL, England
Penguin Group (USA) Inc., 375 Hudson Street, New York, New York 10014, USA
Penguin Group (Canada), 90 Eglinton Avenue East, Suite 700, Toronto, Ontario, Canada M4P 2Y3
(a division of Pearson Penguin Canada Inc.)
Penguin Ireland, 25 St Stephen's Green, Dublin 2, Ireland
(a division of Penguin Books Ltd)
Penguin Group (Australia), 250 Camberwell Road, Camberwell, Victoria 3124, Australia
(a division of Pearson Australia Group Pty Ltd)
Penguin Books India Pvt Ltd, 11 Community Centre, Panchsheel Park, New Delhi – 110 017, India
Penguin Group (NZ), 67 Apollo Drive, Rosedale, North Shore 0632, New Zealand
(a division of Pearson New Zealand Ltd)
Penguin Books (South Africa) (Pty) Ltd, 24 Sturdee Avenue, Rosebank, Johannesburg 2196, South Africa

Penguin Books Ltd, Registered Offices: 80 Strand, London WC2R 0RL, England

www.penguin.com

Published in the United States of America by Metropolitan Books 2003
Published in Great Britain by Hamish Hamilton 2003
Published in Penguin Books 2004
Reissued in this edition 2007
1

Copyright © Aviva Chomsky, Diane Chomsky and Harry Chomsky, 2003
All rights reserved

The moral right of the author has been asserted

Please see www.hegemonyorsurvival.net or www.americanempireproject.com for expanded
endnotes and an e-book with additional background, discussion and sources.

Printed in England by Clays Ltd, St Ives plc

Except in the United States of America, this book is sold subject
to the condition that it shall not, by way of trade or otherwise, be lent,
re-sold, hired out, or otherwise circulated without the publisher's
prior consent in any form of binding or cover other than that in
which it is published and without a similar condition including this
condition being imposed on the subsequent purchaser

ISBN: 978–0–141–03506–2

Contents

Chapter 1

Priorities and Prospects

A few years ago, one of the great figures of contemporary biology, Ernst Mayr, published some reflections on the likelihood of success in the search for extraterrestrial intelligence.[1] He considered the prospects very low. His reasoning had to do with the adaptive value of what we call "higher intelligence," meaning the particular human form of intellectual organization. Mayr estimated the number of species since the origin of life at about fifty billion, only one of which "achieved the kind of intelligence needed to establish a civilization." It did so very recently, perhaps 100,000 years ago. It is generally assumed that only one small breeding group survived, of which we are all descendants.

Mayr speculated that the human form of intellectual organization may not be favored by selection. The history of life on Earth, he wrote, refutes the claim that "it is better to be smart than to be stupid," at least judging by biological success: beetles and bacteria, for example, are vastly more successful than humans in terms of survival. He also made the rather somber observation that "the average life expectancy of a species is about 100,000 years."

We are entering a period of human history that may provide an answer to the question of whether it is better to be smart than stupid. The most hopeful prospect is that the question will *not* be

1

answered: if it receives a definite answer, that answer can only be that humans were a kind of "biological error," using their allotted 100,000 years to destroy themselves and, in the process, much else.

The species has surely developed the capacity to do just that, and a hypothetical extraterrestrial observer might well conclude that humans have demonstrated that capacity throughout their history, dramatically in the past few hundred years, with an assault on the environment that sustains life, on the diversity of more complex organisms, and with cold and calculated savagery, on each other as well.

TWO SUPERPOWERS

The year 2003 opened with many indications that concerns about human survival are all too realistic. To mention just a few examples, in the early fall of 2002 it was learned that a possibly terminal nuclear war was barely avoided forty years earlier. Immediately after this startling discovery, the Bush administration blocked UN efforts to ban the militarization of space, a serious threat to survival. The administration also terminated international negotiations to prevent biological warfare and moved to ensure the inevitability of an attack on Iraq, despite popular opposition that was without historical precedent.

Aid organizations with extensive experience in Iraq and studies by respected medical organizations warned that the planned invasion might precipitate a humanitarian catastrophe. The warnings were ignored by Washington and evoked little media interest. A high-level US task force concluded that attacks with weapons of mass destruction (WMD) within the United States are "likely," and would become more so in the event of war with Iraq. Numerous specialists and intelligence agencies issued similar warnings, adding that Washington's belligerence, not only with regard to Iraq, was increasing the long-term threat of international terrorism and proliferation of WMD. These warnings too were dismissed.

In September 2002 the Bush administration announced its

National Security Strategy, which declared the right to resort to force to eliminate any perceived challenge to US global hegemony, which is to be permanent. The new grand strategy aroused deep concern worldwide, even within the foreign policy elite at home. Also in September, a propaganda campaign was launched to depict Saddam Hussein as an imminent threat to the United States and to insinuate that he was responsible for the 9-11 atrocities and was planning others. The campaign, timed to the onset of the midterm congressional elections, was highly successful in shifting attitudes. It soon drove American public opinion off the global spectrum and helped the administration achieve electoral aims and establish Iraq as a proper test case for the newly announced doctrine of resort to force at will.

President Bush and his associates also persisted in undermining international efforts to reduce threats to the environment that are recognized to be severe, with pretexts that barely concealed their devotion to narrow sectors of private power. The administration's Climate Change Science Program (CCSP), wrote *Science* magazine editor Donald Kennedy, is a travesty that "included no recommendations for emission limitation or other forms of mitigation," contenting itself with "voluntary reduction targets, which, even if met, would allow US emission rates to continue to grow at around 14% per decade." The CCSP did not even consider the likelihood, suggested by "a growing body of evidence," that the short-term warming changes it ignores "will trigger an abrupt nonlinear process," producing dramatic temperature changes that could carry extreme risks for the United States, Europe, and other temperate zones. The Bush administration's "contemptuous pass on multilateral engagement with the global warming problem," Kennedy continued, is the "stance that began the long continuing process of eroding its friendships in Europe," leading to "smoldering resentment."[2]

By October 2002 it was becoming hard to ignore the fact that the world was "more concerned about the unbridled use of American power than . . . about the threat posed by Saddam Hussein," and "as intent on limiting the giant's power as . . . in taking away the despot's weapons."³ World concerns mounted in the months that followed, as the giant made clear its intent to attack Iraq even if the UN inspections it reluctantly tolerated failed to unearth weapons that would provide a pretext. By December, support for Washington's war plans scarcely reached 10 percent almost anywhere outside the US, according to international polls. Two months later, after enormous worldwide protests, the press reported that "there may still be two superpowers on the planet: the United States and world public opinion" ("the United States" here meaning state power, not the public or even elite opinion).⁴

By early 2003, studies revealed that fear of the United States had reached remarkable heights throughout the world, along with distrust of the political leadership. Dismissal of elementary human rights and needs was matched by a display of contempt for democracy for which no parallel comes easily to mind, accompanied by professions of sincere dedication to human rights and democracy. The unfolding events should be deeply disturbing to those who have concerns about the world they are leaving to their grandchildren.

Though Bush planners are at an extreme end of the traditional US policy spectrum, their programs and doctrines have many precursors, both in US history and among earlier aspirants to global power. More ominously, their decisions may not be irrational within the framework of prevailing ideology and the institutions that embody it. There is ample historical precedent for the willingness of leaders to threaten or resort to violence in the face of significant risk of catastrophe. But the stakes are far higher today. The choice between hegemony and survival has rarely, if ever, been so starkly posed.

Let us try to unravel some of the many strands that enter into this complex tapestry, focusing attention on the world power that proclaims global hegemony. Its actions and guiding doctrines must be a primary concern for everyone on the planet, particularly, of course, for Americans. Many enjoy unusual advantages and freedom, hence the ability to shape the future, and should face with care the responsibilities that are the immediate corollary of such privilege.

ENEMY TERRITORY

Those who want to face their responsibilities with a genuine commitment to democracy and freedom—even to decent survival—should recognize the barriers that stand in the way. In violent states these are not concealed. In more democratic societies barriers are more subtle. While methods differ sharply from more brutal to more free societies, the goals are in many ways similar: to ensure that the "great beast," as Alexander Hamilton called the people, does not stray from its proper confines.

Controlling the general population has always been a dominant concern of power and privilege, particularly since the first modern democratic revolution in seventeenth-century England. The self-described "men of best quality" were appalled as a "giddy multitude of beasts in men's shapes" rejected the basic framework of the civil conflict raging in England between king and Parliament, and called for government "by countrymen like ourselves, that know our wants," not by "knights and gentlemen that make us laws, that are chosen for fear and do but oppress us, and do not know the people's sores." The men of best quality recognized that if the people are so "depraved and corrupt" as to "confer places of power and trust upon wicked and undeserving men, they forfeit their power in this behalf unto those that are good, though but a few." Almost three centuries later, Wilsonian idealism, as it is standardly termed, adopted a rather similar stance. Abroad, it is Washington's responsibility to ensure that government is in the hands of "the good, though but a few." At home, it is necessary to safeguard a system of elite decision-making and public ratification—"polyarchy," in the terminology of political science—not democracy.[5]

As president, Woodrow Wilson himself did not shrink from severely repressive policies even within the United States, but such measures are not normally available in places where popular struggles have won a substantial measure of freedom and rights. By Wilson's day it was widely recognized by elite sectors in the US and Britain that within their societies, coercion was a tool of diminishing utility, and that it would be necessary to devise new means to tame the beast, primarily through control of opinion and attitude. Huge industries have since developed devoted to these ends.

Wilson's own view was that an elite of gentlemen with "elevated ideals" must be empowered to preserve "stability and righteousness."[6] Leading public intellectuals agreed. "The public must be put in its place," Walter Lippmann declared in his progressive essays on democracy. That goal could be achieved in part through "the manufacture of consent," a "self-conscious art and regular organ of popular government." This "revolution" in the "practice of democracy" should enable a "specialized class" to manage the "common interests" that "very largely elude public opinion entirely." In essence, the Leninist ideal. Lippmann had observed the revolution in the practice of democracy firsthand as a member of Wilson's Committee on Public Information, which was established to coordinate wartime propaganda and achieved great success in whipping the population into war fever.

The "responsible men" who are the proper decision-makers, Lippmann continued, must "live free of the trampling and the roar of a bewildered herd." These "ignorant and meddlesome outsiders" are to be "spectators," not "participants." The herd does have a "function": to trample periodically in support of one or another element of the leadership class in an election. Unstated is that the responsible men gain that status not by virtue of any special talent or knowledge but by willing subordination to the systems of actual power and loyalty to their operative principles—crucially, that basic decisions over social and economic life are to be kept within institutions with top-down authoritarian control, while the participation of the beast is to be limited to a diminished public arena.

Just how diminished the public arena should be is a matter of debate. Neoliberal initiatives of the past thirty years have been designed to restrict it, leaving basic decision-making within largely unaccountable private tyrannies, linked closely to one another and to a few powerful states. Democracy can then survive, but in sharply reduced form. The Reagan-Bush sectors have taken an extreme position in this regard, but the policy spectrum is fairly narrow. Some argue that it scarcely exists at all, mocking the pundits who "actually make a living contrasting the finer points of the sitcoms on NBC with those broadcast on CBS" during election campaigns: "Through tacit agreement the two major parties approach the contest for the presidency [as] political kabuki [in which] the players know their roles and everyone sticks to the script," "striking poses" that cannot be taken seriously.[7]

If the public escapes its marginalization and passivity, we face a "crisis of democracy" that must be overcome, liberal intellectuals explain, in part through measures to discipline the institutions responsible for "the indoctrination of the young"—schools, universities, churches, and the like—and perhaps even through government control of the media, if self-censorship does not suffice.[8]

In taking these views, contemporary intellectuals are drawing on good constitutional sources. James Madison held that power must be delegated to "the wealth of the nation," "the more capable set of men," who understand that the role of government is "to protect the minority of the opulent against the majority." Precapitalist in his worldview, Madison had faith that the "enlightened Statesman" and "benevolent philosopher" who were to exercise power would "discern the true interest of their country" and guard the public interest against the "mischief" of democratic majorities. The mischief would be avoided, Madison hoped, under the system of fragmentation he devised. In later years he came to fear that severe problems would arise with the likely increase of those who "will labor under all the hardships of life, and secretly sigh for a more equal distribution of its benefits." A good deal of modern history reflects these conflicts over who will make decisions, and how.

Recognition that control of opinion is the foundation of government, from the most despotic to the most free, goes back at least to David Hume, but a qualification should be added. It is far more important in the more free societies, where obedience cannot be maintained by the lash. It is only natural that the modern institutions of thought control—frankly called propaganda before the word became unfashionable because of totalitarian associations—should have originated in the most free societies. Britain pioneered with its Ministry of Information, which undertook "to direct the thought of most of the world." Wilson followed soon after with his Committee on Public Information. Its propaganda successes inspired progressive democratic theorists and the modern public-relations industry. Leading participants in the CPI, like Lippmann and Edward Bernays, quite explicitly drew from these achievements of thought control, which Bernays called "the engineering of consent, ... the very essence of the democratic process." The term *propaganda* became an entry in the *Encyclopaedia Britannica* in 1922 and in the *Encyclopedia of Social Sciences* a decade later, with Harold Lasswell's scholarly endorsement of the new techniques for controlling the public mind. The methods of the pioneers were particularly significant, Randal Marlin writes in his history of propaganda, because of their "widespread imitation ... by Nazi Germany, South Africa, the Soviet Union, and the US Pentagon," though the achievements of the PR industry dwarf them all.[9]

Problems of domestic control become particularly severe when the governing authorities carry out policies that are opposed by the general population. In those cases, the political leadership may be tempted to follow the path of the Reagan administration, which established an Office of Public Diplomacy to manufacture consent for its murderous policies in Central America. One high government official described its Operation Truth as "a huge psychological operation of the kind the military conducts to influence a population in denied or enemy territory"—a frank characterization of pervasive attitudes toward the domestic population.[10]

ENEMY TERRITORY ABROAD

While the enemy at home often has to be controlled by intensive propaganda, beyond the borders more direct means are available. The leaders of the current Bush administration—mostly recycled from more reactionary sectors of the Reagan–Bush I administrations—provided sufficiently clear illustrations during their earlier stints in office. When the traditional regime of violence and repression was challenged by the Church and other miscreants in the Central American domains of US power, the Reagan administration responded with a "war on terror," declared as soon as it took office in 1981. Not surprisingly, the US initiative instantly became a terrorist war—a campaign of slaughter, torture, and barbarism—that soon extended to other regions of the world as well.

In one country, Nicaragua, Washington had lost control of the armed forces that had traditionally subdued the region's population, one of the bitter legacies of Wilsonian idealism. The US-backed Somoza dictatorship was overthrown by the Sandinista rebels, and the murderous National Guard was dismantled. Therefore Nicaragua had to be subjected to a campaign of international terrorism that left the country in ruins. Even the psychological effects of Washington's terrorist war are severe. The spirit of exuberance, vitality, and optimism that followed the overthrow of the dictatorship could not long survive as the reigning superpower intervened to dash the hopes that a grim history might finally take a different course.

In the other Central American countries targeted by the Reaganite "war on terror," forces equipped and trained by the United States maintained control. Without an army to defend the population against the terrorists—that is, the security forces themselves—atrocities were even worse. The record of murder, torture, and devastation was extensively reported by human rights organizations, church groups, Latin American scholars, and many others, but it remained little known to citizens of the state that bore prime responsibility, and was quickly effaced.[11]

By the mid-1980s, the US-backed state terrorist campaigns had created societies "affected by terror and panic . . . collective intimidation and generalized fear," in the words of a leading Church-based Salvadoran human rights organization: the population had "internalized acceptance" of "the daily and frequent use of violent means" and "the frequent appearance of tortured bodies." Returning from a brief visit to his native Guatemala, journalist Julio Godoy wrote that "one is tempted to believe that some people in the White

House worship Aztec gods—with the offering of Central American blood." He had fled a year earlier when his newspaper, *La Epoca*, was blown up by state terrorists, an operation that aroused no interest in the United States: attention was carefully focused on the misdeeds of the official enemy, real no doubt but hardly detectable given the scale of US-backed state terror in the region. The White House, Godoy wrote, installed and supported forces in Central America that could "easily compete against Nicolae Ceausescu's Securitate for the World Cruelty Prize."[12]

After the terrorist commanders had achieved their goals, the consequences were reviewed at a conference in San Salvador of Jesuits and lay associates, who had more than enough personal experience to draw on, quite apart from what they had observed through the grisly decade of the 1980s. The conference concluded that it does not suffice to focus on the terror alone. It is no less important "to explore . . . what weight the culture of terror has had in domesticating the expectations of the majority," preventing them from considering "alternatives to the demands of the powerful."[13] Not only in Central America.

Destroying hope is a critically important project. And when it is achieved, formal democracy is allowed—even preferred, if only for public-relations purposes. In more honest circles, much of this is conceded. Of course, it is understood much more profoundly by the beasts in men's shapes who endure the consequences of challenging the imperatives of stability and order.

These are all matters that the second superpower, world public opinion, should make every effort to understand if it hopes to escape the containment to which it is subjected and to take seriously the ideals of justice and freedom that come easily to the lips but are harder to defend and advance.

Chapter 2

Imperial Grand Strategy

High on the global agenda by fall 2002 was the declared intention of the most powerful state in history to maintain its hegemony through the threat or use of military force, the dimension of power in which it reigns supreme. In the official rhetoric of the National Security Strategy, "Our forces will be strong enough to dissuade potential adversaries from pursuing a military build-up in hopes of surpassing, or equaling, the power of the United States."[1]

One well-known international affairs specialist, John Ikenberry, describes the declaration as a "grand strategy [that] begins with a fundamental commitment to maintaining a unipolar world in which the United States has no peer competitor," a condition that is to be "permanent [so] that no state or coalition could ever challenge [the US] as global leader, protector, and enforcer." The declared "approach renders international norms of self-defense—enshrined by Article 51 of the UN Charter—almost meaningless." More generally, the doctrine dismisses international law and institutions as of "little value." Ikenberry continues: "The new imperial grand strategy presents the United States [as] a revisionist state seeking to parlay its momentary advantages into a world order in which it runs the show," prompting others to find ways to "work around, undermine, contain and retaliate against U.S. power." The strategy threatens to "leave the world more dangerous and divided—and the United States less secure,"[2] a view widely shared within the foreign policy elite.

ENFORCING HEGEMONY

The imperial grand strategy asserts the right of the United States to undertake "preventive war" at will: *Preventive,* not preemptive.[3] Preemptive war might fall within the framework of international law. Thus if Russian bombers had been detected approaching the US from the military base in Grenada conjured up by the Reagan administration in 1983, with the clear intent to bomb, then, under a reasonable interpretation of the UN Charter, a preemptive attack destroying the planes and perhaps even the Grenadan base would have been justifiable. Cuba, Nicaragua, and many others could have exercised the same right for many years while under attack from the US, though of course the weak would have to be insane to implement their rights. But the justifications for preemptive war, whatever they might be, do not hold for preventive war, particularly as that concept is interpreted by its current enthusiasts: the use of military force to eliminate an imagined or invented threat, so that even the term *preventive* is too charitable.

Preventive war falls within the category of war crimes. If indeed it is an idea "whose time has come,"[4] then the world is in deep trouble.

As the invasion of Iraq began, the prominent historian and Kennedy adviser Arthur Schlesinger wrote that

> The president has adopted a policy of "anticipatory self-defense" that is alarmingly similar to the policy that imperial Japan employed at Pearl Harbor, on a date which, as an earlier American president said it would, lives in infamy. Franklin D. Roosevelt was right, but today it is we Americans who live in infamy.[5]

He added that "the global wave of sympathy that engulfed the United States after 9-11 has given way to a global wave of hatred of American arrogance and militarism," and even in friendly countries the public regards Bush "as a greater threat to peace than Saddam Hussein." International law specialist Richard Falk finds it "inescapable" that the Iraq war was a "Crime against Peace of the sort for which surviving German leaders were indicted, prosecuted, and punished at the Nuremberg trials."[6]

Some defenders of the strategy recognize that it runs roughshod over international law but see no problem in that. The whole framework of international law is just "hot air," legal scholar Michael Glennon writes: "The grand attempt to subject the rule of force to the rule of law" should be deposited in the ashcan of history—a convenient stance for the one state able to adopt the new non-rules for its purposes, since it spends almost as much as the rest of the world combined on means of violence and is forging new and dangerous paths in developing means of destruction, over near-unanimous world opposition. The proof that the system is all "hot air" is straightforward: Washington "made it clear that it intends to do all it can to maintain its preeminence," then "announced that it would ignore" the UN Security Council over Iraq and declared more broadly that "it would no longer be bound by the [UN] Charter's rules governing the use of force." QED. Accordingly, the rules have "collapsed" and "the entire edifice came crashing down." This, Glennon concludes, is a good thing, since the US is the leader of the "enlightened states" and therefore "must resist [any effort] to curb its use of force."[7]

The enlightened leader is also free to change the rules at will. When the military forces occupying Iraq failed to discover the weapons of mass destruction that allegedly justified the invasion, the administration's stance shifted from "absolute certainty" that Iraq possessed WMD on a scale that required immediate military action to the assertion that American accusations had been "justified by the discovery of equipment that potentially could be used to produce weapons." Senior officials suggested a "refinement in the controversial concept of a 'preventive war' " that entitles Washington to take military action "against a country that has deadly weapons in mass quantities." The revision "suggests instead that the administration will act against a hostile regime that has nothing more than the intent and ability to develop [WMD]."[8]

Virtually any country has the potential and ability to produce WMD, and intent is in the eye of the beholder. Hence the refined version of the grand strategy effectively grants Washington the right of arbitrary aggression. Lowering the bar for the resort to force is the most significant consequence of the collapse of the proclaimed argument for the invasion.

The goal of the imperial grand strategy is to prevent any challenge to the "power, position, and prestige of the United States." The quoted words are not those of Dick Cheney or Donald Rumsfeld, or any of the other statist reactionaries who formulated the National Security Strategy of September 2002. Rather, they were spoken by the respected liberal elder statesman Dean Acheson in 1963. He was justifying US actions against Cuba in full knowledge that Washington's international terrorist campaign aimed at "regime change" had been a significant factor in bringing the world close to nuclear war only a few months earlier, and that it was resumed immediately after the Cuban missile crisis was resolved. Nevertheless, he instructed the American Society of International Law that no "legal issue" arises when the US responds to a challenge to its "power, position, and prestige."

Acheson's doctrine was subsequently invoked by the Reagan administration, at the other end of the political spectrum, when it rejected World Court jurisdiction over its attack on Nicaragua, dismissed the court order to terminate its crimes, and then vetoed two Security Council resolutions affirming the court judgment and calling on all states to observe international law. State Department legal adviser Abraham Sofaer explained that most of the world cannot "be counted on to share our view" and that "this same majority often opposes the United States on important international questions." Accordingly, we must "reserve to ourselves the power to determine" which matters fall "essentially within the domestic jurisdiction of the United States"—in this case, the actions that the court condemned as the "unlawful use of force" against Nicaragua; in lay terms, international terrorism.[9]

Contempt for international law and institutions was particularly flagrant in the Reagan-Bush years—the first reign of Washington's current incumbents—and their successors continued to make it clear that the US reserved the right to act "unilaterally when necessary," including the "unilateral use of military power" to defend such vital interests as "ensuring uninhibited access to key markets, energy supplies, and strategic resources."[10] But the posture was not exactly new.

The basic principles of the imperial grand strategy of September 2002 go back to the early days of World War II. Even before the US entered the war, high-level planners and analysts concluded that in the postwar world the US would seek "to hold unquestioned power," acting to ensure the "limitation of any exercise of sovereignty" by states that might interfere with its global designs. They recognized further that "the foremost requirement" to secure these ends was "the rapid fulfillment of a program of complete rearmament"—then, as now, a central component of "an integrated policy to achieve military and economic supremacy for the United States." At the time, these ambitions were limited to "the non-German world," which was to be organized under the US aegis as a "Grand Area," including the Western Hemisphere, the former British Empire, and the Far East. After it became fairly clear that Germany would be defeated, the plans were extended to include as much of Eurasia as possible.[11]

The precedents, barely sampled here, reveal the narrow range of the planning spectrum. Policy flows from an institutional framework of domestic power, which remains fairly stable. Economic decision-making power is highly centralized, and John Dewey scarcely exaggerated when he described politics as "the shadow cast on society by big business." It is only natural that state policy should seek to construct a world system open to US economic penetration and political control, tolerating no rivals or threats.[12] A crucial corollary is vigilance to block any moves toward independent development that might become a "virus infecting others," in the terminology of planners. That is a leading theme of postwar history, often disguised under thin Cold War pretexts that were also exploited by the super-power rival in its narrower domains.

The basic missions of global management have endured from the early postwar period, among them: containing other centers of global power within the "overall framework of order" managed by the United States; maintaining control of the world's energy supplies; barring unacceptable forms of independent nationalism; and over-coming "crises of democracy" within domestic enemy territory. The missions assume different forms, notably in periods of fairly sharp transition: the changes in the international economic order from about 1970; the restoration of the superpower enemy to something like its traditional quasi-colonial status twenty years later; the threat of international terrorism aimed at the United States itself from the early 1990s, shockingly consummated on 9-11. Over the years, tac-tics have been refined and modified to deal with these shifts, pro-gressively ratcheting up the means of violence and driving our endangered species closer to the edge of catastrophe.

Nevertheless, the September 2002 unveiling of the imperial grand strategy justifiably sounded alarm bells. Acheson and Sofaer were *describing* policy guidelines, and within elite circles. Their stands are known only to specialists or readers of dissident literature. Other cases may be regarded as worldly-wise reiterations of the maxim of Thucydides that "large nations do what they wish, while small nations accept what they must." In contrast, Cheney-Rumsfeld-Powell and their associates are officially *declaring* an even more extreme policy, one aimed at permanent global hegemony by reli-ance on force where necessary. They intend to be heard, and took action at once to put the world on notice that they mean what they say. That is a significant difference.

NEW NORMS OF INTERNATIONAL LAW

The declaration of the grand strategy was rightly understood to be an ominous step in world affairs. It is not enough, however, for a great power to declare an official policy. It must go on to establish the policy as a new norm of international law by carrying out exemplary actions. Distinguished specialists and public intellectuals may then soberly explain that law is a flexible living instrument so that the new norm is now available as a guide to action. Accordingly, as the new imperial strategy was announced, the war drums began to beat to rouse public enthusiasm for an attack on Iraq. At the same time the midterm election campaign opened. The conjunction, already noted, should be kept in mind.

The target of preventive war must have several characteristics:

1. It must be virtually defenseless.
2. It must be important enough to be worth the trouble.
3. There must be a way to portray it as the ultimate evil and an imminent threat to our survival.

Iraq qualified on all counts. The first two conditions are obvious. The third is easy to establish. It is only necessary to repeat the impassioned orations of Bush, Blair, and their colleagues: the dictator "is assembling the world's most dangerous weapons [in order to] dominate, intimidate, or attack"; and he "has already used them on whole villages—leaving thousands of his own citizens dead, blind, or transfigured. . . . If this is not evil, then evil has no meaning."[13]

The president's eloquent denunciation in his January 2003 State of the Union address surely rings true. And certainly those who contribute to enhancing evil should not enjoy impunity—among them, the speaker of those lofty words and his current associates, who long supported the man of ultimate evil in full awareness of his crimes. It is impressive to see how easy it is, while recounting the monster's worst offenses, to suppress the crucial words "with our help, which continued because we didn't care." Praise and support shifted to denunciation as soon as the monster committed his first authentic crime: disobeying (or perhaps misunderstanding) orders by invading Kuwait in 1990. Punishment was severe—for his subjects. The tyrant, however, escaped unscathed and was further strengthened by the sanctions regime then imposed by his former friends.

As the time approached to demonstrate the new norm of preventive war in September 2002, National Security Adviser Condoleezza Rice warned that the next evidence of Saddam Hussein's intentions might be a mushroom cloud—presumably in New York; Hussein's neighbors, including Israeli intelligence, dismissed the allegations, which were later undermined by the UN inspectors, though Washington continued to claim otherwise. From the first moments of the propaganda offensive, it was apparent that the pronouncements lacked credibility. " 'This administration is capable of any lie . . . in order to advance its war goal in Iraq,' says a US government source in Washington with some two decades of experience in intelligence." Washington opposed inspections, he suggested, because it feared that nothing much would be found. The president's claims about Iraqi threats "should be viewed as transparent attempts to scare Americans into supporting a war," two leading international-relations scholars added. That is standard operating procedure. Washington still refuses to provide evidence to support its 1990 claims of a huge Iraqi military buildup on the Saudi border, the primary justification offered for the 1991 war, claims instantly undermined by the one journal that investigated them, but to no effect.[14]

Evidence or not, the president and his associates issued grim warnings about the dire threat Saddam posed to the United States and to his neighbors, and his links to international terrorists, hinting broadly that he was involved in the 9-11 attacks. The government-media propaganda assault had its effects. Within weeks, some 60 percent of Americans came to regard Saddam Hussein as "an immediate threat to the US" who must be removed quickly in self-defense. By March, almost half believed that Saddam Hussein was personally involved in the 9-11 attacks and that the hijackers included Iraqis. Support for the war was strongly correlated with these beliefs.[15]

Abroad, "public diplomacy . . . failed badly," the international press reported, but "at home it has succeeded brilliantly in linking the war on Iraq with the trauma of September 11. . . . [N]early 90 percent believe [Saddam's] regime is aiding and abetting terrorists who are planning future strikes against the US." Political analyst Anatol Lieven commented that most Americans had been "duped . . . by a propaganda programme which for systematic mendacity has few parallels in peacetime democracies."[16] The September 2002 propaganda campaign also proved sufficient to give the administration a bare majority in the midterm elections, as voters put aside their immediate concerns and huddled under the umbrella of power in fear of the demonic enemy.

Public diplomacy worked its magic with Congress instantaneously. In October, Congress granted the president authority to go to war "to defend the national security of the United States against the continuing threat posed by Iraq." This particular script is familiar. In 1985, President Reagan declared a national emergency, renewed annually, because "the policies and the actions of the government of Nicaragua constitute an unusual and extraordinary threat to the national security and foreign policy of the United States." In 2002, Americans again had to tremble in fear, this time before Iraq.

The brilliant success of public diplomacy at home was revealed once again when the president "provided a powerful Reaganesque finale to a six-week war" on the deck of the aircraft carrier *Abraham Lincoln* on May 1, 2003. He was free to declare—without concern for skeptical domestic comment—that he had won a "victory in a war on terror" by having "removed an ally of Al Qaeda."[17] It is immaterial that the alleged link between Saddam Hussein and Osama bin Laden, in fact, his bitter enemy, was based on no credible evidence and largely dismissed by competent observers. Also immaterial is the only known connection between the Iraq invasion and the threat of terror: that the invasion enhanced the threat, as had been widely predicted; it appears to have been a "huge setback in the 'war on terror' " by sharply increasing Al Qaeda recruitment.[18]

The propaganda impact persisted past the end of the war. After the failure of intense efforts to discover WMD, a third of the population believed that US forces had found WMD and more than 20 percent believed Iraq had used them during the war.[19] These may simply be the reactions of people who are subject to fear of just about anything after many years of intense propaganda designed to tame the "great beast" by inducing panic.

The phrase "powerful Reaganesque finale" is presumably a reference to Reagan's proud announcement that the US was "standing tall" after having overcome the terrible threat posed by Grenada. Astute commentators added that Bush's carefully staged USS *Abraham Lincoln* extravaganza marked "the beginning of his 2004 re-election campaign," which the White House hopes "will be built as much as possible around national-security themes, a staple of the campaign being the removal of Iraqi leader Saddam Hussein." To further drive home the message, the official campaign opening was delayed until mid-September 2004 so that the Republican Convention, meeting in New York, would be able to celebrate the wartime leader who alone can save Americans from a reenactment of 9-11, as he did in Iraq. The electoral campaign will focus on "the *battle* of Iraq, not the war," chief Republican political strategist Karl Rove explained. This is part of a "far larger and longer war against terrorism that [Rove] sees clearly, perchance fortuitously, stretching well toward Election Day 2004."[20] And surely beyond.

By September 2002, then, all three necessary factors for establishing the new norm of international law were in place: Iraq was defenseless, extremely important, and an imminent threat to our very existence. There was always the possibility that things might go wrong. But it was unlikely, at least for the invaders. The disparity of force was so phenomenal that overwhelming victory was assured, and any humanitarian consequences could be blamed on Saddam Hussein. If unpleasant, they would not be investigated, and traces would disappear from view, at least if the past is any guide. Victors do not investigate their own crimes, so that little is known about them, a principle that brooks few exceptions: the death toll of the US wars in Indochina, for example, is not known within a range of millions. The same principle underlay the war crimes trials after World War II. The operational definition of *crimes of war* and *crimes against humanity* was straightforward:

crimes qualified as crimes if they were carried out by the enemy, not by the Allies. Destruction of urban civilian concentrations, for example, was excluded. The principle has been applied in subsequent tribunals, but only to defeated enemies or others who can be safely despised.

After the invasion of Iraq was declared a success, it was publicly recognized that one motive for the war had been to establish the imperial grand strategy as a new norm: "Publication of the [National Security Strategy] was the signal that Iraq would be the first test, not the last," the *New York Times* reported. "Iraq became the petri dish in which this experiment in pre-emptive policy grew." A high official added that "we will not hesitate to act alone, if necessary, to exercise our right of self-defense by acting pre-emptively," now that the norm has been established. "The exemplary nature of the whole exercise [in Iraq] is well recognized by the rest of the world," Harvard Middle East historian Roger Owen observed. Peoples and regimes will have to change the way they see the world "from a view based on the United Nations and international law to one based on an identification" with Washington's agenda. They are being instructed by the display of force to put aside "any serious considerations of national interest" in favor of reflecting "American goals."[21]

The need for a demonstration of strength to "maintain credibility" in the eyes of the world may have tipped the balance on the war with Iraq. In a review of planning, the *Financial Times* traced the decision to go to war to mid-December 2002, after Iraq's submission of its declaration on armaments to the UN. " 'There was a feeling that the White House was being mocked,' says one person who worked closely with the National Security Council during those days after the declaration was delivered on December 8. 'A tinpot dictator was mocking the president. It provoked a sense of anger inside the White House. After that point, there was no prospect of a diplomatic solution.' "[22] What followed was just diplomatic theater for obfuscation while military forces were put in place.

With the grand strategy not only officially declared but also implemented, the new norm of preventive war takes its place in the canon. The US may now find it possible to turn to harder cases. There are many tempting possibilities: Iran, Syria, the Andean region, and a number of others. The prospects depend in large part on whether the "second superpower" can be intimidated and contained.

The modalities for establishing norms merit further reflection. Most important, only those with the guns and the faith have the authority to impose their demands on the world. A revealing example of the prerogatives of power is the widely hailed "normative revolution" that ended the millennium. After a few false starts, the 1990s became "the decade of humanitarian intervention." The new right to intervene on "humanitarian" grounds was established by the courage and altruism of the US and its allies, particularly in Kosovo and East Timor, the two jewels in the diadem. The Kosovo bombing in particular is understood by distinguished authorities to have established the norm of resort to force without Security Council authorization.

A simple question arises: Why were the 1990s considered "the decade of humanitarian intervention" but not the 1970s? Since World War II there have been two major examples of resort to force that really did put an end to terrible crimes, in both cases arguably in self-defense: India's invasion of East Pakistan in 1971, ending a mass slaughter and other horrors, and Vietnam's invasion of Cambodia in December 1978, terminating Pol Pot's atrocities as they were picking up through 1978. Nothing remotely comparable took place under the Western aegis in the 1990s. Accordingly, someone who does not understand the conventions might be pardoned for asking why "the new norm" was not recognized as such in the 1970s.

The idea is unthinkable, and the reasons seem clear. The real examples of intervention that terminated huge atrocities were carried out by the wrong people. Still worse, in both cases the US was adamantly opposed to intervention and moved instantly to punish the offender, particularly Vietnam, by subjecting it to a US-backed Chinese invasion, then even harsher sanctions than before, while the US and UK offered direct support for the ousted Khmer Rouge. It follows that the 1970s cannot have been the decade of humanitarian intervention, and no new norms could have been established then.

The essential insight was formulated by a unanimous vote of the International Court of Justice in one of its earliest rulings, in 1949:

> The Court can only regard the alleged right of intervention as the manifestation of a policy of force, such as has, in the past, given rise to most serious abuses and such as cannot, whatever be the defects in international organization, find a place in international law . . . ; from the nature of things, [intervention] would be reserved for the most powerful states, and might easily lead to perverting the administration of justice itself.[23]

While Western powers and intellectuals were admiring themselves for having established the new norm of humanitarian intervention in the late 1990s, the rest of the world also had some thoughts on the matter. It is illuminating to see how they reacted, say, to Tony Blair's repetition of the official reasons for the bombing of Serbia in 1999: failure to bomb "would have dealt a devastating blow to the credibility of NATO" and "the world would have been less safe as a result of that." The objects of NATO's solicitude did not seem overly impressed by the need to safeguard the credibility of those who had been crushing them for centuries. Nelson Mandela, for example, condemned Blair for "encouraging international chaos, together with America, by ignoring other nations and playing 'policeman of the world' " in their attacks on Iraq in 1998 and Serbia the next year. In the world's largest democracy—which, after independence, began to recover from the grim effects of centuries of British rule—the Clinton-Blair efforts to shore up NATO's credibility and make the world safe were also not appreciated, but official and press condemnations in India remained unheard. Even in Israel, the client state par excellence, the pretensions of Clinton-Blair and a host of domestic admirers were ridiculed by leading military and political analysts as a return to old-fashioned "gunboat diplomacy" under the familiar "cloak of moralistic righteousness," and as a "danger to the world."[24]

Another source of information might have been the nonaligned movement, the governments of about 80 percent of the world's population at the time of their South Summit in April 2000. The meeting was the most important in their history, the first ever at the level of heads of state, who, in addition to issuing a detailed and sophisticated critical analysis of the neoliberal socioeconomic programs called "globalization" by Western ideologues, also firmly rejected "the so-called 'right' of humanitarian intervention." That stand was reiterated in the summit of nonaligned countries in Malaysia in February 2003, in the same words.[25] Perhaps they had learned too much history, the hard way, to be comforted by exalted rhetoric and had heard enough about "humanitarian intervention" over the centuries.

It is an exaggeration to say that only the most powerful are granted the authority to establish norms of appropriate behavior—for themselves. The authority is sometimes delegated to reliable clients. Thus, Israel's crimes are permitted to establish norms: for example, its regular resort to "targeted killings" of suspects—called "terrorist atrocities" when carried out by the wrong hands. In May 2003, two leading Israeli civil rights attorneys provided "a detailed list of all of the liquidations and all of the attempted assassinations that Israel's security forces carried out" during the al-Aqsa Intifada, from November 2000 through April 2003. Using official and semi-official records, they found that "Israel carried out no less than 175 liquidation attempts"—one attempt every five days—killing 235 people, of whom 156 were suspected of crimes. "It greatly pains us to say the following," the lawyers wrote, but "the consistent, widespread policy of targeted liquidations bounds on a crime against humanity."[26]

Their judgment is not quite accurate. Liquidation is a crime in the wrong hands, but it is a justified, if regrettable, act of self-defense when carried out by a client, and even establishes norms for the "the boss-man called 'partner,' "[27] who provides authorization. The "boss-man" himself made use of Israel's precedent with the assassination by missile of a suspect in Yemen, along with five other people who happened to be nearby, to much acclaim. The hit was "conveniently timed [as an] October surprise . . . to show the incumbent in his finest hour, on the eve of the midterm elections," and offer "a taste of what is to come."[28]

A more far-reaching example of establishing norms was Israel's bombing of the Osirak reactor in Iraq in June 1981. At first the attack was criticized as a violation of international law. Later, after Saddam Hussein was transformed from favored friend to unspeakable fiend in August 1990, the reaction to the Osirak bombing also shifted. Once a (minor) crime, it was now considered an honored norm, and was greatly praised for having impeded Saddam Hussein's nuclear weapons program.

The norm, however, required the evasion of a few inconvenient facts. Shortly after the 1981 bombing, the Osirak site was inspected by a prominent nuclear physicist, Richard Wilson, then chair of the physics department at Harvard University. He concluded that the installation bombed was not suited for plutonium production, as Israel had charged, unlike Israel's own Dimona reactor, which had reportedly produced several hundred nuclear weapons. His conclusions were supported by the Iraqi nuclear physicist Imad Khadduri, who was in charge of experimental work at the reactor before the bombing and later fled the country. He too reported that the Osirak reactor was unsuitable for the production of plutonium, though after the Israeli bombing in 1981, Iraq took the "solid decision to go full speed ahead with weaponization." Khadduri estimated that it would have taken Iraq decades to obtain the required amount of weapons-grade material, had the program not been sharply accelerated as a result of the bombing. "Israel's action increased the determination of Arabs to produce nuclear weapons," Kenneth Waltz concluded. "Israel's strike, far from foreclosing Iraq's nuclear career, gained Iraq support from some other Arab states to pursue it."[29]

Whatever the facts, thanks to Iraq's invasion of Kuwait a decade later, the norm that Israel established in 1981 is now firmly in place.

And if indeed the 1981 bombing accelerated the proliferation of WMD, that in no way tarnishes the deed, and teaches no lessons about the consequences of resort to force in violation of old-fashioned conceptions of international law—conceptions that must be discarded now that they have been demonstrated to be "hot air" by the boss-man's contempt for them. In the future, the US and its Israeli client and perhaps some highly favored others can resort to the norm as they see fit.

THE RULE OF LAW

The grand strategy extends to domestic US law. As in many other countries, the government used the occasion of the terrorist atrocities of 9-11 to discipline its own population. After 9-11, often with questionable relation to terror, the Bush administration claimed, and exercised, the right to declare people—including US citizens—to be "enemy combatants" or "suspected terrorists" and to imprison them without charge or access to lawyers or family until the White House determines that its "war on terror" has been successfully concluded: that is, indefinitely. The Ashcroft Justice Department takes it to be "fundamental [that] if you hold someone as an enemy combatant, obviously you hold them without access to family members and without access to counsel." These claims of executive authority have been partially upheld by the courts, which have ruled "that a wartime president can indefinitely detain a United States citizen captured as an enemy combatant on the battlefield and deny that person access to a lawyer."[30]

The treatment of "enemy combatants" in Washington's Guantánamo prison camp in a still-occupied part of Cuba elicited substantial protest from human rights organizations and others, even the Justice Department's own inspector general, in a scathing report that the department disregarded. After the conquest of Iraq, evidence soon surfaced that Iraqi prisoners were being subjected to similar treatment: gagged, bound, hooded, beaten "in the manner of the Afghans and other captives held at Guantánamo Bay in Cuba—

treatment in itself questionable under international law," to put it mildly. The Red Cross strongly protested the refusal of the US command to allow it access to prisoners of war, in violation of the Geneva Conventions, and to captured civilians.[31] Moreover, the designations are capricious. An enemy combatant can be anyone that the US chooses to attack, with no credible evidence, as Washington concedes.[32]

Justice Department thinking is illuminated by a confidential plan leaked to the Center for Public Integrity, entitled "Domestic Security Enhancement Act of 2003." This "new assault on our civil liberties" vastly expands state power, Yale Law professor Jack Balkin writes. It undermines constitutional rights by granting the state the authority to rescind citizenship on the charge of providing "material support" to an organization on the attorney general's blacklist even if the accused has no idea that the organization has been blacklisted. "Give a few dollars to a Muslim charity Ashcroft thinks is a terrorist organization," Balkin writes, "and you could be on the next plane out of this country." The plan states that "an intent to relinquish nationality need not be manifested in words, but can be inferred from conduct"; inferred by the attorney general, whose judgment we must honor, on faith. Analogies have been drawn to the darkest days of McCarthyism, but these new proposals are more extreme. The plan also extends powers of surveillance without court authorization, permits secret arrests, and further protects the state from the scrutiny of citizens, a matter of great significance to the reactionary statists of the Bush II regime. "There is no civil right—not even the precious right of citizenship—that this Administration will not abuse to secure ever greater control over American life," Balkin concludes.[33]

President Bush is said to have on his desk a bust of Winston Churchill, a gift from his friend Tony Blair. Churchill had a few things to say on these topics:

> The power of the executive to cast a man into prison without formulating any charge known to the law, and particularly to

deny him the judgment of his peers, is in the highest degree odious, and the foundation of all totalitarian government whether Nazi or Communist.[34]

The powers the Bush administration is demanding go well beyond even these odious practices. Churchill's warning against such abuse of executive power for intelligence and preventive purposes was issued in 1943, when Britain was facing possible destruction at the hands of the most vicious mass murder machine in human history. Perhaps someone in the Justice Department might want to contemplate the thoughts of the man whose image faces their leader every day.

INTERNATIONAL LAW AND INSTITUTIONS

The imperial grand strategy effectively dispenses with "the international rule of law as an overarching goal of policy," a critical review by the American Academy of Arts and Sciences points out, noting that neither international law nor the UN Charter is even mentioned in the National Security Strategy. "The primacy of law over force [that] has been a major thread in American foreign policy since the end of World War II" disappears from the new strategy. Also "all but disappeared" are the international institutions "that extend the reach of law, and seek to constrain the powerful as well as to grant the weak a voice." From now on, force reigns, and the US will exercise that force as it sees fit. The analysts conclude that the strategy will increase "the motivation of U.S. enemies to act [in reaction to their growing] resentment of perceived intimidation." They will seek "cheap and easy ways of exploiting U.S. vulnerabilities," which abound. Lack of concern with this on the part of Bush planners is also illustrated by the fact that the National Security Strategy contains just a single sentence on enhancing arms control efforts, for which the administration has only contempt.[35] Writing in the Academy's journal, two international affairs specialists describe the plans for "extended confrontation, not political accommodation," as

"inherently provocative." They warn that "the apparent commitment of the United States to active military confrontation for decisive national advantage" carries immense risks.[36] Many concur, even
on narrow grounds of self-interest.

The Academy's assessment of the primacy of law over force in
American policy requires serious qualifications. Since World War II,
the US government has adopted the standard practice of powerful
states, regularly choosing force over law when that was considered
expedient for "the national interest," a technical term referring to
the special interests of domestic sectors that are in a position to
determine policy. For the Anglo-American world, that truism is as
old as Adam Smith. He bitterly condemned the "merchants and
manufacturers" in England who were "by far the principal architects" of policy and made sure their own interests were "most peculiarly attended to," no matter how "grievous" the effect on others,
including the victims of their "savage injustice" abroad and the people of England as well.[37] Truisms have a way of remaining true.

The dominant elite view with regard to the UN was well
expressed in 1992 by Francis Fukuyama, who had served in the
Reagan-Bush State Department: the UN is "perfectly serviceable as
an instrument of American unilateralism and indeed may be the primary mechanism through which that unilateralism will be exercised
in the future." His prediction proved accurate, presumably because
it was based on consistent practice going back to the early days of
the UN. At that time, the state of the world guaranteed that the UN
would be virtually an instrument of US power. The institution was
greatly admired, though elite distaste for it increased notably in subsequent years. The shift of attitude roughly traced the course of
decolonization, which opened a small window for "the tyranny of
the majority": that is, for concerns emanating from outside the centers of concentrated power that the business press calls the "de facto
world government" of "the masters of the universe."[38]

When the UN fails to serve as "an instrument of American unilateralism" on issues of elite concern, it is dismissed. One of many
illustrations is the record of vetoes. Since the 1960s the US has been

far in the lead in vetoing Security Council resolutions on a wide
range of issues, even those calling on states to observe international
law. Britain is second, France and Russia far behind. Even that record is skewed by the fact that Washington's enormous power often
compels the weakening of resolutions to which it objects, or keeps
crucial matters off the agenda entirely—Washington's wars in Indochina, to cite one example that was of more than a little concern to
the world.

Saddam Hussein was rightly condemned for his failure to comply
fully with numerous Security Council resolutions, though less was
said about the fact that the US rejected the same resolutions. The
most important of them, Resolution 687, called for ending sanctions
when Iraqi compliance was determined by the Security Council, and
moving on to eliminate WMD and delivery systems from the Middle
East (Article 14, a coded reference to Israel). There was never a
possibility that the US would accept Article 14, and it was removed
from discussion.

President Bush I and his secretary of state, James Baker,
announced at once that the US would reject the primary condition
of 687 as well, barring even "relaxation of sanctions as long as
Saddam Hussein is in power." Clinton concurred. His secretary of
state, Warren Christopher, wrote in 1994 that Iraqi compliance is
not "enough to justify lifting the embargo," thus "changing the rules
unilaterally," Dilip Hiro points out.[39] Washington's use of UN
inspectors (UNSCOM) to spy on Iraq also undermined inspections,
which were terminated by Iraq after Clinton and Blair bombed the
country in December 1998 in defiance of the UN. The likely outcome of these inspections is known with confidence only to ideologues on all sides. It was clear enough throughout, however, that
disarmament through international inspectors was not the US-UK
objective and that the two warrior states would not comply with
the relevant UN resolutions.

Some commentators have pointed out that Israel has the lead in
violating resolutions. US-backed Turkey and Morocco have also violated more Security Council resolutions than Iraq. These resolutions

have to do with highly significant matters: aggression, harsh and brutal practices during decades-long military occupations, grave breaches of the Geneva Conventions (war crimes, in terms of US law), and other matters that rank higher than incomplete disarmament. The resolutions concerning Iraq also refer to internal repression, and in this respect Saddam Hussein's record was horrendous, but that was (regrettably) only a side issue, as revealed by the support for him by the current incumbents in Washington well past his worst crimes and the war with Iran. Resolutions concerning Israel do not come under Chapter VII, which would carry the threat of force, but any such proposal would instantly be vetoed by the US.

The veto brings up another important matter missing from the discussions of Iraq's incomplete compliance with Security Council resolutions. Plainly, if Iraq had had the right of veto, it would have been in defiance of no UN resolutions. No less plainly, any serious discussion of defiance of the Security Council must take into account vetoes, the most extreme form of noncompliance. That exercise is excluded, however, because of the conclusions that would follow at once.

The issue of the veto was not entirely ignored during the preparation for the Iraq invasion. France's threat to veto a UN declaration of war was bitterly condemned. "They said they are going to veto anything that held Saddam to account," Bush declared, with his familiar concern for truth, as he delivered his ultimatum to the Security Council on March 16, 2003. There was much fury about France's iniquity, and talk of actions to punish the country that did not follow orders from Crawford, Texas. In general, threat of veto by others is a scandal, revealing the "failure of diplomacy" and the miserable behavior of the UN. To select virtually at random, "If lesser powers contrive to turn the council into a forum for counterbalancing American power with votes, words, and public appeals, they will further erode its legitimacy and credibility," according to Edward Luck, director of the Center on International Organization at Columbia University.[40] Routine resort to the veto by the world champion is generally ignored or downplayed, occasionally hailed as demonstrating the principled stand of embattled Washington. But there is no concern that this erodes the legitimacy and credibility of the UN.

There should have been little reason for surprise, therefore, when a senior Bush administration official explained in October 2002 that "we don't need the Security Council," so if it "wants to stay relevant, then it has to give us similar authority" to that just granted by Congress—authority to use force at will. The stand was endorsed by the president and by Secretary of State Colin Powell, who added that "obviously, the Council can always go off and have other discussions," but "we have the authority to do what we believe is necessary." Washington agreed to submit a resolution to the Security Council (UN 1441), leaving no doubt, however, that the exercise was meaningless. "Whatever the diplomatic niceties, Mr. Bush made it clear that he regarded the resolution to be all the authority he needed to act against Iraq should Mr. Hussein balk," diplomatic correspondents observed. "Though Washington would consult other members of the Security Council, it would not feel it necessary to win their approval." Echoing Powell, White House chief of staff Andrew Card explained that "the UN can meet and discuss, but we don't need their permission."[41]

The administration's "decent respect for the opinion of mankind [in declaring] the causes which impel" it to action was reemphasized when Powell addressed the Security Council a few months later, announcing Washington's intention to go to war. "US officials were adamant that his briefing should not be interpreted as part of a protracted effort to garner support for a resolution authorizing the use of force," the international press reported. A US official said, "We're not going to negotiate on a second resolution because we don't need to. . . . If the rest of the Council wants to catch up to us we might stop briefly to sign on the dotted line," but nothing more.[42] The world was placed on notice that Washington will use force as it chooses; the debating society can "catch up" and join the enterprise or suffer the consequences that befall those who are not "with us" and are therefore "with the terrorists," as the president laid out the options.

Bush and Blair underscored their contempt for international law and institutions at their subsequent summit meeting at a US military base in the Azores, where they were joined by Spain's prime minister, José Maria Aznar. The US-UK leaders "issued an ultimatum" to the United Nations Security Council: capitulate in twenty-four hours or we will invade Iraq and impose the regime of our choice without your meaningless seal of approval, and we will do so—crucially—whether or not Saddam Hussein and his family leave the country. Our invasion is legitimate, Bush declared, because "the United States of America has the sovereign authority to use force in assuring its own national security," threatened by Iraq with or without Saddam. The UN is irrelevant because it "has not lived up to its responsibilities"—that is, to follow Washington's orders. The US will "enforce the just demands of the world" even if the world overwhelmingly objects.[43]

Washington also took pains to ensure that the essential hollowness of official declarations was in plain view, for all the world to see. At a news conference on March 6, the president stated that there is only "a single question: Has the Iraqi regime fully and unconditionally disarmed as required by 1441, or has it not?" He then immediately went on to make it clear that the answer to the single question did not matter, announcing that "when it comes to our security we really don't need anyone's permission." UN inspections and Security Council deliberations were therefore a farce, and even completely verified compliance was irrelevant. A few days earlier Bush had declared the answer to the "single question" immaterial: the US will institute the regime of its choice even if Saddam disarms completely, and even if he and his cohorts disappear, as underscored at the Azores summit.[44]

The president's disregard of the single question was in fact already on the record. A few months earlier, White House spokesman Ari Fleischer had informed the press that "the policy of the United States is regime change, with or without inspectors"; "regime change" does not mean a regime that Iraqis might prefer, but one that the conqueror will impose, calling it "democratic," which is standard practice; even Russia installed "people's democracies."

Later, with the war winding down, Fleischer restored the "single question" to its primary status: Iraq's possession of WMD "is what this war was about and is about." As Bush was presenting his self-contradictory stance at his news conference, British Foreign Minister Jack Straw announced that if Saddam Hussein disarmed, "we accept that the government of Iraq stays in place," so that the "single question" is disarmament: talk about "liberation" and "democracy" is mere fluff, and Britain will not support Bush's resort to war on his grounds—except that Britain made it clear that it would do as it was told.[45]

Meanwhile Colin Powell contradicted the president's declaration that the US will take control of Iraq no matter what: "The question simply is: has Saddam Hussein made a strategic, political decision to comply with the United Nations Security Council resolutions [and] to get rid of his weapons of mass destruction? That's it in a nutshell. . . . That's the question. There is no other question." Back to the "single question," rejected by the president five days earlier and again the following day. As the invasion began, Powell returned to the "single question." Iraq "was being attacked because it had violated its 'international obligations' under its 1991 surrender agreement, which required the disclosure and disarmament of its dangerous weapons."[46] Everything else that has been claimed is therefore irrelevant: the US will unilaterally decide that the inspectors should not be permitted to do their work, and the 1991 agreement entitles the US to resort to violence, contrary to its explicit wording.

Pick some other day and audience and the goal is "liberation" and "democracy" not only for Iraq but for the region, a "noble dream." The message is clear: We will do what we choose, giving whatever pretext happens to be on hand. You will "catch up," or else.

Unexplained is why the threat of WMD became so severe after September 2002, while before National Security Adviser Rice had accepted the consensus that "if they do acquire WMD, their weapons will be unusable because any attempt to use them will bring national obliteration."[47]

Punishment for being "against us" can be severe, and the benefits of catching up and remaining "relevant" are substantial. Senior US officials were dispatched to Security Council members to "urge leaders to vote with the United States on Iraq or risk 'paying a heavy price,' " not an insignificant concern for fragile countries "whose concerns drew little attention before they landed seats on the council." Mexican diplomats tried to explain to Washington's emissaries that the people "are overwhelmingly opposed to a war," but that plea was dismissed as ridiculous.[48]

A special problem arose for "countries that have succumbed to popular pressure to embrace democracy [and] now have a public to answer to." For them, repercussions for taking democratic forms seriously may include economic strangulation. In contrast, "Mr. Powell made clear that US political and military allies will benefit from handouts." Ari Fleischer meanwhile "hotly denied" that Bush was offering quid pro quos in exchange for votes, "evoking peals of laughter from the press corps," the *Wall Street Journal* reported.[49]

Rewards for following orders include not only financial handouts but also authorization to escalate terrorist atrocities. Russian president Vladimir Putin, whose relations with Bush are reported to be particularly soulful, was awarded "a diplomatic nod for Russia's crackdown on Chechen separatists—a move that some analysts here and in the Middle East contend could damage long-term US interests." One might imagine some other reasons to be concerned about Washington's support for state terrorism. To make it clear that such reactions are "irrelevant," the head of a Muslim charity was sentenced in federal court on the charge of having diverted funds to Chechens resisting the vicious Russian military occupation, just as Putin was receiving his green light. The head of the same charity was also charged with funding ambulances for Bosnia; in that case, the crime was apparently committed at about the same time that Clinton was flying Al Qaeda and Hezbollah operatives to Bosnia to support the US side in the ongoing wars.[50]

Turkey was offered similar inducements: a huge financial package and the right to invade Kurdish northern Iraq. Remarkably, Turkey did not fully submit, teaching a lesson in democracy to the West that aroused great ire and, as Secretary of State Powell sternly announced at once, instant punishment for the misdeed.[51]

The "diplomatic niceties" are for those who prefer to be deluded, as is the apparent support of Security Council members for the US-initiated Resolution 1441. The support is in fact submission; signers understood what the alternative would be. In systems of law that are intended to be taken seriously, coerced acquiescence is invalid. In international affairs, however, it is honored as diplomacy.

After the Iraq war, the UN again proved "irrelevant," because its "complicated trade system for Iraq" caused problems for US companies granted contracts under US military rule. The complicated trade system was in fact imposed by the US as part of its sanctions regime, for which there was virtually no support outside the UK. But now it was in the way. Hence, in the words of a "coalition diplomat," the US wanted "the message to be, 'We're coming here [to the Security Council] because we want to, not because we have to.' " The background issue, diplomats on all sides agree, is "how much of a free hand the U.S. should be given to manage Iraqi oil and establish a successor government." Washington demands a free hand. Other countries, a large majority of the US population, and (to the extent that we have information) the people of Iraq prefer "to extend U.N. oversight there" and "to normalize Iraq's diplomatic and economic relations," as well as its internal affairs, within that framework.[52]

Through all the shifts of justifications and pretexts, one principle remains invariant: the US must end up in effective control of Iraq, under some façade of democracy if that proves feasible.

That "America's imperial ambition" should extend to the whole world after the collapse of its sole major rival should hardly elicit surprise—and there are, needless to say, numerous predecessors, with consequences not too pleasant to recall. The current situation, however, is different. There has never in history been anything remotely like the near-monopoly of means of large-scale violence in the hands of one state—all the more reason for subjecting its practices and operative doctrines to extra-careful scrutiny.

ELITE CONCERNS

Within establishment circles, there has been considerable concern that "America's imperial ambition" is a serious threat even to its own population. Their alarm reached new heights as the Bush administration declared itself to be a "revisionist state" that intends to rule the world permanently, becoming, some felt, "a menace to itself and to mankind" under the leadership of "radical nationalists" aiming for "unilateral world domination through absolute military superiority."[53] Many others within the mainstream spectrum have been appalled by the adventurism and arrogance of the radical nationalists who have regained the power they wielded through the 1980s, but now operate with fewer external constraints.

The concerns are not entirely new. During the Clinton years, the prominent political analyst Samuel Huntington observed that for much of the world the US is "becoming the rogue superpower, [considered] the single greatest external threat to their societies." Robert Jervis, then president of the American Political Science Association, warned that "in the eyes of much of the world, in fact, the prime rogue state today is the United States." Like others, they anticipated that coalitions might arise to counterbalance the rogue superpower, with threatening implications.[54]

Several leading figures of the foreign policy elite have pointed out that the potential targets of America's imperial ambition are not likely simply to await destruction. They "know that the United States can be held at bay only by deterrence," Kenneth Waltz has written, and that "weapons of mass destruction are the only means to deter the United States." Washington's policies are therefore leading to proliferation of WMD, Waltz concludes, tendencies accelerated by its commitment to dismantle international mechanisms to control the resort to violence. These warnings were reiterated as Bush prepared to attack Iraq: one consequence, according to Steven Miller, is that others "are likely to draw the conclusion that weapons of mass destruction are necessary to deter American intervention." Another well-known specialist warned that the "general strategy of preventive war" is likely to provide others with "overwhelming incentives to wield weapons of terror and mass destruction" as a deterrent to "the unbridled use of American power." Many have noted the likely impetus to Iranian nuclear weapons programs. And "there is no question that the lesson that the North Koreans have learned from Iraq is that it needs a nuclear deterrent," Selig Harrison commented.[55]

As the year 2002 drew to a close, Washington was teaching an ugly lesson to the world: if you want to defend yourself from us, you had better mimic North Korea and pose a credible military threat, in this case, conventional: artillery aimed at Seoul and at US troops near the DMZ. We will enthusiastically march on to attack Iraq, because we know that it is devastated and defenseless; but North Korea, though an even worse tyranny and vastly more dangerous, is not an appropriate target as long as it can cause plenty of harm. The lesson could hardly be more vivid.

Still another concern is the "second superpower," public opinion. Not only was the "revisionism" of the political leadership without precedent; so too was the opposition to it. Comparisons are often drawn to Vietnam. The common query "What happened to the tradition of protest and dissent?" makes clear how effectively the historical record has been cleansed and how little sense there is, in many circles, of the changes in public consciousness over the past four decades. An accurate comparison is revealing: In 1962, public protest was nonexistent, despite the announcement that year that the Kennedy administration was sending the US Air Force to bomb South Vietnam, as well as initiating plans to drive millions of people into what amounted to concentration camps and launching chemical warfare programs to destroy food crops and ground cover. Protest did not reach any meaningful level until years later, after hundreds of thousands of US troops had been dispatched, densely populated areas had been demolished by saturation bombing, and the aggression had spread to the rest of Indochina. By the time protest became significant, the bitterly anticommunist military historian and Indochina specialist Bernard Fall had warned that "Vietnam as a cultural and historic entity . . . is threatened with extinction" as "the countryside literally dies under the blows of the largest military machine ever unleashed on an area of this size."[56]

In 2002, forty years later, in striking contrast, there was large-scale, committed, and principled popular protest before the war had been officially launched. Absent the fear and illusion about Iraq that were unique to the US, prewar opposition would probably have reached much the same levels as elsewhere. That reflects a steady increase over these years in unwillingness to tolerate aggression and atrocities, one of many such changes.

The leadership is well aware of these developments. By 1968, fear of the public was so serious that the Joint Chiefs of Staff had to consider whether "sufficient forces would still be available for civil disorder control" if more troops were sent to Vietnam. The Department of Defense feared that further troop deployments ran the risk of "provoking a domestic crisis of unprecedented proportions."[57] The Reagan administration at first tried to follow Kennedy's South Vietnam model in Central America but backed down in the face of an unanticipated public reaction that threatened to undermine more important components of the policy agenda, turning instead to clandestine terror—clandestine in the sense that it could be more or less concealed from the general public. When Bush I took office in 1989, public reaction was again very much on the agenda. Incoming administrations typically commission a review of the world situation from the intelligence agencies. These reviews are secret, but in 1989 a passage was leaked concerning "cases where the U.S. confronts much weaker enemies." The analysts advised that the US must "defeat them decisively and rapidly." Any other outcome would be "embarrassing" and might "undercut political support," understood to be thin.[58]

We are no longer in the 1960s, when the population would tolerate a murderous and destructive war for years without visible protest. The activist movements of the past forty years have had a significant civilizing effect in many domains. By now, the only way to attack a much weaker enemy is to construct a propaganda offensive depicting it as an imminent threat or perhaps engaged in genocide, with confidence that the military campaign will scarcely resemble an actual war.

Elite concerns extend to the impact of Bush administration radical nationalists on world public opinion, which was overwhelmingly opposed to their war plans and militant posturing. These have surely been factors in the general decline of trust in leadership revealed by a World Economic Forum poll released in January 2003. According to the poll, only NGO leaders had the trust of a clear majority, followed by UN and spiritual/religious leaders, then leaders of Western Europe and economic managers, and right below them, corporate executives. Far below, at the very bottom, were the leaders of the United States.[59]

A week after the poll was released, the annual World Economic Forum opened in Davos, Switzerland, but without the exuberance of earlier years. "The mood has darkened," the press noted: for the "movers and shakers," it was not "global party time" anymore. The founder of the WEF, Klaus Schwab, identified the most pressing reason: "Iraq will be the overwhelming theme of all the discussions." Powell's aides warned him before his presentation that the mood was "ugly" at Davos, the Wall Street Journal reported. "A chorus of international complaints about the American march toward war with Iraq was reaching a crescendo at this gathering of some 2,000 corporate executives, politicians and academics." They were not overwhelmed by Powell's "sharp new message": in his own words, "when we feel strongly about something we will lead," even if no one is following us. "We will act even if others are not prepared to join us."[60]

The theme of the WEF was "Building Trust," for good reasons.

In his speech, Powell stressed that the US reserves the "sovereign right to take military action" when and how it chooses. He said further that no one "trusts Saddam and his regime," which was certainly true, though his comment left out some other leaders who are not trusted. Powell also assured his audience that Saddam Hussein's weapons were "meant to intimidate Iraq's neighbors," failing to explain why those neighbors did not seem to perceive the threat.[61]

Much as they despised the murderous tyrant, Iraq's neighbors joined the "many outside the United States mystified at why Washington is so obsessed and fearful of what is, in the end, a minor power whose wealth and power have been truncated by internationally imposed constraints." Aware of the dire effects of the sanctions on the general population, they also knew that Iraq was one of the weakest states in the region: its economy and military expenditures were a fraction of Kuwait's, which has 10 percent of Iraq's population, and much farther below those of others nearby.[62] For these and other reasons, the neighboring countries had been mending fences with Iraq for some years over strong US opposition. Like the US Department of Defense and the CIA, they knew "perfectly well that today's Iraq poses no threat to anyone in the region, let alone in the United States," and that "To argue otherwise is dishonest."[63]

By the time they met, the "movers and shakers" at Davos had heard even more unpleasant news about "building trust." An opinion poll in Canada found that more than "36 percent of Canadians viewed the US as the biggest threat to world peace, against just 21 percent naming Al Qaeda, 17 percent choosing Iraq and 14 percent North Korea." That despite the fact that the general image of the US had improved to 72 percent in Canada, in contrast to dropping sharply in Western Europe. An informal poll run by *Time* magazine found that more than 80 percent of respondents in Europe regarded the US as the greatest threat to world peace. Even if these numbers were wrong by some substantial factor, they are dramatic. Their significance is magnified by contemporaneous international polls on the US-UK drive for war with Iraq.[64]

"The messages from U.S. embassies around the globe have become urgent and disturbing," the *Washington Post* noted in a lead story. "Many people in the world increasingly think President Bush is a greater threat to world peace than Iraqi President Saddam Hussein." "The debate has not been about Iraq," a State Department official was quoted as saying. "There is real angst in the world about our power, and what they perceive as the rawness, the arrogance, the unipolarity" of the administration's actions. The headline read,

"Danger Ahead? The World Sees President Bush as a Threat." A cover story in *Newsweek* three weeks later, by its senior foreign affairs editor, also warned that the global debate was not about Saddam: "It is about America and its role in the new world. . . . A war with Iraq, even if successful, might solve the Iraq problem. It doesn't solve the America problem. What worries people around the world above all else is living in a world shaped and dominated by one country—the United States. And they have come to be deeply suspicious and fearful of us."[65]

After 9-11, at a time of enormous global sympathy and solidarity with the United States, George Bush asked, "Why do they hate us?" The question was wrongly put, and the right question was scarcely addressed. But within a year, the administration succeeded in providing an answer: "Because of you and your associates, Mr. Bush, and what you have done. And if you continue, the fear and hatred you have inspired may extend to the country you have shamed as well." On that, the evidence is hard to ignore. For Osama bin Laden, it is a victory probably beyond his wildest dreams.

INTENTIONAL IGNORANCE

The fundamental assumption that lies behind the imperial grand strategy, often considered unnecessary to formulate because its truth is taken to be so obvious, is the guiding principle of Wilsonian idealism: We—at least the circles who provide the leadership and advise them—are good, even noble. Hence our interventions are necessarily righteous in intent, if occasionally clumsy in execution. In Wilson's own words, we have "elevated ideals" and are dedicated to "stability and righteousness," and it is only natural, then, as Wilson wrote in justifying the conquest of the Philippines, that "our interest must march forward, altruists though we are; other nations must see to it that they stand off, and do not seek to stay us."[66]

In the contemporary version, there is a guiding principle that "defines the parameters within which the policy debate occurs," a consensus so broad as to exclude only "tattered remnants" on the right and left and "so authoritative as to be virtually immune to challenge." The principle is *"America as historical vanguard"*: "History has a discernible direction and destination. Uniquely among all the nations of the world, the United States comprehends and manifests history's purpose." Accordingly, US hegemony is the realization of history's purpose, and what it achieves is for the common good, the merest truism, so that empirical evaluation is unnecessary, if not faintly ridiculous. The primary principle of foreign policy, rooted in Wilsonian idealism and carried over from Clinton to Bush II, is *"the imperative of America's mission as the vanguard of history, transforming the global order and, in doing so, perpetuating its own dominance,"* guided by *"the imperative of military supremacy, maintained in perpetuity and projected globally."*[67]

By virtue of its unique comprehension and manifestation of history's purpose, America is entitled, indeed obligated, to act as its leaders determine to be best, for the good of all, whether others understand or not. And like its noble predecessor and current junior partner, Great Britain, America should not be deterred in realizing history's transcendent purpose even if it is "held up to obloquy" by the foolish and resentful, as was its predecessor in global rule, according to its most prestigious advocates.[68]

To still any qualms that might arise, it suffices to refresh our understanding that "Providence summons Americans" to the task of reforming global order: the "Wilsonian tradition . . . to which all recent occupants of the Oval Office, regardless of party, have adhered"—as have, commonly, their predecessors, their counterparts elsewhere, and their most reviled enemies, with required change of names.[69] But to reassure ourselves that the powerful are motivated by "elevated ideals" and "altruism" in the quest of "stability and righteousness," we have to adopt the stance called "intentional ignorance" by a critic of the terrible atrocities in Central America in the 1980s backed by the political leadership that is again at the helm in Washington.[70] Adopting that stance, not only can we tidy up the past, conceding the inevitable flaws that accompany even the best of intentions, but more recently, since the advent of the new

norm of humanitarian intervention, we can even go on to portray
US foreign policy as having entered a "noble phase" with a "saintly
glow." Washington's "post–Cold War interventions were, on the
whole, noble but half-hearted; they were half-hearted *because* they
were noble," historian Michael Mandelbaum assures us. Perhaps we
are even too saintly: we must beware of "granting idealism a near
exclusive hold on our foreign policy," more sober voices warn, thus
neglecting our own legitimate interests in our dedicated service to
others.[71]

Somehow, Europeans have failed to understand the unique idealism of American leaders. How can this be, since it is the merest
truism? Max Boot suggests an answer. Europe has "often been
driven by avarice," and the "cynical Europeans" cannot comprehend the "strain of idealism" that animates US foreign policy: "After
200 years, Europe still hasn't figured out what makes America tick."
Their ineradicable cynicism leads Europeans to attribute base
motives to Washington and to fail to join its noble ventures with
sufficient enthusiasm. Another respected historian and political commentator, Robert Kagan, offers a different explanation. Europe's
problem is that it is consumed with "paranoid, conspiratorial anti-
Americanism," which has "reached a fevered intensity," though fortunately a few figures, like Berlusconi and Aznar, brave the storm.[72]

Unwittingly, no doubt, Boot and Kagan are plagiarizing John
Stuart Mill's classic essay on humanitarian intervention, in which
he urged Britain to undertake the enterprise vigorously—specifically,
to conquer more of India. Britain must pursue this high-minded
mission, Mill explained, even though it will be "held up to obloquy"
on the continent. Unmentioned was that by doing so, Britain was
striking still further devastating blows at India and extending the
near-monopoly of opium production that it needed both to force
open Chinese markets by violence and to sustain the imperial system
more broadly by means of its immense narcotrafficking enterprises,
all well known in England at the time. But such matters could not
be the source of the "obloquy." Rather, Europeans are "exciting
odium against us," Mill wrote, because they are unable to compre-

hend that England is truly "a novelty in the world," a remarkable nation that acts only "in the service of others." It is dedicated to peace, though if "the aggressions of barbarians force it to a successful war," it selflessly bears the cost while "the fruits it shares in fraternal equality with the whole human race," including the barbarians it conquers and destroys for their own benefit. England is not only peerless but near perfect, in Mill's view, with no "aggressive designs," desiring "no benefit to itself at the expense of others." Its policies are "blameless and laudable." England was the nineteenth-century counterpart of the "idealistic new world bent on ending inhumanity," motivated by pure altruism and uniquely dedicated to the highest "principles and values," though also sadly misunderstood by the cynical or perhaps paranoid Europeans.[73] Mill's essay was written as Britain engaged in some of the worst crimes of its imperial reign. It is hard to think of a more distinguished and truly honorable intellectual—or a more disgraceful example of apologetics for terrible crimes. Such facts might inspire some reflection as Boot and Kagan illustrate Marx's dictum about tragedy replayed as farce. It is also worth recalling that the record of continental imperialism is even worse, and the rhetoric that accompanied it no less glorious, as when France gained Mill's approval by carrying out its civilizing mission in Algeria—while "exterminating the indigenous population," the French minister of war declared.[74]

Kagan's concept of "anti-Americanism," while conventional, also merits reflection. In such pronouncements, the term *anti-American* and its variants ("hating America," and the like) are regularly employed to defame critics of state policy who may admire and respect the country, its culture, and its achievements, indeed think it is the greatest place on earth. Nevertheless, they "hate America" and are "anti-American" on the tacit assumption that the society and its people are to be identified with state power. This usage is drawn directly from the lexicon of totalitarianism. In the former Russian empire, dissidents were guilty of "anti-Sovietism." Perhaps critics of Brazil's military dictatorship were labeled "anti-Brazilian." Among people with some commitment to freedom and democracy, such attitudes are inconceivable. It would only arouse ridicule in Rome or Milan if a critic of Berlusconi's policies were condemned as "anti-Italian," though perhaps it would have passed in Mussolini's day.

It is useful to remember that no matter where we turn, there is rarely any shortage of elevated ideals to accompany the resort to violence. The words accompanying the "Wilsonian tradition" may be stirring in their nobility, but should also be examined in practice, not just rhetoric: for example, Wilson's call for conquest of the Philippines, already mentioned; or as president, his interventions in Haiti and the Dominican Republic that left both countries in ruins; or what Walter LaFeber calls the "Wilson corollary" to the Monroe Doctrine, which dictated "that only American oil interests receive concessions" within the reach of its power.[75]

The same is true of the worst tyrants. In 1990, Saddam Hussein warned Kuwait of possible retribution for actions that were undermining Iraq's battered economy after Iraq had protected Kuwait during the war with Iran. But he assured the world that he wanted not "permanent fighting, but permanent peace . . . and a dignified life."[76] In 1938, President Roosevelt's close confidant Sumner Welles praised the Munich agreement with the Nazis and felt that it might lead to a "new world order based upon justice and upon law." Shortly after, they carried the project forward by occupying parts of Czechoslovakia, while Hitler explained that they were "filled with earnest desire to serve the true interests of the peoples dwelling in this area, to safeguard the national individuality of the German and Czech peoples, and to further the peace and social welfare of all." Mussolini's concerns for the "liberated populations" of Ethiopia were no less exalted. The same was true of Japan's aims in Manchuria and North China and its sacrifices to create an "earthly paradise" for the suffering people and to defend their legitimate governments from Communist "bandits." What could be more moving than Japan's "exalted responsibility" to establish a "New Order" in 1938 to "insure the permanent stability of East Asia" based on "mutual aid" of Japan, Manchuria, and China "in politi-

cal, economic, and cultural fields," their "joint defence against Communism," and their cultural, economic, and social progress?[77]

After the war, interventions were routinely declared to be
"humanitarian" or in self-defense and therefore in accord with the
UN Charter: for example, Russia's murderous invasion of Hungary
in 1956, justified by Soviet lawyers on the grounds that it was undertaken at the invitation of the government of Hungary as a "defensive
response to foreign funding of subversive activities and armed bands
within Hungary for purposes of overthrowing the democratically
elected government"; or, with comparable plausibility, the US attack
against South Vietnam a few years later, undertaken in "collective
self-defense" against "internal aggression" by the South Vietnamese
and their "assault from the inside" (Adlai Stevenson and John F.
Kennedy, respectively).[78]

We need not assume that these protestations are disingenuous,
no matter how grotesque they may be. Often one finds the same
rhetoric in internal documents, where there is no obvious reason to
dissemble: for example, the argument by Stalin's diplomats that "to
create real democracies, some outside pressure would be necessary.
. . . We should not hesitate to use this kind of 'interference into the
domestic affairs' of other nations . . . since democratic government
is one of the main guarantees of durable peace."[79]

Others agree, doubtless with no less sincerity, urging that

> we should not hesitate before police repression by the local
> government. This is not shameful since the Communists are
> essentially traitors. . . . It is better to have a strong regime in
> power than a liberal government if it is indulgent and relaxed
> and penetrated by Communists.

George Kennan, in this case, briefing US ambassadors in Latin
America on the need to be guided by a pragmatic concern for "the
protection of our raw materials"—ours, wherever they happen to
be located, to which we must preserve our inherent "right of access,"
by conquest if necessary, in accord with the ancient law of nations.[80]

It requires a heavy dose of intentional ignorance and loyalty to power to delete from memory the human consequences of instituting and sustaining "strong regimes." The same talents are needed to sustain faith in the appeal to national security invoked to justify the use of force, a pretext that can rarely be upheld for any state, on inspection of the historical and documentary record.

As these few examples illustrate, even the harshest and most shameful measures are regularly accompanied by profession of noble intent. An honest look would only generalize Thomas Jefferson's observation on the world situation of his day:

> We believe no more in Bonaparte's fighting merely for the liberties of the seas, than in Great Britain's fighting for the liberties of mankind. The object is the same, to draw to themselves the power, the wealth, and the resources of other nations.[81]

A century later, Woodrow Wilson's secretary of state, Robert Lansing (who also appears to have had few illusions about Wilsonian idealism), commented scornfully on "how willing the British, French or Italians are to accept a mandate" from the League of Nations, as long as "there are mines, oil fields, rich grain fields or railroads" that will "make it a profitable undertaking." These "unselfish governments" declare that mandates must be accepted "for the good of mankind": "they will do their share by administering the rich regions of Mesopotamia, Syria, &c." The proper assessment of these pretensions is "so manifest that it is almost an insult to state it."[82]

And manifest indeed it is, when declarations of noble intent are proferred by others. For oneself, different standards apply.

One may choose to have selective faith in the domestic political leadership, adopting the stance that Hans Morgenthau, one of the founders of modern international relations theory, condemned as "our conformist subservience to those in power," the regular stance of most intellectuals throughout history.[83] But it is important to recognize that profession of noble intent is predictable, and therefore carries no information, even in the technical sense of the term. Those who are seriously interested in understanding the world will adopt the same standards whether they are evaluating their own political and intellectual elites or those of official enemies. One might fairly ask how much would survive this elementary exercise of rationality and honesty.

It should be added that there are occasional departures from the common stance of subordination to power on the part of the educated classes. Some of the most important current illustrations are to be found in two countries whose harsh and repressive regimes have been sustained by US military aid: Turkey and Colombia. In Turkey, prominent writers, journalists, academics, publishers, and others not only protest atrocities and draconian laws but also carry out regular civil disobedience, facing and sometimes enduring severe and prolonged punishment. In Colombia, courageous priests, academics, human rights and union activists, and others face the constant threat of assassination in one of the world's most violent states.[84] Their actions should elicit humility and shame among their Western counterparts, and would if the truth were not veiled by the intentional ignorance that makes a crucial contribution to ongoing crimes.

Chapter 3

The New Era of Enlightenment

The final years of the millennium witnessed a display of exuberant self-adulation that may even have surpassed its none-too-glorious predecessors, with awed acclaim for the leaders of an "idealistic new world bent on ending inhumanity," dedicated to "principles and values" for the first time in history. An era of enlightenment and benevolence was upon us, in which the civilized nations, led by the United States, then "at the height of its glory," acted out of "altruism" and "moral fervor" in pursuit of exalted ideals.[1]

Such a shift would be a comforting development indeed. But to join the chorus of self-congratulation, we would need to overlook some recalcitrant facts.

The first and most striking is the record of terror and criminal atrocities carried out with the decisive support of the reigning superpower and its allies in very recent years, continuing without noticeable change, and suppressed as effectively as in the past within the prevailing intellectual culture, matters of great significance, which do not disappear from actual history merely because that is the preference of its caretakers.

Taking a longer view, we would also be compelled to disregard the fact that over the last millennium, "war has been the dominant activity of European states." And we would have to put aside the basic reason for that unpleasant reality: "the central, tragic fact is simple: coercion *works;* those who apply substantial force to their fellows get compliance, and from that compliance draw the multiple advantages of money, goods, deference, [and] access to pleasures denied to less powerful people"[2]—a fact of life understood all too well by most of the people of the world, but a principle of statecraft that has been rescinded, so we are now told, not for the first time.

One more immediate way to evaluate the prospects that were hailed with such enthusiasm is to consider the flow of US military aid. A good starting point is the year 1997, when the US foreign policy was lauded for entering a "noble phase" with a "saintly glow," setting the tone for the rhetorical flights that ensued. At the mundane level of fact, 1997 was of some significance for the human rights movement. In that single year the flow of US arms to Turkey exceeded the combined total of US military aid to Turkey for the entire Cold War period prior to the onset of its counterinsurgency campaign against its miserably repressed Kurdish population. By 1997 the campaign had driven millions of people from the devastated countryside, with tens of thousands killed and every imaginable form of barbaric torture, ranking high among the crimes of the grisly 1990s. As atrocities escalated, Turkey became the leading recipient of US arms worldwide, Israel and Egypt aside, with 80 percent of its supply coming from Washington.

In the same year, US military aid to Colombia began to skyrocket, increasing from $50 million to $290 million two years later, and rapidly growing since. By 1999 Colombia had replaced Turkey as the world leader in US military aid. Further militarization of Colombia's internal conflicts, deeply rooted in the awful history of a rich society with extreme poverty and violence, had the predictable consequences for the tortured population and also led guerrilla forces to become yet another army terrorizing the peasantry and, more recently, the urban population as well. The most prominent Colombian human rights organization estimates the number of people forcefully displaced at 2.7 million, increasing by 1,000 a day. They estimate that more than 350,000 people were driven from their homes by violence in the first nine months of 2002, more than in all of 2001. Political killings were reported to have risen to twenty a day, double the level of 1998.

In the case of the leading recipients of US military aid, the reaction is silence, and increased support for the atrocities.

Consider, for comparison, the most demonic and dangerous member of the "axis of evil." The *New York Times* reports that "as many as a million people have been relocated inside Iraq," concluding accurately that "one element of the misery caused by President Saddam Hussein's rule" is the internally displaced population.[3] The article was headlined "Uprooted Iraqis See War as Path to Lost Homes." There has been no inquiry into whether Kurds and Colombians, uprooted with extreme violence, apparently in even greater numbers, might also see war as a path to lost homes. The proposal would, in fact, be outlandish. Washington could alleviate the misery and perhaps clear the way to a more substantial solution to deeply rooted problems by simply withdrawing its support for atrocities. But that would require at the very least a willingness on the part of the educated classes to look into the mirror instead of restricting themselves to lamentations on the crimes of official enemies, about which there is often little that can be done.

EAST TIMOR AND KOSOVO

Just as Colombia was replacing Turkey as the leading recipient of US military aid, another tale of horror was unfolding that Washington could easily have brought to a quick end: East Timor. In 1999, Indonesia escalated the atrocities in the territory they had invaded in 1975, killing perhaps 200,000 people with the military and diplomatic support of the US and Britain, assisted by "intentional ignorance." In the early months of 1999, Indonesian forces and their paramilitary associates added several thousand more to the death toll,[4] while the ruling generals announced that worse would come if the population voted the wrong way in an August 30 referendum on independence—as they did, with amazing courage. The Indonesian military made good on its promise, driving hundreds of thousands from their homes and destroying most of the country. For the first time, the atrocities were well publicized in the United States. On September 8, the Clinton administration reacted by reiterating its position that East Timor is "the responsibility of the Government of Indonesia, and we don't want to take that responsibility away from them." A few days later, under strong international and domestic pressure, Clinton reversed the 25-year policy of support for Indonesia's crimes in East Timor, and informed the Indonesian military that Washington would no longer directly support their crimes. They immediately withdrew from the territory, allowing an Australian-led UN peacekeeping force to enter unopposed.[5]

The lesson was crystal clear: as a handful of activists and critics had been saying for almost twenty-five years, there had never been any need for threats or forceful measures. It would have sufficed to withdraw from participation for some of the worst crimes of the late twentieth century to have come to a halt. But that was not the lesson that was drawn. Instead, the doctrinal system, rising to the challenge, drew the required conclusion: the events in East Timor demonstrated that foreign policy had entered into a "noble phase," as the leaders of the civilized West pursued their dedication to "principles and values."

That recasting is an impressive achievement. One wonders whether it would be possible to contrive a hypothetical series of events that could not be adapted to prove the required thesis.

East Timor was offered as a crucial example of the era of enlightenment with its new "norms of humanitarian intervention." There was no intervention, let alone humanitarian intervention.[6] Those who were at the height of their glory were still persisting in their decades-old participation in Indonesia's crimes just at the moment when these accolades appeared.

The prime illustration of the new era, however, was Kosovo, where the US and its allies acted out of "altruism" and "moral fervor" alone, forging "a new kind of approach to the use of power in world politics," as they "reacted to the deportation of more than a million Kosovars from their homeland" by bombing so as to save them "from horrors of suffering, or from death."[7] This description, from a scholarly source, is the standard version. Accounts in the media, journals of opinion, and scholarship rarely depart from it. To select some typical examples, we read that after "violence surged" in Kosovo in 1998, Serb forces "responded with an ethnic-cleansing campaign and drove more than half the Albanian popu-lation into exile . . . The growing bloodshed led the U.S. and its allies . . . to launch a massive bombing campaign, . . . allowing Albanian refugees to return."[8] "In the spring of 1999 [Serbs] appeared to be conducting an ethnic cleansing campaign"; Albanian Kosovars "fled the assault, . . . recounting stories of summary executions and forced expulsions" when they reached neighboring countries, and these expulsions and atrocities "elicited the NATO bombing campaign" on March 24.[9] Hence the intervention in Kosovo was "purely for the benefit of the people of the region, . . . an act of altruism," like all US interventions in the region.[10] It was "absolutely right," Tim-othy Garton Ash concludes, because it passed the "very high . . . threshold for such humanitarian intervention, . . . something approaching genocide, by the killing or 'ethnic cleansing' of large numbers of its people" by the Serbian government.[11]

Surely this establishes the case and justifies the praise for the altruistic leaders opening a new era of enlightenment. And so it might, if the claims had any relation to the facts.

The small sample of quotes presented above is typical in several interesting respects. First, the accounts are given without any evi-dence, though an enormous amount was available from impeccable Western sources. Second, the standard picture reverses the order of events. Uncontroversially, the bombing preceded the ethnic cleansing and atrocities, which were, in fact, its anticipated consequence.

Kosovo was an ugly place before the NATO bombing, with an estimated 2,000 killed on all sides during the preceding year. However, the rich Western documentary record reveals no changes

of significance until the March 24 bombing began, apart from a
slight increase in Serbian atrocities two days earlier, when monitors
were withdrawn in anticipation of the NATO attack. The UN began
registering refugees a week later. These basic facts were well known
by May 1999, when the Milosevic indictment was presented; it
detailed a series of terrible crimes, which had, however, virtually
without exception taken place after the bombing.

On March 24, as the bombing began, British defense minister
George Robertson (later NATO secretary-general) testified before
the House of Commons that until mid-January 1999, "the Kosovo
Liberation Army (KLA) was responsible for more deaths in Kosovo
than the Serbian authorities had been." He was referring to the
Albanian guerrillas, by then CIA-backed—who had explained
frankly that their goal was to kill Serbs so as to elicit a harsh reaction that would lead to public support in the West for NATO intervention. A subsequent parliamentary inquiry revealed that Foreign
Secretary Robin Cook had told the House on January 18 that the
KLA had "committed more breaches of the ceasefire, and until this
weekend was responsible for more deaths than the [Yugoslav] security forces."[12]

Robertson and Cook are specifically referring to a massacre carried out by the security forces at Racak on January 15, in which
forty-five people were reported killed. But since Western
documentation reveals no notable change in the distribution of violence after Racak, their conclusions, if valid in mid-January, essentially remained so in late March. It was clear at the time that such
massacres were of no concern to the US or UK leadership. Thus, the
Liquica massacre in East Timor shortly after was apparently far
worse, was only one of many, and had no pretext of self-defense.
Still, this and other massacres led to no change in US-UK support
for the Indonesian invaders. Putting aside such selective concerns,
however, the voluminous Western evidence does not reveal any significant shift in Kosovo before the bombing.

Serious scholarship reaches similar conclusions. Nicholas
Wheeler, who does not invert the chronology, estimates that Serbs

had killed 500 Albanians before the NATO bombing, implying that 1,500 had been killed by the KLA. Nevertheless, he concludes that bombing Serbia was a genuine case of humanitarian intervention because "though only a few hundred Albanians were killed" prior to the bombing, "intelligence points to this as a precursor to a major campaign of killing and ethnic cleansing." Again, no credible sources are provided.[13] This is one of the few serious attempts to provide any justification for the NATO bombing apart from the inverted chronology.

On March 27, three days after the bombing of Serbia began, NATO commander Wesley Clark informed the press that the vicious Serbian reaction was "entirely predictable." He added that it had been "fully anticipated" and was "not in any way" a concern of the political leadership. In his memoirs, Clark reports that on March 6 he had informed Secretary of State Madeleine Albright that if NATO proceeded to bomb Serbia, "almost certainly" the Serbs would "attack the civilian population" and NATO would be able to do nothing to prevent that reaction on the ground. Reviewing Clark's book, Michael Ignatieff recognizes that according to the NATO commander, "the really decisive impulse" propelling the NATO bombing campaign "was not Milosevic's human rights violations in Kosovo before March 1999; nor was it his wholesale eviction after the bombing began. What mattered most was the need to impose NATO's will on a leader whose defiance, first in Bosnia and then in Kosovo, was undermining the credibility of American and European diplomacy and of NATO's willpower."[14]

That the primary concern was the "credibility" of the masters had already been made clear by Clinton and Blair. The point was reiterated in Defense Secretary William Cohen's subsequent report to Congress, once the usual chronological falsifications are disregarded, and it is confirmed by Clark's memoirs.

Andrew Bacevich gives an even more cynical interpretation, dismissing all humanitarian motives. Clinton's resort to force in Bosnia in 1995 and his bombing of Serbia in 1999 were "not, as claimed, to put a stop to ethnic cleansing or in response to claims of conscience, but to preempt threats to the cohesion of NATO and the credibility of American power." The plight of the Kosovars," he alleges, was not a concern. The intent of the NATO bombing was "to provide an object lesson to any European state fancying that it was exempt from the rules of the post–Cold War era" established by Washington. What counted was "affirming the dominant position of the United States in a Europe that was unified, integrated, and open." From the outset, "the war's architects understood [that] its purpose had been to sustain American primacy" in Europe and "to forestall the intolerable prospect of Europe's backsliding," presumably out of US control.[15]

Four years later, Europe and the US had lost interest. Half of the Kosovars live in poverty. Radical Islamists have capitalized "on the ill feelings produced by the international community's negligent behavior," monopolizing the distribution of "food, clothing, and shelter," as well as the tools for the cultural survival of those in rural areas, giving rise to a "Taliban phenomenon." Postwar Western policies "may prove to be directly responsible for the production of Europe's own Taliban."[16]

Kosovo and East Timor are conventionally offered not only as the prime illustration of the new era of humanitarian intervention but also as a demonstration of how new norms are evolving "toward a redefined role for the United Nations." The norms that Western powers established in these two cases render the UN Charter obsolete. With these norms established, it becomes legitimate to invade a country without Security Council authorization. As approvingly noted by the dean of the Woodrow Wilson School of Public and International Affairs at Princeton, "That is the lesson that the United Nations and all of us should draw" from the invasion of Iraq, firmly grounded in the new norms.[17]

The record suggests that we should draw rather different lessons: about how norms are established by the powerful to provide justification for their claimed "sovereign right to take military action" at will (Colin Powell); and how even very recent history can be reconstructed by well-functioning doctrinal systems. These are the crucial lessons, and those concerned with the future would be well advised to take them seriously.

THE NEED FOR COLONIZATION

As the tragedies of East Timor and Kosovo unfolded in 1999, Turkey relinquished to Colombia its place as leading recipient of US arms. The reason is not hard to discern: Turkish state terror was by then a success, Colombia's was not. Throughout the 1990s and the new era of enlightenment, Colombia had by far the worst human rights record in the Western Hemisphere and was at the same time by far the hemisphere's leading recipient of US arms and military training, a correlation that is well-established and would be of no slight concern if it were known outside of scholarship and dissident circles.

Atrocities in Colombia include displacement of the population through chemical warfare (called "fumigation") under the guise of a drug war that is hard to take seriously. One of the leading academic authorities notes that "a provocative case can be made that US drug policy contributes effectively to the control of an ethnically distinct and economically deprived underclass at home and serves US economic and security interests abroad."[18] Many criminologists and observers of the international scene regard that as a considerable understatement. The analysis helps explain why the US-sponsored actions are carried out with ever greater enthusiasm and zeal even as they increasingly fail to achieve the alleged goal of dealing with domestic drug use, and why measures that are known to be far more effective, specifically prevention and treatment, are scarcely funded.

The governors of Colombia's targeted southern provinces, along with peasants and human rights activists, have proposed plans relying on manual eradication of coca and poppies and support for alternative crops, but to little effect. Meanwhile the land is poisoned by fumigation, children die, and the uprooted and scattered victims suffer from sickness and injury.

Peasant agriculture is based on a rich tradition of knowledge and experience gained over many centuries, commonly passed on from mother to daughter. Though a remarkable human achievement, it is very fragile and can be destroyed forever in a single generation. It is being destroyed, and along with it, some of the richest biodiversity in the world. Campesinos, indigenous people, and Afro-Colombians are now joining the millions in rotting slums and camps. And with the people gone, multinationals can strip the mountains for coal, extract oil and other resources, and probably convert what is left of the land to ranching by the rich or agroexport in an environment shorn of its treasures and variety. Informed analysts and observers describe Washington's fumigation programs as another stage in the historical process of driving poor peasants from the land for the benefit of foreign investors and Colombian elites.

Like many other centers of turmoil and state terror, Colombia is part of an important oil-producing region, and a significant producer itself: much the same is true of Chechnya, Western China, the Central Asian dictatorships, and other places where state violence was intensified after 9-11 on the pretext of a "war on terror," and with the expectation that there would be a nod from Washington. Human rights organizations and the State Department agree that the overwhelming majority of atrocities in Colombia can be attributed to the military and paramilitaries, the "sixth division" of the five-division Colombian army, because of their close links, according to Human Rights Watch. The proportion of atrocities attributed to the paramilitaries has been increasing as crimes are privatized in accord with neoliberal practice, a familiar development elsewhere as well: Serbia used private militias in the former Yugoslavia, as did Indonesia in East Timor, and Turkey in the southeast, and many other places. There is a corresponding privatization of international atrocities. Fumigation is being taken over by "private" companies consisting of US military officers under contract to the Pentagon, also a pattern that is worldwide, and useful for evading accountability.

Even if one were to give credence to the US arguments in favor of the drug war, the underlying assumptions are scandalous. Imagine the reaction to a proposal that Colombia or China should undertake fumigation programs in North Carolina to destroy government-subsidized crops used for more lethal products—which, furthermore, they not only must import at risk of trade sanctions, but for which they must allow advertising aimed at vulnerable populations.

There is a new and highly regarded literary genre inquiring into the cultural defects that keep us from responding properly to the crimes of others. An interesting question no doubt, though by any reasonable standard it ranks well below a different one: Why do we persist in our own crimes, either directly or through crucial support for murderous clients? It is instructive to ask how often, or how accurately, one finds reference to Turkey, Colombia, East Timor, and many similar examples in the contemporary literature on the flaws in our character. There is much self-congratulation about the new "ruling ideology" in the moral universe of the enlightened states, grounded in the principle that "all states have a responsibility to protect their citizens; if their leaders are unable or unwilling to do so, they render their countries liable to military intervention—authorized by the Security Council or, failing that (as in the case of Kosovo), by individual countries in 'conscience-shocking situations.' "[19] Atrocities comparable to or much worse than anything charged to Milosevic in Kosovo before the NATO bombing were not "conscience-shocking" when responsibility traced back home, as it often did—and even when the crimes took place *within*, not just *near*, the borders of NATO.

In the case of Turkey, "conscience-shocking situations" went virtually unheeded in the United States until the moment in early 2003 when the Turkish government defied Washington's demands and followed the wishes of 95 percent of its population by refusing to allow an attack on Iraq from its borders. At that point, one began to read about "Turkey's ghastly record of torturing, killing, and 'disappearing' Turkish Kurds and destroying more than 3,000 of their villages," with citations from human rights organizations reiterating what they had reported in far more detail years before while the crimes were in progress, thanks to US aid, and could easily have been stopped. To this day, the decisive US role remains under wraps.

As before, the most that can be said is that we "tolerated" the abuses suffered by the Kurds (Aryeh Neier).[20]

Massive contribution to major atrocities is not "toleration." The time to expose the suffering of the Kurds is while Washington is providing the means to carry out the crimes that are found shocking in retrospect, with responsibility safely displaced far away. Such performances, which are routine, would be deplored among official enemies. Their easy acceptance in the most powerful state in history again does not bode well for the future.

Another currently fashionable formulation of the mission of the enlightened states holds that "the need . . . for colonisation is as great as it ever was in the nineteenth century" to bring to the rest of the world the principles of order, freedom, and justice to which "postmodern" societies are dedicated; the version offered by Tony Blair's key foreign policy adviser, Robert Cooper.[21] He did not elaborate on the "need for colonisation" in the nineteenth century and the consequences as that obligation was shouldered by Britain, France, Belgium, and other standard-bearers of Western civilization, but an honest look at the real world may well support his judgment that the need for colonization is as compelling now as it was in the days Cooper recalls with nostalgia. To rephrase, we can learn a good deal about today's enlightened states by paying a little attention to their record and how they portrayed it, both as events were unfolding and in historical retrospect.

We should not, however, overlook the changes in world order that have occurred since World War II. One of these Robert Jervis calls a "change of spectacular proportions, perhaps the single most striking discontinuity that the history of international politics has anywhere provided": that the states of Europe now live in peace— and, some argue more controversially, democracies do not go to war with one another.[22] It is this striking discontinuity to which Cooper alludes in joining those who hail the birth of a "postmodern world system" of law, justice, and civility, though the West must "revert to the rougher methods of an earlier era—force, preemptive attack, deception, whatever is necessary, when it comes to dealing with those who still live in the nineteenth-century world of every state for itself." The West must revert to "the laws of the jungle . . . when we are operating in the jungle"—exactly as it has done in the disgraceful past.

PROTECTING NAUGHTY CHILDREN
FROM INFECTION

The enlightened states of the late nineteenth century were not the first to laud themselves for liberating barbarians from their sad fate—by violence, destruction, and plunder. They were drawing from a rich tradition of distinguished leaders who were troubled by the rising "flood of evil doctrines and pernicious examples" and asked "what would become of our religious and political institutions, of the moral force of our governments, and of that conservative system which has saved [us] from complete dissolution [if] the contagion and the invasion of vicious principles" is not deterred or overcome. In expressing these concerns, the Czar and Metternich were referring to "the pernicious doctrines of republicanism and popular self-rule [spread by] the apostles of sedition" in the New World—in the rhetoric of contemporary planners, a rotten apple that might spoil the barrel, a domino that might topple others. The contagion of these doctrines, they warned, "crosses the seas, and often appears with all the symptoms of destruction which characterize it, in places where not even any direct contact, any relation of proximity might give ground for apprehension." Worse yet, the apostles of sedition had just announced their intention to expand their dominion by proclaiming the Monroe Doctrine—"a species of arrogance, peculiarly American and inexcusable," as Bismarck later described it.[23]

Bismarck did not have to await the era of Wilsonian idealism to learn the meaning of the Monroe Doctrine, explained by Secretary of State Robert Lansing to President Wilson, who found his description "unanswerable," though advising that it would be "impolitic" to let it reach the public:

> In its advocacy of the Monroe Doctrine the United States considers its own interests. The integrity of other American nations is an incident, not an end. While this may seem based on self-ishness alone, the author of the Doctrine had no higher or more generous motive in its declaration.[24]

The doctrine could not yet be implemented fully because of the balance of world power, though Wilson did secure US domination of the Caribbean region by force, leaving a terrible legacy that remains to this day, and was able to move somewhat beyond, driving the British enemy out of oil-rich Venezuela and supporting the vicious and corrupt dictator Juan Vicente Gómez, who opened the country to US corporations. Open-door/free-trade policies were instituted in the usual way: by pressuring Venezuela to bar British concessions while continuing to demand—and secure—US oil rights in the Middle East, where the British and French were in the lead. By 1928 Venezuela had become the world's leading oil exporter, with US companies in charge. The story continues right to the front pages of 2003, with enormous poverty in a country of rich resources and potential, yielding great wealth to foreign investors and a small sector of the population.

The reach of US power was still limited in Wilson's time, but as President William Howard Taft had presciently observed, "the day is not far distant [when] the whole hemisphere will be ours in fact as, by virtue of our superiority of race, it already is ours morally." Latin Americans may not understand, the Wilson administration added, but that is because "they are naughty children who are exercising all the privileges and rights of grown-ups" and require "a stiff hand, an authoritative hand." More gentle means should not be overlooked, however. It may be useful to "pat them a little bit and make them think that you are fond of them," Secretary of State John Foster Dulles advised President Eisenhower.[25]

There are naughty children everywhere. Wilson regarded Filipinos as "children [who] must obey as those who are in tutelage"— at least, those who survived the liberation he had called for while extolling his altruism. His State Department also regarded Italians as "like children [who] must be [led] and assisted more than almost any other nation." It was therefore right and proper for his successors to offer enthusiastic support for the "fine young revolution" of Mussolini's Fascism that crushed the threat of democracy among Italians who "hunger for strong leadership and enjoy . . . being dramatically governed." The conception remained in place through the 1930s and was revived immediately after the war. As the US undertook to subvert Italian democracy in 1948 by withholding food from starving people, restoring the Fascist police, and threatening worse, the State Department's Italian desk officer explained that policies must be designed so that "even the dumbest wop would sense the drift." Haitians were "little more than primitive savages," according to Franklin Delano Roosevelt, who claimed to have rewritten the Haitian Constitution during Wilson's military occupation—so as to permit US corporations to take over Haiti's land and resources after its recalcitrant Parliament had been sent packing by the marines. When the Eisenhower administration was seeking to overthrow the newly established Castro government in Cuba in 1959, CIA chief Allen Dulles complained that "there was in Cuba no opposition to Castro who were capable of action," in part because "in these primitive countries where the sun shone, the demands of the people were far less than in the more advanced societies," so they were unaware of how much they were suffering.[26]

The need for discipline has been reiterated forcefully over the years. To mention another case of contemporary relevance, when Iran's conservative parliamentary government sought to gain control of its own resources, the US and Britain instigated a military coup to install an obedient regime that ruled with terror for twenty-five years. The coup sent a more far-reaching message, spelled out by the editors of the New York Times: "Underdeveloped countries with rich resources now have an object lesson in the heavy cost that must be paid by one of their number which goes berserk with fanatical nationalism . . . Iran's experience [may] strengthen the hands of more reasonable and more far-seeing leaders [elsewhere], who will have a clear-eyed understanding of the principles of decent behavior."[27]

The same lesson had been taught nearer home, at the Chapulte-pec (Mexico) Conference in February 1945 that laid the basis for the postwar order now that the Monroe Doctrine could be enforced in the Wilsonian sense. Latin Americans were then under the influence of what the State Department called "the philosophy of the New Nationalism, [which] embraces policies designed to bring about a broader distribution of wealth and to raise the standard of living of the masses." Washington was concerned that "economic nationalism is the common denominator of the new aspirations for industrialization"—just as it had been for England, the United States, and in fact every other country that succeeded in industrializing. "Latin Americans are convinced that the first beneficiaries of the development of a country's resources should be the people of that country." That was unacceptable: the "first beneficiaries" must be US investors, while Latin America fulfills its service function. The US therefore imposed an "Economic Charter for the Americas" designed to eliminate economic nationalism "in all its forms."[28] With an exception, however: economic nationalism remained a crucial feature of the US economy, which relied far more than in the past on a dynamic state sector, often operating under the cover of defense.

It is useful to recall that even at the peak of the Cold War more perceptive observers understood that the primary threat posed by Communism was the economic transformation of the Communist countries "in ways that reduce their willingness and ability to complement the industrial economies of the West," another version of "the philosophy of the new nationalism," in this case dating from 1917.[29]

The same concerns account for the persistence into the postwar period of "the analytical framework American policymakers had developed and employed during the interwar years for relations with right-wing dictatorships" of European fascism, historian David Schmitz notes.[30] The point has been to control the "threat of Communism," understood not as a military threat, but very much in the terms just described. The "analytical framework" of relations with the fascist states is eminently worth recalling, if only because it has reappeared with such consistency right to the present and therefore can teach us a good deal about the world that has been shaped in no small measure by the most powerful states and the private institutions that are their "tools and tyrants," to borrow the words of James Madison when he contemplated with much unease the fate of the democratic experiment of which he was the leading framer.

The rise of fascism in the interwar period elicited concern, but was generally regarded rather favorably by the US and British governments, the business world, and a good deal of elite opinion. The reason was that the fascist version of extreme nationalism permitted extensive Western economic penetration and also destroyed the much-feared labor movements and the left, and the excessive democracy in which they could function. Support for Mussolini was effusive. Across a broad range of opinion, "that admirable Italian gentleman" (as President Roosevelt described him in 1933) enjoyed great respect until World War II broke out. Support extended to Hitler's Germany as well. It is, incidentally, well to bear in mind that the most monstrous regime in history came to power in the country that by reasonable measures represented the highest peak of Western civilization in the sciences and the arts, and had been considered a model of democracy before international conflict took forms that could not accommodate this conception;[31] and—rather like Saddam Hussein half a century later—retained substantial Anglo-American support until Hitler launched direct aggression that infringed too seriously on US and UK interests.

Support for fascism began at once. Praising the Fascist takeover in Italy, which quickly destroyed the parliamentary system and violently suppressed labor and political opposition, Ambassador Henry Fletcher articulated the assumptions that were to guide US policy there and elsewhere in years to come. Italy faced a stark choice, he wrote the secretary of state: either "Mussolini and Fascism" or "Giolitti and Socialism"; Giolitti was a leading figure of Italian liberalism. A decade later, in 1937, the State Department continued to regard European fascism as a moderate force that "must succeed or the masses, this time reinforced by the disillusioned middle classes, will again turn to the Left." That same year, US Ambassador to Italy William Philips was "greatly impressed by the efforts of Mussolini to improve the conditions of the masses" and found "much evidence" in favor of the Fascists' view that "they represent a true democracy in as much as the welfare of the people is their principal objective." He considered Mussolini's accomplishments "astounding [and] a source of constant amazement," and enthusiastically praised his "great human qualities." The State Department vigorously concurred, also lauding Mussolini's "magnificent" achievements in Ethiopia, and hailing Fascism for having "brought order out of chaos, discipline out of license, and solvency out of bankruptcy." In 1939, FDR continued to regard Italian fascism as "of great importance to the world [though] still in the experimental stage."

In 1938, FDR and his close confidant Sumner Welles approved of Hitler's Munich settlement, which dismembered Czechoslovakia. As noted earlier, Welles felt that it "presented the opportunity for the establishment by the nations of the world of a new world order based upon justice and upon law," in which the Nazi moderates would play a leading role. In April 1941, George Kennan wrote from his consular post in Berlin that German leaders have no wish to "see other people suffer under German rule," are "most anxious that their new subjects should be happy in their care," and are making "important compromises" to assure this benign outcome.

The business world, too, was highly enthusiastic about European fascism. Investment boomed in Fascist Italy; "the wops are unwopping themselves," *Fortune* magazine declared in 1934. After the rise of Hitler, investment boomed in Germany for similar reasons: a stable climate had been established for business operations, with the threat of "the masses" contained. Until war broke out in 1939, Scott Newton writes, Britain was even more supportive of Hitler, for reasons deeply rooted in Anglo-German industrial, commercial, and financial relations, and "a policy of self-preservation for the British establishment" in the face of rising popular democratic pressures.[32]

Even after the US entered the war, attitudes remained ambivalent. By 1943, the US and Britain had begun their efforts, which intensified after the war, to dismantle the antifascist resistance worldwide and restore something like the traditional order, often rewarding some of the worst war criminals with prominent roles.[33] Reviewing the record, Schmitz points out that "the ideological basis and fundamental assumptions of American policy remained remarkably consistent" through the rest of the century; the Cold War "demanded new approaches and tactics" but otherwise left interwar priorities unchanged.[34]

The "analytical framework" Schmitz illustrates in detail has persisted until the present, leaving immense suffering and devastation. Throughout, policy planners have faced the "agonizing problem" of how to reconcile a formal commitment to democracy and freedom with the overriding fact that "the United States may often need to do terrible things to get what it has always wanted," Alan Tonelson observes. What the US wanted was "economic policies that would enable American business to operate as freely as possible and often as monopolistically as possible," with the aim of creating "an integrated, United States–dominated capitalist world economy."[35]

Still more ominous than the "philosophy of the new nationalism" was the threat that it could become a "virus" that might infect others, not by conquest but by example. That was understood from the earliest days. Secretary of State Lansing warned President Wilson that the Bolshevik disease might spread, "a very real danger in view of the process of social unrest throughout the world." Wilson was particularly concerned that "the American negro [soldiers] returning from abroad" might be infected by the example of the soldiers' and workers' councils that were being set up in Germany as the war ended, establishing a form of democracy that was as intolerable to the West as it was to Lenin and Trotsky. Similar fears were expressed by Lloyd George's government in Britain, which found "hostility to Capitalism" to be widespread among the working people of England, who were paying close attention to the popular councils that developed in Russia before the Bolshevik takeover destroyed them—counterrevolutionary violence that did not alleviate elite concerns in the West.

Within the United States, social unrest was largely suppressed by Wilson's "Red Scare," though only temporarily. Business leaders remained alert to "the hazard facing industrialists [with] the newly realized political power of the masses" and the constant need for shaping public opinion "if we are to avoid disaster."[36] Concern over Soviet economic development and its demonstration effect persisted into the 1960s, when the Soviet economy began to stagnate, in large measure because of the escalating arms race that Soviet Premier Khrushchev had sought desperately to prevent.

The Cold War itself from its origins in 1917 was in significant respects a "North-South" conflict writ large. Russia had been Europe's original "third world," declining relative to the West up to World War I while serving the standard function of providing resources, markets, and investment opportunities. Russia was a special case because of its scale and military power, a factor of growing importance after it played the leading role in defeating Nazi Germany and achieved superpower status in the military dimension. But the primary threats remained as they have been throughout the non–Western World: independent nationalism and the virus effect.

On these grounds it is possible to explain the "logical illogicality" noted by the War Department in 1945, when it prepared plans for the US to take control of most of the world and surround Russia with military force while denying the adversary any comparable rights. The illogicality they perceived dissolves as soon as we realize that the Soviet Union might have "flirted with the thought" of associating itself with "a rising tide all over the world wherein the common man aspires to higher and wider horizons."[37] The plans were therefore logical and necessary, however illogical they may appear on the surface.

Leading scholars basically agree. John Lewis Gaddis realistically traces the Russia-US conflict back to 1917, and explains that the immediate Western invasion was a justified act of self-defense. It was undertaken "in response to a profound and potentially far-reaching intervention by the new Soviet government in the internal affairs, not just of the West, but of virtually every country in the world," namely, "the Revolution's challenge . . . to the very survival of the capitalist order."[38] Change in the social order in Russia and the possibility that Russian development might infect others therefore justified the invasion of Russia.

Attack is therefore defense, another "logical illogicality" that becomes coherent once the doctrinal apparatus is properly understood. On the same grounds, we can understand the persistence of basic policies of the US and other leading Western powers before, during, and after the Cold War, always in self-defense. Note that the defensive invasion of Russia in 1918 is another precursor for the doctrine of preventive war declared in September 2002 by radical nationalists pursuing their imperial vision.

Let's return to the "striking discontinuity in international politics" at the end of World II (Robert Jervis). One element is that the US became a global actor for the first time, displacing its European rivals and using its incomparable wealth and power to organize the world system, with care and skill. What Jervis had in mind, however, is the "democratic peace." For centuries, Europeans had devoted themselves to slaughtering one another, meanwhile conquering most of the world. By 1945 they realized that the game was over: the next time it was played would be the last. Western powers can still resort to violence against the weak and defenseless, but not against one another. The Cold War superpower conflict, too, kept to that understanding, though not without extreme hazard.

The standard interpretation is different: the "democratic peace" reflects "some happy combination of liberal norms and institutions such as representative democracy and market economies."[39] Though these factors are real enough, their contribution to the striking discontinuity cannot be properly assessed without due attention to the realization that Western civilization was on the verge of self-annihilation, thanks to the rational pursuit of its traditional practices. Now Europe is internally at peace, just as North America has been since the native population was virtually annihilated, half of

Mexico conquered, the US-Canada border established, and the phrase "United States" transformed from plural to singular 150 years ago. On a global scale, however, the practices, institutions, and dominant culture remain largely unchanged. The portents cannot be lightly dismissed.

Chapter 4

Dangerous Times

Concern about current threats is widespread and realistic. In February 2002 the famous "doomsday clock" of the *Bulletin of the Atomic Scientists* was advanced two minutes toward midnight, even before the release of the Bush administration's National Security Strategy and Nuclear Posture Review, which elicited shudders worldwide. With different threats in mind, strategic analyst Michael Krepon regarded the final days of 2002 as "the most dangerous time since the 1962 Cuban missile crisis." A high-level task force concluded that "we are entering a time of especially grave danger [as we] are preparing to attack a ruthless adversary [Iraq] who may well have access to [weapons of mass destruction]." Such dangers are likely to become even more grave in the longer term as a consequence of the easy resort to violence, as many have pointed out.[1]

The reasons behind these concerns merit close attention, but too narrow a focus can be misleading. We can gain a more realistic perspective on them by asking why the Cuban missile crisis was such a "dangerous time." The answers bear directly on the perils ahead.

ONE WORD AWAY FROM NUCLEAR WAR

The missile crisis "was the most dangerous moment in human history," Arthur Schlesinger commented in October 2002 at a conference in Havana on the fortieth anniversary of the crisis, attended by a number of those who witnessed it from within as it unfolded. Decision-makers at the time undoubtedly understood that the fate of the world was in their hands. Nevertheless, attendees at the conference may have been shocked by some of the revelations. They were informed that in October 1962 the world was "one word away" from nuclear war. "A guy named Arkhipov saved the world," said Thomas Blanton of the National Security Archive in Washington, which helped organize the event. He was referring to Vasili Arkhipov, a Soviet submarine officer who blocked an order to fire nuclear-armed torpedoes on October 27, at the tensest moment of the crisis, when the submarines were under attack by US destroyers. A devastating response would have been a near certainty, leading to a major war.[2]

Participants in the decisions at the time, and at the retrospective forty years later, did not have to be reminded of President Eisenhower's warning that "a major war would destroy the Northern Hemisphere."[3] "The parallel between Kennedy's handling of the crisis and President Bush's deliberations over Iraq was a recurrent theme at the meeting," the press reported, "with many participants accusing Bush of ignoring history," saying "they had come to make sure it does not happen again, and to offer lessons for today's crises, most notably President George W. Bush's deliberations about whether to strike Iraq."[4] Schlesinger was surely not the only one to bring up the fact that "Kennedy chose quarantine as an alternative to military action [while] Bush is committed to military action"; nor, presumably, was he the only one to have been taken aback to learn just how close the world came to destruction even under the less aggressive choice.

In his authoritative account of the missile crisis, Raymond Garthoff observes that "in the United States, there was almost universal approbation for President Kennedy's handling of the crisis." That's a fair assessment, though whether the approval is warranted is a separate question.

The confrontation finally came down to two basic issues: (1) Would Kennedy pledge that the US would not invade Cuba? And (2) would he make a public announcement that the US would withdraw its Jupiter nuclear missiles from Turkey, on the border of Russia and aimed at its heartland? On both issues, Kennedy ultimately refused. He agreed only to a secret commitment to withdraw the missiles, which had in any case already been scheduled to be replaced by Polaris nuclear submarines. He refused to make any formal commitment not to invade Cuba. Rather, he continued "to conduct an active policy of seeking to undermine and displace the Castro regime, including covert operations against Cuba," Garthoff observes.

In a highly provocative gesture as the crisis intensified, the missiles were turned over to Turkish command "with ceremonial fanfare" on October 22. Garthoff comments: the event was "certainly noted in Moscow, *but* not in Washington."[5] There it was presumably regarded as just another exercise of "logical illogicality."

As history is crafted by the powerful, the most dramatic moment of the missile crisis was provided by UN Ambassador Adlai Stevenson at the Security Council on October 25, when he exposed Soviet deception by unveiling a photograph of a missile site in Cuba taken by US spy planes. The concept "Stevenson moment" has entered into historical memory, in celebration of this victory over a vicious foe aiming to destroy us.

As an intellectual exercise, let's imagine how the "Stevenson moment" might be viewed by a hypothetical extraterrestrial observer. Call him Martian, and assume that he is free from earthly systems of doctrine and ideology. Martian would surely note that there is no "Khrushchev moment" in history: no moment at which Soviet Premier Nikita Khrushchev or his UN ambassador dramatically unveiled photographs of the Jupiter missiles placed in Turkey in 1961–62, or of the provocative transfer of the missiles to the Turkish military with "ceremonial fanfare" just as the most dangerous moment in human history approached. Reflecting on this distinction, Martian should recall that the Jupiter missiles were only a small element of a far greater threat to Russia, and that Russia had repeatedly been invaded and almost destroyed in the preceding half-century—twice by newly rearmed Germany, its richer Western part now within a hostile military alliance led by the world's mightiest superpower; once in 1918 by Britain, the US, and their allies. And he might observe that there was, of course, no Russian threat to invade Turkey, nor any large-scale Russian terrorist campaign or economic warfare against Turkey, nor even a lesser counterpart to the crimes that the Kennedy administration was carrying out against Cuba at the time.

Despite all this, only the "Stevenson moment" exists in historical memory. Martian would surely grasp how the distinction reflects the balance of global power. He would also presumably recall a principle that must be close to a historical universal of intellectual culture: *We* are "good" (whoever *we* happen to be), and *they* are "evil" if they stand in our way. Therefore, the radical asymmetry makes perfect sense, within the framework of established doctrine.

The contours of the asymmetry become even sharper when we consider the occasional effort at extenuation: the crime of the Russians in Cuba was stealth, while the US surrounded Russia with lethal offensive weapons quite openly. That is true. The world ruler not only has no need to conceal its intent, but prefers to advertise it, to "maintain credibility." The subordination of the ideological system to power ensures that virtually any action—international terrorism (as in Cuba), overt aggression (as in South Vietnam at the same time), participation in mass slaughter to destroy the only mass-based political party (as in South Vietnam and Indonesia), and many others—will either be dispatched to oblivion or reshaped into an act of legitimate self-defense or an act of benevolence that perhaps went astray.[6]

The importance of owning a properly crafted "history" was revealed once again in February 2003, when Colin Powell addressed the UN Security Council, informing its members that the US would go to war with or without UN authorization. The question pondered by commentators was whether Powell would be able to provide a Stevenson moment.

Some thought he had. *New York Times* columnist William Safire triumphantly reported Powell's "Adlai Stevenson moment": a satellite image of trucks next to a bunker allegedly storing chemical weapons, then another with the trucks gone[7]—clear proof that Iraq had deceived the inspectors by removing the illegal weapons before they arrived, and that the devious Iraqis had penetrated the inspection team, confirming the US thesis that the team was unreliable and hence could not be provided with intelligence data that Washington claimed to have. It was later conceded, with Powell's silent nod of agreement, that for a range of reasons—the time lapse between the taking of the photos, the uncertain use of the site in question—the photographs proved nothing, one of a series of similar cases, which later became a torrent. Still, this was deemed a "Stevenson moment," though Adam Clymer pointed out that there was a "stark difference" between the two: Stevenson's moment was "one of real fear about Soviet missiles, of imminent nuclear confrontation." Apparently, there could have been no fear, anywhere, about missiles on the Russian border.

Stevenson's son felt that the differences were even starker. His father had presented the Security Council with proof that "a nuclear superpower was installing missiles in Cuba and threatening to upset the world's 'balance of terror' "—or, from Martian's standpoint, threatening to shift the world's balance of terror to be a little less extreme in Washington's favor. And, he continued, "That 'moment' had an obvious purpose: containing the Soviet Union and maintaining peace."[8] In Martian translation, the Stevenson moment did contribute to a partial containment, but of Washington, not the USSR. A possible invasion of Cuba was averted, though Washington's international terrorist campaign and economic warfare were resumed at once, and the threat to Russia was escalated—all of which takes on greater significance against the background of superpower interchanges at the time, to which we return.

Kennedy had no doubts about the threat of the Russian missiles in Cuba. Meeting with his high-level advisers (ExComm), he said, "It's just as if we suddenly began to put a major number of [medium-range ballistic missiles] in Turkey. . . . Now that'd be god-dam dangerous." His national security adviser, McGeorge Bundy, responded: "Well, we *did,* Mr. President." Surprised, JFK said, "But that was five years ago"—actually, one year ago, during his admin-istration. He later expressed concern that if the facts were known, his decision to risk war rather than agree publicly to joint with-drawal of missiles from Cuba and Turkey would not play well in Peoria: he feared most people would consider it "a very fair trade."[9]

Whatever one's judgment about the actions of Khrushchev and Kennedy, there should be universal agreement that Khrushchev's decision to dispatch the missiles to Cuba was an act of criminal lunacy, in the light of the possible consequences. It would pass beyond lunacy to condemn those who warned of the dangers and criticized Khrushchev bitterly for proceeding despite the risks. It is the merest truism that choices are assessed in terms of the range of likely consequences. We understand the truism very well when con-sidering the actions of official enemies but find it hard to apply to ourselves. There are many illustrations, including recent US military exercises. Aid agencies, scholars, and others who properly warned of the risks in Afghanistan and Iraq were ridiculed when the worst, fortunately, did not come to pass. At the same level of moral imbe-cility, one would rush into the streets every October to sing praises to the Kremlin, while ridiculing those who warned of the dangers of placing missiles in Cuba and persist in condemning the criminal lunacy of the act.

Kennedy officials state that the president had not authorized an invasion of Cuba. Secretary of Defense Robert McNamara, how-ever, informed his cabinet associates on October 22, 1962, that "the President ordered us to prepare an invasion months ago. . . . And we have developed plans in great detail," fully enough so that an invasion could be launched in a week.[10] At the fortieth anniversary conference, McNamara reiterated his view that "Cuba was justified in fearing an attack. 'If I were in Cuban or Soviet shoes, I would have thought so, too,' he said."

What took place, and the background for it, most definitely does "offer lessons for today's crises," as participants in the October 2002 retrospective insisted. While this may well have been "the most dangerous moment in human history," it is not the only such case of flirting with catastrophe. More generally, it is far from the only illustration of unanticipated and unpredictable consequences of the resort to, or even the threat of, force, among the many reasons why sane people understand it to be a last resort, facing a very heavy burden of proof.

Other lessons bear directly on conflicted US relations with Europe, another topical matter at the anniversary meeting. The missile crisis suggests some reasons why Europeans might be wary of the US political leadership—in that case, not radical right nationalists but those at the liberal, multilateral end of the political spectrum. Europe's fate was hanging in the balance as the president and his advisers decided to reject what they feared would be regarded as a "fair trade" if it were known. But Europe was kept in the dark and treated with disdain. Kennedy's ExComm "summarily dismissed any idea of sharing with the allies decisions that could have led to the nuclear destruction of Western Europe as well as North America," Frank Costigliola writes in a rare study of the topic.

Kennedy told his secretary of state privately that allies "must come along or stay behind. . . . We cannot accept a veto from any other power," words heard again forty years later from Bush and Powell. The US commander of NATO put its air forces on alert without consultation with Europe. Kennedy's closest ally, British prime minister Harold Macmillan, told his associates that Kennedy's actions were "escalating into war" but he could do nothing "to stop it"; he knew only what he could learn from British intelligence. Washington's perception of the US-UK "special relationship" was articulated by a senior Kennedy adviser in internal discussion at the peak of the crisis: Britain will "act as our lieutenant (the fashionable word is partner)." McGeorge Bundy suggested that some effort be made to encourage Europeans to "feel that they're a part of it . . . feel that they know," but only in order to keep them quiet. Europeans are not capable of the "rational and logical" approach of

American decision-makers, his aide Robert Komer advised. If European leaders found out what was happening, Bundy added, they might make "noise ... saying that they can live with Soviet [medium-range ballistic missiles], why can't we." The word *noise* connotes "discordant, unintelligent clamor," Costigliola adds.[11]

Perhaps many Europeans might not be too happy about the significance accorded their survival, even if respected US commentators are confident that their reluctance to "come along" is a sign of "paranoid anti-Americanism," "ignorance and avarice," and other "cultural deficiencies."

International terrorism dominated the headlines as the retrospective conference took place; so did Washington's allegedly novel doctrine of regime change. But there is little novel here: The Cuban missile crisis grew directly out of a campaign of international terrorism aimed at forceful regime change. Historian Thomas Paterson concludes, quite plausibly, that "the origins of the October 1962 crisis derived largely from the concerted U.S. campaign to quash the Cuban revolution" by violence and economic warfare.[12] We can gain a better insight into current implications by looking at how the crisis evolved, and the guiding principles that motivated policy.

INTERNATIONAL TERRORISM AND REGIME CHANGE: CUBA

The Batista dictatorship was overthrown in January 1959 by Castro's guerrilla forces. In March, the National Security Council (NSC) considered means to institute regime change. In May, the CIA began to arm guerrillas inside Cuba. "During the Winter of 1959–1960, there was a significant increase in CIA-supervised bombing and incendiary raids piloted by exiled Cubans" based in the US.[13] We need not tarry on what the US or its clients would do under such circumstances. Cuba, however, did not respond with violent actions within the United States for revenge or deterrence. Rather, it followed the procedure required by international law. In July 1960, Cuba called on the UN for help, providing the Security Council with records of some twenty bombings, including names of pilots, plane registration numbers, unexploded bombs, and other specific details, alleging considerable damage and casualties and calling for resolution of the conflict through diplomatic channels. US Ambassador Henry Cabot Lodge responded by giving his "assurance [that] the United States has no aggressive purpose against Cuba." Four months before, in March 1960, his government had made a formal decision in secret to overthrow the Castro government, and preparations for the Bay of Pigs invasion were well advanced.[14]

Washington was concerned that Cubans might try to defend themselves. CIA chief Allen Dulles therefore urged Britain not to provide arms to Cuba. His "main reason," the British ambassador reported to London, "was that this might lead the Cubans to ask for Soviet or Soviet bloc arms," a move that "would have a tremendous effect," Dulles pointed out, allowing Washington to portray Cuba as a security threat to the hemisphere, following the script that had worked so well in Guatemala.[15] Dulles was referring to Washington's successful demolition of Guatemala's first democratic experiment, a ten-year interlude of hope and progress, greatly feared in Washington because of the enormous popular support reported by US intelligence and the "demonstration effect" of social and economic measures to benefit the large majority. The Soviet threat was routinely invoked, abetted by Guatemala's appeal to the Soviet bloc for arms after the US had threatened attack and cut off other sources of supply. The result was a half-century of horror, even worse than the US-backed tyranny that came before.

For Cuba, the schemes devised by the doves were similar to those of CIA director Dulles. Warning President Kennedy about the "inevitable political and diplomatic fall-out" from the planned invasion of Cuba by a proxy army, Arthur Schlesinger suggested efforts to trap Castro in some action that could be used as a pretext for invasion: "One can conceive a black operation in, say, Haiti which might in time lure Castro into sending a few boatloads of men on to a Haitian beach in what could be portrayed as an effort to overthrow the Haitian regime, . . . then the moral issue would be clouded, and the anti-US campaign would be hobbled from the start."[16] Reference is to the regime of the murderous dictator "Papa Doc" Duvalier, which was backed by the US (with some reservations), so that an effort to help Haitians overthrow it would be a crime.

Eisenhower's March 1960 plan called for the overthrow of Castro in favor of a regime "more devoted to the true interests of the Cuban people and more acceptable to the U.S.," including support for "military operation on the island" and "development of an adequate paramilitary force outside of Cuba." Intelligence reported that popular support for Castro was high, but the US would determine the "true interests of the Cuban people." The regime change was to be carried out "in such a manner as to avoid any appearance of U.S. intervention," because of the anticipated reaction in Latin America and the problems of doctrinal management at home.

The Bay of Pigs invasion came a year later, in April 1961, after Kennedy had taken office. It was authorized in an atmosphere of "hysteria" over Cuba in the White House, Robert McNamara later testified before the Senate's Church Committee. At the first cabinet meeting after the failed invasion, the atmosphere was "almost savage," Chester Bowles noted privately: "there was an almost frantic reaction for an action program." At an NSC meeting two days later, Bowles found the atmosphere "almost as emotional" and was struck by "the great lack of moral integrity" that prevailed. The mood was reflected in Kennedy's public pronouncements: "The complacent, the self-indulgent, the soft societies are about to be swept away with the debris of history. Only the strong . . . can possibly survive," he told the country, sounding a theme that would be used to good effect by the Reaganites during their own terrorist wars.[17] Kennedy was aware that allies "think that we're slightly demented" on the subject of Cuba, a perception that persists to the present.[18]

Kennedy implemented a crushing embargo that could scarcely be endured by a small country that had become a "virtual colony" of the US in the sixty years following its "liberation" from Spain.[19] He also ordered an intensification of the terrorist campaign: "He asked his brother, Attorney-General Robert Kennedy, to lead the top-level interagency group that oversaw Operation Mongoose, a program of paramilitary operations, economic warfare, and sabotage he launched in late 1961 to visit the 'terrors of the earth' on Fidel Castro and, more prosaically, to topple him."[20]

The terrorist campaign was "no laughing matter," Jorge Domínguez writes in a review of recently declassified materials on operations under Kennedy, materials that are "heavily sanitized" and "only the tip of the iceberg," Piero Gleijeses adds.[21]

Operation Mongoose was "the centerpiece of American policy toward Cuba from late 1961 until the onset of the 1962 missile crisis," Mark White reports, the program on which the Kennedy brothers "came to pin their hopes." Robert Kennedy informed the CIA that the Cuban problem carries "the top priority in the United States Government—all else is secondary—no time, no effort, or manpower is to be spared" in the effort to overthrow the Castro regime. The chief of Mongoose operations, Edward Lansdale, provided a timetable leading to "open revolt and overthrow of the Communist regime" in October 1962. The "final definition" of the program recognized that "final success will require decisive U.S. military intervention," after terrorism and subversion had laid the basis. The implication is that US military intervention would take place in October 1962—when the missile crisis erupted.[22]

In February 1962, the Joint Chiefs of Staff approved a plan more extreme than Schlesinger's: to use "covert means . . . to lure or provoke Castro, or an uncontrollable subordinate, into an overt hostile reaction against the United States; a reaction which would in turn create the justification for the US to not only retaliate but destroy Castro with speed, force and determination."[23] In March, at the request of the DOD Cuba Project, the Joint Chiefs of Staff submitted a memorandum to Defense Secretary Robert McNamara outlining "pretexts which they would consider would provide justification for US military intervention in Cuba." The plan would be undertaken if "a credible internal revolt is impossible of attainment during the next 9–10 months," but before Cuba could establish relations with Russia that might "directly involve the Soviet Union."

A prudent resort to terror should avoid risk to the perpetrator.

The March plan was to construct "seemingly unrelated events to camouflage the ultimate objective and create the necessary impression of Cuban rashness and responsibility on a large scale, directed at other countries as well as the United States," placing the US "in the apparent position of suffering defensible grievances [and developing] an international image of Cuban threat to peace in the Western Hemisphere." Proposed measures included blowing up a US ship in Guantánamo Bay to create "a 'Remember the Maine' incident," publishing casualty lists in US newspapers to "cause a helpful wave of national indignation," portraying Cuban investigations as "fairly compelling evidence that the ship was taken under attack," developing a "Communist Cuban terror campaign [in Florida] and even in Washington," using Soviet bloc incendiaries for cane-burning raids in neighboring countries, shooting down a drone aircraft with a pretense that it was a charter flight carrying college students on a holiday, and other similarly ingenious schemes—not implemented, but another sign of the "frantic" and "savage" atmosphere that prevailed.[24]

On August 23 the president issued National Security Memorandum No. 181, "a directive to engineer an internal revolt that would be followed by U.S. military intervention," involving "significant U.S. military plans, maneuvers, and movement of forces and equipment" that were surely known to Cuba and Russia.[25] Also in August, terrorist attacks were intensified, including speedboat strafing attacks on a Cuban seaside hotel "where Soviet military technicians were known to congregate, killing a score of Russians and Cubans"; attacks on British and Cuban cargo ships; the contamination of sugar shipments; and other atrocities and sabotage, mostly carried out by Cuban exile organizations permitted to operate freely in Florida.[26] A few weeks later came "the most dangerous moment in human history."

Terrorist operations continued through the tensest moments of the missile crisis. They were formally canceled on October 30, several days after the Kennedy and Khrushchev agreement, but went on nonetheless. On November 8, "a Cuban covert action sabotage team dispatched from the United States successfully blew up a Cuban industrial facility," killing 400 workers, according to the Cuban government. Raymond Garthoff writes that "the Soviets could only see [the attack] as an effort to backpedal on what was, for them, the key question remaining: American assurances not to attack Cuba." These and other actions reveal again, he concludes, "that the risk and danger to both sides could have been extreme, and catastrophe not excluded."[27]

After the crisis ended, Kennedy renewed the terrorist campaign. Ten days before his assassination he approved a CIA plan for "destruction operations" by US proxy forces "against a large oil refinery and storage facilities, a large electric plant, sugar refineries, railroad bridges, harbor facilities, and underwater demolition of docks and ships." A plot to kill Castro was initiated on the day of the Kennedy assassination. The campaign was called off in 1965, but "one of Nixon's first acts in office in 1969 was to direct the CIA to intensify covert operations against Cuba."[28]

Of particular interest are the perceptions of the planners. In his review of recently released documents on Kennedy-era terror, Domínguez observes that "only once in these nearly thousand pages of documentation did a U.S. official raise something that resembled a faint moral objection to U.S.-government sponsored terrorism": a member of the NSC staff suggested that it might lead to some Russian reaction, and raids that are "haphazard and kill innocents . . . might mean a bad press in some friendly countries." The same attitudes prevail throughout the internal discussions, as when Robert Kennedy warned that a full-scale invasion of Cuba would "kill an awful lot of people, and we're going to take an awful lot of heat on it."[29]

Terrorist activities continued under Nixon, peaking in the mid-1970s, with attacks on fishing boats, embassies, and Cuban offices overseas, and the bombing of a Cubana airliner, killing all seventy-three passengers. These and subsequent terrorist operations were carried out from US territory, though by then they were regarded as criminal acts by the FBI.

So matters proceeded, while Castro was condemned by editors for maintaining an "armed camp, despite the security from attack promised by Washington in 1962."[30] The promise should have sufficed, despite what followed; not to speak of the promises that preceded, by then well documented, along with information about how well they could be trusted: e.g., the "Lodge moment" of July 1960.

On the thirtieth anniversary of the missile crisis, Cuba protested a machine-gun attack against a Spanish-Cuban tourist hotel; responsibility was claimed by a group in Miami. Bombings in Cuba in 1997, which killed an Italian tourist, were traced back to Miami. The perpetrators were Salvadoran criminals operating under the direction of Luis Posada Carriles and financed in Miami. One of the most notorious international terrorists, Posada had escaped from a Venezuelan prison, where he had been held for the Cubana airliner bombing, with the aid of Jorge Mas Canosa, a Miami businessman who was the head of the tax-exempt Cuban-American National Foundation (CANF). Posada went from Venezuela to El Salvador, where he was put to work at the Ilopango military air base to help organize US terrorist attacks against Nicaragua under Oliver North's direction.

Posada has described in detail his terrorist activities and the funding for them from exiles and CANF in Miami, but felt secure that he would not be investigated by the FBI. He was a Bay of Pigs veteran, and his subsequent operations in the 1960s were directed by the CIA. When he later joined Venezuelan intelligence with CIA help, he was able to arrange for Orlando Bosch, an associate from his CIA days who had been convicted in the US for a bomb attack on a Cuba-bound freighter, to join him in Venezuela to organize further attacks against Cuba. An ex–CIA official familiar with the Cubana bombing identifies Posada and Bosch as the only suspects in the bombing, which Bosch defended as "a legitimate act of war." Generally considered the "mastermind" of the airline bombing, Bosch was responsible for thirty other acts of terrorism, according to the FBI. He was granted a presidential pardon in 1989 by the incoming Bush I administration after intense lobbying by Jeb Bush

and South Florida Cuban-American leaders, overruling the Justice
Department, which had found the conclusion "inescapable that it
would be prejudicial to the public interest for the United States to
provide a safe haven for Bosch [because] the security of this nation
is affected by its ability to urge credibly other nations to refuse aid
and shelter to terrorists."[31]

Cuban offers to cooperate in intelligence-sharing to prevent terrorist attacks have been rejected by Washington, though some did
lead to US actions. "Senior members of the FBI visited Cuba in 1998
to meet their Cuban counterparts, who gave [the FBI] dossiers about
what they suggested was a Miami-based terrorist network: information which had been compiled in part by Cubans who had infiltrated exile groups." Three months later the FBI arrested Cubans
who had infiltrated the US-based terrorist groups. Five were sentenced to long terms in prison.[32]

The national security pretext lost whatever shreds of credibility
it might have had after the collapse of the Soviet Union in 1991,
though it was not until 1998 that US intelligence officially informed
the country that Cuba no longer posed a threat to US national security. The Clinton administration, however, insisted that the military
threat posed by Cuba be reduced to "negligible," but not completely
removed. Even with this qualification, the intelligence assessment
eliminated a danger that had been identified by the Mexican ambassador in 1961, when he rejected JFK's attempt to organize collective
action against Cuba on the grounds that "if we publicly declare that
Cuba is a threat to our security, forty million Mexicans will die
laughing."[33]

In fairness, however, it should be recognized that missiles in Cuba
did pose a threat. In private discussions the Kennedy brothers
expressed their fears that the presence of Russian missiles in Cuba
might deter a US invasion of Venezuela. So "the Bay of Pigs was
really right," JFK concluded.[34]

The Bush I administration reacted to the elimination of the security
pretext by making the embargo much harsher, under pressure from
Clinton, who outflanked Bush from the right during the 1992 election

campaign. Economic warfare was made still more stringent in 1996, causing a furor even among the closest US allies. The embargo came under considerable domestic criticism as well, on the grounds that it harms US exporters and investors—the embargo's only victims, according to the standard picture in the US; Cubans are unaffected. Investigations by US specialists tell a different story. Thus, a detailed study by the American Association for World Health concluded that the embargo had severe health effects, and only Cuba's remarkable health care system had prevented a "humanitarian catastrophe"; this has received virtually no mention in the US.[35]

The embargo has effectively barred even food and medicine. In 1999 the Clinton administration eased such sanctions for all countries on the official list of "terrorist states," apart from Cuba, singled out for unique punishment. Nevertheless, Cuba is not entirely alone in this regard. After a hurricane devastated West Indian islands in August 1980, President Carter refused to allow any aid unless Grenada was excluded, as punishment for some unspecified initiatives of the reformist Maurice Bishop government. When the stricken countries refused to agree to Grenada's exclusion, having failed to perceive the threat to survival posed by the nutmeg capital of the world, Carter withheld all aid. Similarly, when Nicaragua was struck by a hurricane in October 1988, bringing starvation and causing severe ecological damage, the current incumbents in Washington recognized that their terrorist war could benefit from the disaster, and therefore refused aid, even to the Atlantic Coast area with close links to the US and deep resentment against the Sandinistas. They followed suit when a tidal wave wiped out Nicaraguan fishing villages, leaving hundreds dead and missing in September 1992. In this case, there was a show of aid, but hidden in the small print was the fact that apart from an impressive donation of $25,000, the aid was deducted from assistance already scheduled. Congress was assured, however, that the pittance of aid would not affect the administration's suspension of over $100 million of aid because the US-backed Nicaraguan government had failed to demonstrate a sufficient degree of subservience.[36]

US economic warfare against Cuba has been strongly condemned in virtually every relevant international forum, even declared illegal by the Judicial Commission of the normally compliant Organization of American States. The European Union called on the World Trade Organization to condemn the embargo. The response of the Clinton administration was that "Europe is challenging 'three decades of American Cuba policy that goes back to the Kennedy Administration,' and is aimed entirely at forcing a change of government in Havana."[37] The administration also declared that the WTO has no competence to rule on US national security or to compel the US to change its laws. Washington then withdrew from the proceedings, rendering the matter moot.

SUCCESSFUL DEFIANCE

The reasons for the international terrorist attacks against Cuba and the illegal economic embargo are spelled out in the internal record. And no one should be surprised to discover that they fit a familiar pattern—that of Guatemala a few years earlier, for example.

From the timing alone, it is clear that concern over a Russian threat could not have been a major factor. The plans for forceful regime change were drawn up and implemented before there was any significant Russian connection, and punishment was intensified after the Russians disappeared from the scene. True, a Russian threat did develop, but that was more a consequence than a cause of US terrorism and economic warfare.

In July 1961 the CIA warned that "the extensive influence of 'Castroism' is not a function of Cuban power. . . . Castro's shadow looms large because social and economic conditions throughout Latin America invite opposition to ruling authority and encourage agitation for radical change," for which Castro's Cuba provided a model. Earlier, Arthur Schlesinger had transmitted to the incoming President Kennedy his Latin American Mission report, which warned of the susceptibility of Latin Americans to "the Castro idea of taking matters into one's own hands." The report did identify a

Kremlin connection: the Soviet Union "hovers in the wings, flour-
ishing large development loans and presenting itself as the model for
achieving modernization in a single generation." The dangers of the
"Castro idea" are particularly grave, Schlesinger later elaborated,
when "the distribution of land and other forms of national wealth
greatly favors the propertied classes" and "the poor and underpriv-
ileged, stimulated by the example of the Cuban revolution, are now
demanding opportunities for a decent living." Kennedy feared that
Russian aid might make Cuba a "showcase" for development, giving
the Soviets the upper hand throughout Latin America.

In early 1964, the State Department Policy Planning Council
expanded on these concerns: "The primary danger we face in Castro
is . . . in the impact the very existence of his regime has upon the
leftist movement in many Latin American countries. . . . The simple
fact is that Castro represents a successful defiance of the US, a nega-
tion of our whole hemispheric policy of almost a century and a
half."[38] To put it simply, Thomas Paterson writes, "Cuba, as symbol
and reality, challenged U.S. hegemony in Latin America."[39] International terrorism and economic warfare to bring about regime
change are justified not by what Cuba does, but by its "very existence," its "successful defiance" of the proper master of the hemisphere. Defiance may justify even more violent actions, as in Serbia,
as quietly conceded after the fact; or Iraq, as also recognized when
pretexts had collapsed.

Outrage over defiance goes far back in American history. Two
hundred years ago, Thomas Jefferson bitterly condemned France for
its "attitude of defiance" in holding New Orleans, which he coveted.
Jefferson warned that France's "character [is] placed in a point of
eternal friction with our character, which though loving peace and
the pursuit of wealth, is high-minded." France's "defiance [requires
us to] marry ourselves to the British fleet and nation," Jefferson
advised, reversing his earlier attitudes, which reflected France's crucial contribution to the liberation of the colonies from British rule.[40]
Thanks to Haiti's liberation struggle, unaided and almost universally
opposed, France's defiance soon ended, but the guiding principles
remain in force, determining friend and foe.

GUIDING PRINCIPLES

The principles illustrated in the missile crisis explain why international law is irrelevant. Domestic law was also declared irrelevant. Rejecting a 1961 legal brief that held the Bay of Pigs invasion to be a violation of US neutrality laws, Attorney General Robert Kennedy determined that the US-run forces were "patriots." Therefore none of their activities "appear to be violations of our neutrality laws," which "clearly . . . were not designed for the kind of situation which exists in the world today."[41]

The world did not suddenly become extraordinarily dangerous on 9-11, requiring "new paradigms" that dismantle international law and institutions and grant the White House the power to disregard the domestic rule of law.

The achievements of international terrorism are excluded from sanitized history, but they are recognized with pride by the perpetrators. The famous School of the Americas, which trains Latin American officers to carry out their missions, proudly announces as one of its "talking points" that the US Army helped to "defeat liberation theology,"[42] the heresy to which the Latin American Church succumbed when it adopted "the preferential option for the poor" and was made to suffer its own "terrors of the earth" for this departure from good order. Symbolically, the grim decade of Reagan–Bush I terror was opened, shortly before they took office, by the assassination of a conservative Salvadoran archbishop who had become a "voice for the voiceless," with thinly veiled complicity of the US-backed security forces; and the decade closed with the murder of six Jesuit Salvadoran intellectuals whose brains were blown out, and their housekeeper and her daughter murdered, by an elite Washington-armed and -trained battalion that had already compiled a record of bloody atrocities.

The significance of these events in Western culture is illustrated by the fact that the work of these troublesome priests is unread and their names unknown, in sharp contrast to their counterparts under Kremlin rule. They were thus doubly assassinated: murdered and forgotten. In fact, the corpses received another kick in the face.

Immediately after the murders, Václav Havel visited Washington to speak at a joint session of Congress, where he received a standing ovation for praising the "defenders of freedom"—who, he and his audience surely knew, had armed and trained the assassins of the six leading Latin American intellectuals, while leaving a bloody trail of the usual victims. His praise for our glorious selves after these achievements won rapturous acclaim from leading liberal commentators, who saw in it more signs that we are entering "a romantic age" (Anthony Lewis), and were awed by his "voice of conscience" that "speaks compellingly of the responsibilities that large and small powers owe each other" (Washington Post editors). But not the responsibility that the US owes to the people of Central America, at least those who survived the murderous onslaught of the 1980s.[43]

In the case of Cuba, "successful defiance" elicited reactions that brought the world close to destruction. But that is unusual. Successful defiance has regularly been overcome by one or another form of violence without any risk to the perpetrators. One strategy from the early 1960s was the installation of neo-Nazi National Security States, which had as their goal "to destroy permanently a perceived threat to the existing structure of socioeconomic privilege by eliminating the political participation of the numerical majority," that is, the "popular classes."[44] The move set off a plague of repression and terror throughout the continent, reaching Central America during the Reaganite phase of the current political leadership. The plague began with the military coup in Brazil set in motion before Kennedy's assassination and carried out shortly after. Washington cooperated with the military forces that overthrew parliamentary democracy in recognition of their "basically democratic and pro–United States orientation," Kennedy's ambassador Lincoln Gordon explained. While the torturers and assassins were carrying out their work, Gordon hailed "the most decisive victory for freedom in the mid-twentieth century." The "democratic rebellion," Gordon cabled Washington, would help in "restraining left-wing excesses" of the former moderate populist elected government, and the "democratic forces" now in charge should "create a greatly improved climate for private investment."[45]

Gordon's view was endorsed by other leading figures of the Kennedy-Johnson administrations, though by the 1980s, as in Chile at the same time, the Brazilian generals were happy to transfer the wreckage to civilian hands. Despite the enormous advantages of the "colossus of the South," the generals had left Brazil in "the same category as the less developed African or Asian countries when it came to social welfare indices" (malnutrition, infant mortality, etc.), with conditions of inequality and suffering rarely matched elsewhere, but a grand success for foreign investors and domestic privilege.[46]

These patterns have not been restricted to the domains of the Monroe Doctrine. To take one of many examples from other parts of the world, while Washington was facilitating the "democratic rebellion" in Brazil and seeking to overcome Cuba's efforts to "take matters into its own hands," elder statesman Ellsworth Bunker was sent to Indonesia to investigate troubling conditions there. He informed Washington that "the avowed Indonesian objective is 'to stand on their own feet' in developing their economy, free from foreign, especially Western, influence." A National Intelligence Estimate in September 1965 warned that if the efforts of the mass-based PKI "to energize and unite the Indonesian nation . . . succeeded, Indonesia would provide a powerful example for the underdeveloped world and hence a credit to communism and a setback for Western prestige." That threat was overcome a few weeks later by a mass slaughter in Indonesia and then the installation of the Suharto dictatorship. From the 1950s, fear of independence and excessive democracy—permitting a popular party of the poor to participate in the electoral arena—had been driving factors in Washington's exercises of subversion and violence, much as in Latin America.[47]

Cuba's crimes became still more immense in 1975 as it extended its reach to Africa, serving as the instrument of Russia's crusade to dominate the world, Washington proclaimed. "If Soviet neocolonialism succeeds" in Angola, UN Ambassador Daniel Patrick Moynihan thundered, "the world will not be the same in the aftermath. Europe's oil routes will be under Soviet control as will the strategic South

Atlantic, with the next target on the Kremlin's list being Brazil."
The theme is again familiar, with changes in the cast of characters.

Washington's fury was roused by another Cuban act of successful
defiance. When a US-backed South African invasion came close to
conquering newly independent Angola, Cuba sent troops on its own
initiative, scarcely even notifying Russia, and beat back the invaders.
The South African press warned of "the blows to South African
pride" and the "boost to African nationalism which has seen South
Africa forced to retreat" by black Cuban soldiers. South Africa's
major black newspaper wrote that "Black Africa is riding the crest
of a wave generated by the Cuban success in Angola" and "tasting
the heady wine of the possibility of realizing the dream of 'total
liberation.' "[48]

The defense of Angola was one of Cuba's most significant contributions to the liberation of Africa. How remarkable these contributions were was unknown before Gleijeses's groundbreaking work
appeared, telling "the story of a small country's vision of defying a
big power's oppression, and, thanks to extraordinary individual her-
oism and self-sacrifice, changing a continent."[49]

Gleijeses observes that "Kissinger did his best to smash the one
movement that represented any hope for the future of Angola," the
MPLA. And though the MPLA "bears a grave responsibility for its
country's plight" in later years, it was "the relentless hostility of the
United States [that] forced it into an unhealthy dependence on the
Soviet bloc and encouraged South Africa to launch devastating military raids in the 1980s."[50]

The many campaigns of international terrorism and economic
warfare to overcome "successful defiance" and "left-wing excesses"
adopting "the philosophy of the new nationalism" and perhaps
even influenced by liberation theology, barely sampled here, are
considered insignificant, or perhaps obviously legitimate, as are
their bitter consequences. Accordingly, they scarcely enter the enormous current literature and public discussion of international terrorism and Washington's supposedly new doctrine of "regime
change." At worst they can be dismissed with comforting euphe-

misms. An occasional casual reference tells us that nothing happened in Cuba beyond "the destabilization campaign known as Operation Mongoose." And fortunately, "with the collapse of the Soviet Union, leftist terrorism has all but dried up. North Korea and Cuba are no longer as busy promoting disorder as they once were."[51] Cuba is listed prominently in scholarly work on terrorism, but typically as a suspect in the crime, not a victim.[52] Reagan-Bush international terrorism in Nicaragua and elsewhere does not exist, or is at worst traceable to inattention or some other understandable departure from the mission assigned by Providence to the leaders of "the idealistic new world bent on ending inhumanity." And the persistence of standard operating procedures after the Cold War also did not occur or doesn't matter. The overriding principle prevails: misdeeds are performed by others; we are culpable only for inadvertent error or oversight.

It is of the utmost significance for the future that in a world-dominant power even the worst crimes are easily effaced. The wars in Indochina are a remarkable example. After years of brutal destruction, much of the US population had come to oppose the wars on principled grounds. Among educated elites, however, objections were typically on narrow grounds of cost and failure. We may concede that there were some flaws in our generally praiseworthy effort, notably My Lai. "When Americans look back with sadness and even shame at the Vietnam war it is horrors like the My Lai *massacre* they have in mind," Jean Bethke Elshtain writes, the only Vietnam example mentioned in her furious denunciation of the crimes of others. My Lai is convenient because the massacre can be blamed on half-educated GIs trying to survive awful conditions in the field, unlike, say, Operation Wheeler Wallawa, to which My Lai was a minor footnote, one of the many post-Tet mass-murder operations planned by respectable people just like us, so that we need feel no "shame," even "sadness," over these huge crimes.[53]

Cuba was added to the official list of terrorist states in 1982, replacing Iraq, which was removed so as to make Saddam Hussein eligible for US aid.

INTERNATIONAL TERRORISM AND REGIME
CHANGE: NICARAGUA

It is instructive to look at another international terrorist campaign
to overcome "successful defiance": the terrorist war against Nicaragua. The case is particularly illuminating because of the scale of
the terrorist campaigns aimed at regime change, the role of the current Washington leadership in executing them, and the way they
were cast when in progress and reshaped in retrospect within the
intellectual culture. The case has further significance because it is so
uncontroversial, in the light of the judgments of the highest international authorities; uncontroversial, that is, among those who have
a minimal commitment to human rights and international law.
There is a simple way to estimate the size of that category: determine
how often these elementary matters are discussed, even mentioned,
in respectable circles in the West, most dramatically after the "war
on terror" was redeclared on 9-11. From that exercise alone one can
draw some conclusions about the future, not very optimistic ones.

The attack against Nicaragua was one of the highest priorities of
the war on terror launched as the Reagan administration came into
office in 1981, targeting primarily "state-sponsored terrorism." Nicaragua was an unusually dangerous agent of the plague because it
was so close to home: "a cancer, right here in our land mass,"
openly renewing the goals of Hitler's *Mein Kampf,* Secretary of State
George Shultz declared to Congress.[54]

Nicaragua was armed by the Soviet Union, which had implanted
there "a privileged sanctuary for terrorists and subversives just two
days' driving time from Harlingen, Texas," the president warned—
"a dagger pointed at the heart of Texas," to paraphrase an illustri-
ous predecessor. This second Cuba would become "a launching pad
for revolution up and down, first of all, Latin America," then who
knows where? "Nicaraguan communists have threatened to carry
their revolution into the United States itself." Soon we may see
"Soviet military bases on America's doorstep," a "strategic disaster." Despite the immense odds he faced, the president bravely told

reporters: "I refuse to give up. I remember a man named Winston Churchill who said, 'Never give in. Never, never, never.' So we won't."[55]

Reagan declared a national emergency because "the policies and the actions of the government of Nicaragua constitute an unusual and extraordinary threat to the national security and foreign policy of the United States." Explaining the bombing of Libya in 1986, Reagan announced that the mad dog Qaddafi was sending arms and advisers to Nicaragua "to bring his war home to the United States," part of his campaign "to expel America from the world." Particularly ominous was Nicaragua's "revolution without borders," regularly brandished though it had immediately been exposed as a fraud. The source was a speech by Sandinista leader Tomás Borge explaining that Nicaragua hoped to develop successfully and provide a model for others, who would have to follow their own paths. The speech was transmuted by Reaganite Public Diplomacy into a design for world conquest, and faithfully relayed by the media.[56]

Even more interesting than the antics of a political leadership seeking to set new records for absurdity and deceit are the actual contents of the document subjected to State Department manipulation. Borge's words probably did strike terror in the hearts of Reagan's planners. They understood very well that the real threat is successful development that might "infect others," renewing the danger of Guatemala's crushed experiment with democracy and social reform, Cuba's "successful defiance," and many other examples, back to the days when the American revolution terrified the Czar and Metternich. The threat had to be recast in terms of aggression and terror for the purposes of Public Diplomacy.

Pursuing that vocation, Secretary of State Shultz warned that "terrorism is a war against ordinary citizens." As he spoke, US planes were bombing Libya, killing dozens of ordinary citizens. The bombing was the first terrorist attack in history scheduled for prime-time TV, exactly when all major networks opened their evening news, no small technical feat given the logistical difficulties. Shultz warned particularly of the Nicaraguan cancer, announcing that we must "cut it out." And not by gentle means: "Negotiations are a euphemism for capitulation if the shadow of power is not cast across the bargaining table," Shultz orated, condemning those who advocate "utopian, legalistic means like outside mediation, the United Nations, and the World Court, while ignoring the power element of the equation."[57]

Washington forcefully blocked such utopian means, beginning with the efforts of Central American presidents to bring a negotiated peace to the region in the early 1980s. Washington proceeded to "cut the cancer out" by violence and, not surprisingly considering the array of forces, with great success. The leading academic historian of Nicaragua, Thomas Walker, points out that after a few years, Washington's terrorist war had reversed the considerable economic growth and social progress that followed the overthrow of the US-backed Somoza dictatorship, driving the highly vulnerable economy to disaster so that the country achieved "the unenviable status of being the poorest country in the Western hemisphere" by the time the administration had achieved its goals. One component of the triumph, Walker continues, was a death toll that would be comparable to 2.25 million dead in the US, relative to population. Reagan State Department official and historian Thomas Carothers observes that for Nicaragua, the toll "in per capita terms was significantly higher than the number of U.S. persons killed in the U.S. Civil War and all the wars of the twentieth century *combined*."[58]

Destruction of Nicaragua was a task of no slight importance. The country's progress during the early 1980s was lauded by the World Bank and other international agencies as "remarkable" and as "laying a solid foundation for long-term socio-economic development" (Inter-American Development Bank). In the health sector, the country enjoyed "one of the most dramatic improvements in child survival in the developing world" (UNICEF, 1986). The real cancer feared by the Reaganites was thus serious: Nicaragua's "remarkable" transformation could have metastasized to a "revolution without borders" in the sense of the speech that was reshaped for propaganda purposes. It was therefore only logical, from Washington's point of view, to eradicate the "virus" before it could "infect others," who must in turn be "inoculated" by terror and repression.[59]

Like Cuba, Nicaragua did not respond to the terrorist attack with bombings in the US, efforts to assassinate the political leadership, and other such measures, which, we are solemnly informed, meet the highest standards when conducted by our leaders. Rather, it approached the World Court for relief. Its legal team was led by the distinguished Harvard University law professor Abram Chayes. Expecting that the US would abide by a court decision, the team prepared a very narrow case, restricted to terrorist acts that required scarcely any argument, because they were conceded: mining of Nicaraguan harbors, in particular.[60]

In 1986, the court found in Nicaragua's favor, dismissing US government claims and condemning Washington for "unlawful use of force"—international terrorism, in lay terms. The court ruling went beyond Nicaragua's narrow charge. Reiterating more forcefully earlier decisions, the court ruled any form of intervention "prohibited" if it interferes with the sovereign right of "choice of a political, economic, social and cultural system, and the formulation of policy": intervention is "wrongful when it uses methods of coercion in regard to such choices." The judgment applies to many other cases. The court also defined "humanitarian aid" explicitly, ruling all US aid to the contras strictly military, hence illegal. US economic warfare was also ruled in violation of valid treaties, therefore unlawful.[61]

The decision had little detectable effect. The World Court was condemned as a "hostile forum" by the editors of the *New York Times,* and therefore irrelevant, like the UN. Legal authorities noted for their defense of world order dismissed the ruling on grounds that America "needs the freedom to defend freedom" (Thomas Franck), as it was doing in devastating Nicaragua and much of the rest of Central America. Others condemned the court because of its "close ties to the Soviet Union" (Robert Leiken, *Washington Post*), a claim not worthy of refutation. Subsequent aid to the contras was uniformly described as "humanitarian" in violation of the explicit court ruling. Congress immediately approved an additional $100 million to escalate what the court had condemned as the "unlawful use of force." Washington continued to undermine "utopian, legalistic means" until it finally achieved its ends by violence.

The World Court further ordered the US to pay indemnities, and Nicaragua sought to estimate the costs, under international supervision. Estimates were in the $17 billion to $18 billion range. The call for reparations was of course dismissed as ridiculous, though just to make sure, after the US regained control, the Nicaraguan government was heavily pressured to abandon the claims for reparations mandated by the court.

Interestingly, the figure of $17 billion is the amount that Iraq has paid to people and companies in compensation for its invasion of Kuwait. The numbers killed in the Iraqi conquest of Kuwait appear to be on the order of the US invasion of Panama a few months earlier (hundreds or thousands, according to various estimates)—a fraction of the deaths in Nicaragua and perhaps 5 percent of those killed in the US-backed Israeli invasion of Lebanon in 1982. There is, of course, no thought of compensation in such cases.

Another relevant comparison in terms of compensation is Vietnam. Here attitudes vary as usual from doves to hawks. At the dovish extreme, President Carter assured Americans that we owe Vietnam no debt and have no responsibility to render it any assistance because "the destruction was mutual." Others thought we should not be so soft-hearted. Taking a moderate view, neither hawk nor dove, President Bush I announced that "it was a bitter conflict, but Hanoi knows today that we seek only answers without the threat of retribution for the past." The crimes the Vietnamese committed against us can never be forgotten, but "we can begin writing the last chapter of the Vietnam war" if they dedicate themselves with sufficient zeal to the MIAs, the sole moral issue that remains after an invasion that left millions dead and three countries in utter ruins, with unknown numbers still dying from unexploded ordinance and the massive chemical warfare attack against the South; the North was spared this particular horror. The adjacent frontpage story in the *New York Times* reports Japan's failure, once again, to "unambiguously" accept the blame "for its wartime aggression."[62]

Given that the invaders were the victims, the Vietnamese are responsible for reparations. Vietnam was therefore compelled to pay to the US the huge debt incurred by the Saigon government that the US had installed as its local agent for its wars in Indochina, which targeted primarily South Vietnam. Clinton, however, magnanimously advocated a plan to allow Vietnam to use some portion of its debt to the US for educational purposes.[63]

Clinton's plan was modeled on a 1908 program that returned to China a portion of the indemnity it was forced to pay for rebelling against its foreign masters (the Boxer Rebellion). There are earlier precedents. Haiti's liberation from French rule in 1804 shocked civilized opinion, which feared that the virus of liberation might spread from "the first *free* nation of *free* men."[64] For obvious reasons, the danger was particularly acute in the US, which took the lead in isolating the criminal state, relenting only in 1862 when destinations were being sought for freed slaves (Liberia was recognized in the same year). In punishment for the crime of liberation, Haiti was compelled to pay France a huge indemnity in 1825, which guaranteed French domination and had a catastrophic effect on the society that France had devastated in the war of liberation in its richest colony.[65]

Half a century before France's punishment of Haiti for its successful defiance, George Washington set forth in 1779 on the conquest of the advanced Iroquois civilization. His goal was to "extirpate them from the Country," he wrote to Lafayette on the Fourth of July, and to expand American boundaries westward toward the Mississippi; conquest of Canada was barred by British force. The "Town destroyer," as Washington was known to the indigenous population, completed his mission successfully. The Iroquois were then informed that they would have to provide compensation for their treacherous resistance to their liberators. Another

Clinton, then governor of New York, informed the defeated tribes that "considering our Losses, the Debts we have incurred, and our former Friendship, it is reasonable that You make to Us a Cession of your Lands as will aid Us in repairing and discharging the same." Having little choice, the Iroquois ceded their territory, only to discover that New York State proceeded at once to violate its solemn treaties and the prohibitions of the Articles of Confederation and to take most of the rest through threats, deception, and guile. A young American soldier later wrote home that "I really feel guilty as I applied the torch to huts that were Homes of Content until we ravagers came spreading desolation everywhere," but perhaps in a good cause: "Our mission here is ostensibly to destroy but may it not transpire that we pillagers are carelessly sowing the seeds of Empire?"[66]

Following the US rejection of the World Court orders, Nicaragua—still eschewing violent retaliation or threat of terror—took its case to the Security Council, which endorsed the court's judgment and called on all states to observe international law. The US vetoed the resolution. Nicaragua then approached the General Assembly, which passed a similar resolution with only the US, Israel, and El Salvador opposed; and another the following year with only the US and Israel opposed. Little of this was even reported, and the matter has disappeared from history.

Washington's reaction to the orders of the World Court and the Security Council was to escalate the terrorist war, while also issuing official orders to its forces to go "after soft targets" and to avoid the Nicaraguan army.[67] State Department spokesperson Charles Redman confirmed and justified the new and more extreme terrorist programs, issuing a statement that "would do credit to George Orwell's Ministry of Truth," Americas Watch responded, adding that Redman's conception of "legitimate target" would justify terrorist attacks on Israeli collectives—or on US civilian targets, for that matter.

New Republic editor Michael Kinsley criticized human rights organizations for becoming too emotional about State Department justifications for terrorist attacks on "soft targets." We should instead adopt a "sensible policy [that meets] the test of cost-benefit analysis," he advised, an analysis of "the amount of blood and misery that will be poured in, and the likelihood that democracy will emerge at the other end"—"democracy" as US elites understand the term, an interpretation illustrated quite clearly in the region. It is taken for granted that they have the right to conduct the analysis and pursue the project if it passes their tests.[68]

And it did pass their tests. In 1990, with a " 'gun to their heads' [as] was clear to many impartial observers" (Walker), Nicaraguans succumbed and voted to turn the country over to the US-backed candidate. US elites celebrated the triumph, entranced by the new "romantic age." Commentators across the spectrum of respectable opinion enthusiastically lauded the success of the methods adopted to "wreck the economy and prosecute a long and deadly proxy war until the exhausted natives overthrow the unwanted government themselves," with a cost to us that is "minimal," leaving the victims "with wrecked bridges, sabotaged power stations, and ruined farms," and thus providing the US candidate with "a winning issue": ending the "impoverishment of the people of Nicaragua" (*Time*). We are "United in Joy" at this outcome, proud of this "Victory for U.S. Fair Play," headlines in the *New York Times* proclaimed.

The official policy of attacking soft targets relied on US control of the skies over Nicaragua and the sophisticated communications equipment provided to the terrorist forces attacking from US bases in Honduras. The Reagan administration tried the technique that was praised by CIA director Allen Dulles in Guatemala and recommended for Cuba: pressuring allies to refuse requests for military aid, so that Nicaragua would turn to the Russians for help and could then be portrayed as a tentacle of the Kremlin-sponsored conspiracy poised to destroy us. The Nicaraguan government did not rise to the bait, however. Reaganite propaganda therefore fabricated lurid tales about Soviet MiGs threatening the US from Nicaraguan bases. That is not surprising; one expects systems of vast power to be committed to lying and deceit. But the reactions are more revealing.

Hawks called for the bombing of Nicaragua in punishment for this new crime. Doves tended to be more cautious, questioning the reliability of the claims but adding that if they were accurate, then we would have to bomb Nicaragua, because the planes would be "capable against the United States" (Senator Paul Tsongas). US security would be at risk if the Nicaraguan air force obtained some vintage 1950s MiGs to defend its airspace. In contrast, there was no threat to Nicaragua's security when US client forces attack undefended civilian targets under the guidance of US planes that controlled the country's skies. Another example of "logical illogicality."

That Nicaragua might have the right to protect its airspace from ongoing US terrorist attack is next to inconceivable. The thought was virtually never voiced—which is reasonable, too, given the principle that US actions are defensive by definition so that any reaction to them is aggression, much like the "internal aggression" of the South Vietnamese in South Vietnam, "assaulting" the American defenders "from the inside," in the rhetoric of Kennedy liberals.

With Washington-style democracy and proper economic practice restored, the country sank more deeply into political and socioeconomic ruin while attention lapsed in the US. A decade after the US had regained control, half the economically active population had left the country, "often the boldest, most capable, most determined," either legally or as illegal migrant workers. Their remittances, estimated at some $800 million annually, "are what keep the damper down on uncontrollable social upheaval," the research journal of the Jesuit University reported. It also estimated that "Nicaragua's gross domestic product would have to grow 5 percent annually for the next fifty years to reattain the productive levels of 1978, before our historic underdevelopment was intensified to the extreme by the US-financed war to destroy the revolution," by the wreckage left by subsequent "globalization," and by the "massive corruption" of the post-1990 US-backed governments. That issue of the journal appeared just as the US suffered its first international terrorist atrocity on home soil.[69]

Another striking illustration of prevailing attitudes toward ter-

rorism is the warning of Bush administration officials two months
later that Nicaragua would be punished if its November 2002 election were to be won by the political forces that had dared to resist
US attack, the FSLN, and thus "do not share the values of the world
community." Washington "cannot forget that Nicaragua ended up
a refuge for violent political extremists" in the 1980s. There is some
truth to that; Managua did serve as a refuge for social democratic
political leaders, poets and writers, prominent religious figures,
human rights activists, and others fleeing the death squads and official security forces of the terrorist states installed and backed by
Washington, rather as Paris became a refuge from fascism and
Stalinism in the 1930s. We are "reminded of [the refuge] daily by
the continuing presence of some members of the FSLN leadership
... who perpetrated these abominations," the State Department
warned Nicaraguan voters. "Given their past record, why should we
believe their statements that they have changed? ... We are confident that the Nicaraguan people will reflect on the nature and history of the candidates and choose wisely."[70]

Nicaraguans hardly needed the warnings. Their history sufficed
to tell them that, should they misbehave by electing the wrong government, as they did in 1984 in an election that the US refused to
recognize because it could not control the outcome (and has
therefore been excised from history),[71] then Nicaragua will again be
considered a state that supports terrorism, with the penalties that
ensue, which are not trivial.

Citing Washington's cynical warnings, the editors of Envío
observed that "it is a safe bet that those who took up arms at a time
when [US] state terrorism was killing, torturing, forcing disappear-
ances and closing all political spaces will now be reclassified as terrorists." The "unimaginable and singular tragedy of September 11
surely felt like the end of the world ... in the targeted country," the
editors observed. But "Nicaragua experiences the end of the world
nearly every day [after] the destruction the US government has
repeatedly wreaked on this country and its people." The atrocities
of 9-11 may be denounced as "Armageddon," but Nicaraguans

recall that their country "lived its own Armageddon in excruciating slow motion [under US assault] and is now submerged in its dismal aftermath," having been reduced to the second poorest country in the hemisphere (after Haiti), vying with Guatemala for the distinction, also enjoying perhaps the world record for concentration of wealth.[72]

Among the victors, all of this has been effaced in the classic fashion. Nicaragua and El Salvador are remembered as "relative success stories—and precisely the kind of success stories we lack in the Middle East," to be remedied by the new crusade for "democratization."[73] One would be hard put to find a phrase within mainstream commentary suggesting that the record of international terrorism of current Bush administration officials might have some bearing on the "war on terror" they redeclared on 9-11. Among the leading figures of the redeclared war is John Negroponte, who ran the Embassy in Honduras that was the main base for the terrorist attacks on Nicaragua. He was duly chosen to oversee the diplomatic component of the current phase of the war on terror at the United Nations. Its military component is run by Donald Rumsfeld, who was Reagan's special envoy to the Middle East during the period of the worst terror there and was also delegated to establish firmer relations with Saddam Hussein. The Central American "war on terror" was supervised by Elliott Abrams. After pleading guilty to misdemeanor counts in the Iran-contra affair, Abrams received a Christmas Eve pardon from President Bush I in 1992, and was appointed by Bush II "to lead the National Security Council's office for Near East and North African affairs, . . . the senior director job [that] oversees Arab-Israeli relations and U.S. efforts to promote peace in the troubled region,"[74] a phrase drawn from Orwell, in light of the record. Abrams is joined by Otto Reich, who was charged with running an illegal covert domestic propaganda campaign against Nicaragua, appointed temporary assistant secretary for Latin American affairs under Bush II, then designated special envoy for Western Hemisphere affairs. To replace Reich as assistant secretary, the administration nominated Roger Noriega, who "served in the

State Department during the Reagan administration, helping forge fiercely anti-Communist policies toward Latin America"; in translation, terrorist atrocities.[75]

Secretary of State Powell, now cast as administration moderate, served as national security adviser during the final stage of the terror, atrocities, and undermining of diplomacy in the 1980s in Central America, and the support for the apartheid regime in South Africa. His predecessor, John Poindexter, was in charge of the Iran-contra crimes and was convicted in 1990 of five felony counts (overturned mostly on technicalities). Bush II placed him in charge of directing the Pentagon's Total Information Awareness program, under which, the ACLU observes, "every American—from the Nebraskan farmer to the Wall Street banker—will find themselves under the accusatory cyber-stare of an all-powerful national security apparatus."[76] The rest of the list is mostly similar.

Nicaraguans were the lucky ones during the first phase of the "war on terror." They at least had an army to defend them against state-supported terrorism. In neighboring states the terrorists *were* the security forces. El Salvador became the leading recipient of US military aid and training (Israel-Egypt aside) by the mid-1980s, as atrocities were peaking. Congress imposed human rights conditions on aid to Guatemala, compelling the Reaganites to resort to their international terror network to take over the task, including Argentine neo-Nazis (until they were overthrown at home), Israel, Taiwan, and others experienced in "counterterror." The torture and destruction of the civilian population were consequently much worse.

The editors of *Envío* add that in December 1989, "the government of George Bush Sr. ordered the invasion of Panama, a military operation that bombed civilian neighborhoods and killed thousands of Panamanians just to flush out a single man, Manuel Noriega. Was that not state terrorism?"[77] A fair question, though much stronger terms are used when those who lack the power to control history carry out such actions.

Though "disappeared" by the victors in routine fashion, the crimes are not forgotten by the victims. Panamanians, too, while condemning the 9-11 attacks, recalled the death of perhaps thousands of poor people in the course of Operation Just Cause, undertaken to kidnap a disobedient thug who was sentenced to life imprisonment in Florida for crimes mostly committed while he was on the CIA payroll. One journalist remarked "how much alike [the victims of 9-11] are to the boys and girls . . . to the mothers and the grandfathers and the little old grandmothers, all of them also innocent . . . [when the] terror was called Just Cause and the terrorist called liberator."[78]

Perhaps such memories help account for the remarkably low level of international support for the US bombing of Afghanistan. In Latin America, where there is the longest experience of US violence, support was least, scarcely detectable. Latin Americans hardly have to be reminded by Carlos Salinas, former director of government relations for Amnesty International, that they "know better than perhaps most people that the U.S. government is one of the biggest sponsors of terrorism."[79]

It is easy to dismiss the world as "irrelevant" or consumed by "paranoid anti-Americanism," but perhaps not wise.

Chapter 5

The Iraq Connection

After eight years, more reactionary sectors of the Reagan-Bush I administrations regained political power in the contested 2000 election. They recognized that the 9-11 atrocities provided them with an opportunity to pursue long-standing goals with even greater intensity, closely following the script of their earlier tenure in office.

THE SCRIPT: INTERNATIONAL

For George Bush the younger, PR specialists and speechwriters have constructed the image of a simple man with a direct line to heaven, who relies on his "gut instincts" as he strides forward to "rid the world of evildoers" while contemplating his "visions" and "dreams," a caricature of ancient epics and children's tales, with an admixture of cowboy fiction. The first time around, the imagery constructed for the leader was not very different, and the rhetoric no less fevered: all states must band together to combat "the evil scourge of terrorism" (Reagan), particularly state-backed international terrorism, a "plague spread by depraved opponents of civilization itself," in a "return to barbarism in the modern age" (George Shultz).[1]

Important questions should have arisen at once: What constitutes terrorism? How does it differ from aggression or resistance? The operative answers are revealing, but the questions never entered the arena of public discussion. A convenient definition was adopted: terrorism is what our leaders declare it to be. Period. The practice continues as the war is redeclared.[2]

In the 1980s the two main foci of the "war on terror" were Central America and the Mideast/Mediterranean region. In Central America, as discussed, the war on terror instantly became a barbaric terrorist war, hailed as a grand success and discarded from history. In the Middle East, as we shall see, the commanders in Washington and their local associates were again responsible for crimes far exceeding anything charged to their official enemies. The facts are particularly noteworthy because the retail terror they were opposing was inflated by their propaganda systems to become the lead story of the year by the mid-1980s, an impressive achievement.

Turning elsewhere, during the Reagan years Washington's South African ally had primary responsibility for more than 1.5 million dead and $60 billion in damage in the newly liberated Portuguese colonies of Angola and Mozambique. A UNICEF study estimated a death toll of 850,000 infants and young children in these two countries—150,000 in 1988 alone, reversing gains of the early post-independence years primarily through the weapon of "mass terrorism." That is putting aside South Africa's practices within its own borders, where it was defending civilization against the onslaughts of Nelson Mandela's African National Congress, one of the "more notorious terrorist groups," according to a 1988 Pentagon report. Meanwhile the Reaganites evaded sanctions, increased trade, and provided valuable diplomatic support for South Africa.[3]

One of the endeavors of the current incumbents has become well known: the success of the CIA and its associates during the 1980s in recruiting radical Islamists and organizing them into a military and terrorist force. The goal, according to Carter's national security adviser, Zbigniew Brzezinski, was "to draw the Russians into the Afghan trap," initially by secret operations that would induce them to invade Afghanistan. The Carter-Brzezinski reaction to the subsequent invasion was based on a complete misinterpretation of the

Russian decision to intervene, according to the very knowledgeable analyst Raymond Garthoff. The Russian decision was undertaken reluctantly and with narrow and defensive objectives, as "is now clearly established in the Soviet archives," he writes. For the Reaganites, who took over a year later, "the single aim," he continues, was "bleeding the Russians and pillorying the Soviets in world opinion." The immediate result was a war that devastated Afghanistan, with even worse consequences after the Russians withdrew and Reagan's jihadis took over. The long-term result was two decades of terror and civil war. In the 1980s there was threat of worse, as "CIA-backed incursions of Afghan guerillas and saboteurs into Soviet territory nearly provoked a major Soviet-Pakistani, if not Soviet-American war," with unforeseeable consequences.[4]

After the Russians withdrew, the terror organizations recruited, armed, and trained by the US and its allies (among them Al Qaeda and similar jihadis) turned their attention elsewhere, inflaming the India-Pakistan conflict with "an unprecedented terrorist offensive in India in March 1993," and repeatedly bringing the region to the brink of nuclear war in later years as the flames spread. A month earlier, related groups had come close to blowing up the World Trade Center, following a "formula taught in CIA manuals." The planning was traced to followers of Sheikh Omar Abdel Rahman, who had been helped to enter the US and was protected within the country by the CIA.[5] Other consequences around the world need not be reviewed.

Also at least partially familiar is the long-standing support of the present incumbents for Saddam Hussein, often attributed to obsession with Iran. That policy continued without change after Iran's capitulation in the Iran-Iraq war, because of "our duty to support U.S. exporters," the State Department explained in early 1990—adding the usual boilerplate about how aiding Saddam would improve human rights, regional stability, and peace. In October 1989, long after the war with Iran was over and more than a year after Saddam's gassing of the Kurds, President Bush I issued a national security directive declaring that "normal relations between the United States and Iraq would serve our longer-term interests and promote stability in both the Gulf and the Middle East." He took the occasion of the invasion of Panama shortly after to lift a ban on loans to Iraq.

The US offered subsidized food supplies that Saddam's regime badly needed after its destruction of Kurdish agricultural production, along with advanced technology and biological agents adaptable to WMD. The warmth of the relations was indicated when a delegation of senators, led by Majority Leader and future Republican presidential candidate Bob Dole, visited Saddam in April 1990. They conveyed President Bush's greetings and assured Saddam that his problems did not lie with the US government but with "the haughty and pampered press." Senator Alan Simpson advised Saddam to "invite them to come here and see for themselves" to overcome their misconceptions. Dole assured Saddam that a commentator on Voice of America who had been critical of him had been removed.[6]

Saddam was not the only monster who won the acclaim of the current incumbents. Among others were Ferdinand Marcos, "Baby Doc" Duvalier, and Nicolae Ceauşescu; all were overthrown from within, despite strong US support until their fate was sealed. Other favorites included Indonesia's President Suharto, who competed with Saddam in barbarism. The first head of state honored with a visit to Bush the elder's White House was Mobutu Sese Seko of Zaire, another high-ranking killer, torturer, and plunderer. The South Korean dictators also received Washington's strong support until US-backed military rule was finally overthrown in 1987 by popular movements. Even minor thugs could be assured of a warm welcome as long as they were performing their function. Secretary of State Shultz was so enamored of Manuel Noriega that he flew to Panama to congratulate him after he had stolen an election by fraud and violence, praising the gangster for "initiating the process of democracy." Later Noriega lost his usefulness in the contra war and other enterprises, and was transferred to the category of "evil"— although, like Saddam, his worst crimes were behind him. He then became the target of invasion and kidnapping from the Vatican

Embassy in Operation Just Cause, with consequences already mentioned.[7]

Some of these rulers easily matched Saddam in internal terror. Ceauşescu provides an instructive case. Under his rule, the population lived in terror of his dread security forces, renowned for their torture and barbarism. A week after he was overthrown in an unanticipated popular revolt in December 1989, the *Washington Post* described how he had "destroy[ed] the economic, intellectual, and artistic fabric of Romania," compiling a "ghastly record in human rights."

President Bush II spoke the truth when he made "a Kennedyesque appearance" at Liberation Square in Bucharest, praising the "nation that just twelve years ago deposed its own iron-fisted ruler, Nicolae Ceauşescu." It was a dramatic occasion: "With a cold rain pelting his black raincoat and uncovered head, Bush said, 'You know the difference between good and evil, because you have seen evil's face. The people of Romania understand that aggressive dictators cannot be appeased or ignored. They must always be opposed.' "[8]

The president and his admirers failed to mention just how his father and his own colleagues had honored the prescription that iron-fisted tyrants like Ceauşescu "must always be opposed." The answer turns out to be a familiar one: by supporting them. We confront "evil's face" by lending it a willing hand, at least if there is something to gain. The immediate post-revolution *Washington Post* article just cited was correct in reporting that "it is nice that President Bush [I] has offered to establish diplomatic relations with [Romania's] hastily organized Council of National Salvation, but that does not absolve the West for its role in helping to maintain this tyrant in recent years"—a message that seems to have gone the way of other unacceptable insights into the real world.

In 1983, Vice President Bush expressed his admiration for Ceauşescu's political and economic progress and "respect for human rights." Two years later Reagan's ambassador resigned because of Washington's objections to his concern for human rights. Shortly after, Secretary of State Shultz praised Romania as among the "good

Communists," rewarding Ceauşescu with a visit and economic favors. So matters continued until the tyrant was overthrown—by Romanians, as in the case of other killers and torturers in the Reagan-Bush entourage.

As soon as its favorite "good Communist" was eliminated, Washington announced that a "terrible burden" had been lifted from Romania, while at the same time lifting its ban on loans to Saddam Hussein in order to achieve the "goal of increasing US exports and put us in a better position to deal with Iraq regarding its human rights record," the State Department explained with a straight face.[9]

As always, the US leadership can confidently take credit for the overthrow of the tyrants it supported until the very end. Saddam Hussein has joined "the pantheon of failed brutal dictators" whom the US has deposed, Donald Rumsfeld proudly announced, including Ceauşescu in the pantheon. On the same day as Rumsfeld's declaration, Paul Wolfowitz explained that his love of democracy was honed "during his formative years in the Reagan administration, when he was the State Department's chief Asia hand," praising the monstrous Suharto and supporting the brutal and corrupt Marcos, whose fall, he now claims, shows that democracy "needs the prodding of the US"[10]— which backed Marcos until he could no longer be sustained in the face of popular opposition joined even by the business classes and the army. The other examples are equally convincing.

As the rogues' gallery of past friends fades into oblivion, new favorites take their place. Among them the Central Asian dictators— Uzbekistan's Islam Karimov, Turkmenistan's Saparmurat Niyazov, and others—who were becoming even more brutal and repressive as they were welcomed as participants in the redeclared "war on terror," also reinforcing the US position in a region of considerable material wealth and strategic significance. Or, in another corner of the world rich in coveted oil, there is Teodoro Obiang of Equatorial Guinea, who ranks high in the competition among bloody tyrants and was duly received with full honors by President Bush in September 2002, shortly before he was reelected to a seven-year term with 97 percent of the vote.

An enthusiastic welcome has also been extended to Algeria,

which had already been singled out for praise by Clinton's State Department for its achievements in combating terror—meaning, its horrendous record of state terrorist atrocities. Bush carried support for terror and torture to new extremes, offering military aid and other assistance to the Algerian government. Washington "has much to learn from Algeria on ways to fight terrorism," we learn from William Burns, US assistant secretary of state for the Middle East. "Mr. Burns is right," Robert Fisk comments. "America has much to learn from the Algerians," including the barbaric techniques of torture that Fisk and a few other journalists have been exposing for years and that are now confirmed by Algerian army defectors in London and Paris. "Up to 200,000 Algerians have been slaughtered in the eleven years since the military cancelled that country's first democratic elections because an Islamist party won," Lara Marlowe writes. "If Algeria is the US model for countering Islamic fundamentalism, heaven help us all."[11]

The sample above illustrates the consistency of the foreign policy record of the current incumbents. The domestic record displays a similar consistency.

THE SCRIPT: DOMESTIC

The Reagan years saw a continuation of the relatively poor economic performance of the 1970s. Growth overwhelmingly benefited the very rich, unlike the "golden age" of the fifties and sixties, when it was evenly spread across the population. During the Reagan-Bush years real wages stagnated or declined along with benefits; working hours increased; and employers were given free rein to ignore protection for labor organizing. The policies were, naturally, unpopular. As the Bush I administration reached its final days, Reagan was ranked alongside Nixon as the least popular living ex-president.[12]

It is not easy, under such conditions, to maintain political power. Only one good method is known: inspire fear. That tactic was employed throughout the Reagan-Bush years, as the leadership conjured up one devil after another to frighten the populace into obedience.

The threats to Americans during the first war on terror were immense. By November 1981, Libyan hit men were roaming the streets of Washington to assassinate the president, who courageously faced down the scoundrel Qaddafi. From the first moment, the administration recognized Libya to be a defenseless punching bag, and therefore set up confrontations in which many Libyans could be killed, hoping for a Libyan response that could be exploited to induce fear.

Before Americans could breathe a sigh of relief over the president's lucky escape from the Libyan hit men, Qaddafi was on the march again, this time invading Sudan across 600 miles of desert, with the air forces of the US and its allies standing by helplessly. Qaddafi also allegedly concocted a plot to overthrow the government of Sudan so subtle that Sudanese and Egyptian intelligence knew nothing about it, as discovered by the few US reporters who took the trouble to investigate. The subsequent US show of force enabled Secretary of State Shultz to announce that Qaddafi "is back in his box where he belongs" because Reagan acted "quickly and decisively," demonstrating "the strength of the cowboy" that so entranced worshipful intellectuals (Paul Johnson, in this case). The episode was quickly relegated to oblivion once its purposes had been served.[13]

Just as the early Libyan threats subsided, another even more dangerous one appeared: an air base in Grenada that the Russians could use to bomb us. Fortunately, our leader came to the rescue in the nick of time. After turning down offers for peaceful settlement on US terms, Washington landed 6,000 elite forces, who were able to overcome the resistance of a few dozen lightly armed, middle-aged Cuban construction workers, and we were at last "standing tall," the gallant cowboy in the White House proclaimed.[14]

But the threats were not over. Soon Nicaraguans were looming on the horizon, only two days' driving time from Harlingen, Texas, waving their copies of *Mein Kampf*. Fortunately, the commander in chief, recalling Churchill's stand against the Nazis, refused to surrender and was able to fend off the threatening hordes, even though they were being supplied by Qaddafi in his campaign to "expel America from the world."[15]

As the White House sought to mobilize congressional support for an intensified attack on Nicaragua in 1986, the Libyan threat was conjured up again with deadly US provocations in the Gulf of Sidra, followed by the bombing of Libya on prime-time TV, killing dozens, on no credible pretext. The official stance was that Article 51 of the UN Charter accords us the right to use violence "in self-defense against future attack." That was perhaps the first explicit formulation of the doctrine of "preventive war," and the end of any hopes of a world of order and law, if taken at all seriously. And it was. *New York Times* legal analyst Anthony Lewis praised the Reagan administration for relying "on a legal argument that violence against the perpetrators of repeated violence is justified as an act of self-defense." Imagine the consequences if others were powerful enough to adopt the Reagan-Lewis doctrine.[16]

So matters continued through the decade. The European tourist industry went into periodic decline, as Americans were too frightened to travel to European cities because they might be attacked by crazed Arabs or other demons. Grave threats were concocted at home as well. Crime in the US is not very different from other industrial countries. Fear of crime, however, is much higher. The same is true of drugs: a problem in other societies, an imminent danger to our very existence in the US. It is easy for political leaders to use the media to whip up fear of these and other menaces. Campaigns are mounted periodically, when required by domestic political needs. Bush I's racist Willie Horton escapade in the 1988 election campaign is a famous example.

The September 1989 redeclaration of the "drug war" was another striking illustration. In the face of substantial evidence to the contrary, the administration dramatically proclaimed that Hispanic narcotraffickers were a menace to our society. Officials could be confident that the tactic would succeed, as explained by journalist and editor Hodding Carter, former assistant secretary of state in the Carter administration. It's a "lead-pipe cinch," he wrote, that "the mass media in America have an overwhelming tendency to jump up and down and bark in concert whenever the White House—any White House—snaps its fingers."

The campaign was a grand success—apart from affecting drug use. Fear of drugs instantly shot to the lead of public concerns. The stage was set for escalating the campaign to remove superfluous people from city streets to the new prisons that were rapidly being built; and to go on to Operation Just Cause, the glorious invasion of Panama on grounds of Noriega's involvement with drug trafficking, among other reasons. At the same time, the Bush administration was threatening Thailand with severe sanctions if it placed barriers on import of a far more lethal US-produced substance, tobacco. But all this passed in silence.

In the case of Panama, too, there was a knockdown legal argument for invasion. UN ambassador Thomas Pickering instructed the Security Council that Article 51 of the UN Charter "provides for the use of armed force to defend a country, to defend our interests and our people," and to prevent "its territory from being used to smuggle drugs into the US"—in this case, by reinstating the white elite of bankers and businessmen, many of whom were themselves suspected of narcotrafficking and money laundering and who soon lived up to their reputation, US government agencies reported.[17]

Throughout, the legal arguments keep to a principle enunciated by the distinguished Israeli statesman Abba Eban: in "determining the legal basis" for some intended action, "one might work backward from the action one wished to take to find a legal justification."[18]

The script has been followed fairly closely as much the same elements gained a hold on political power in the 2000 election. In 1981 they had combined a vast increase in military spending with tax cuts, calculating "that growing hysteria over the ensuing deficit would create powerful pressures to cut federal [social] spending, and thus, perhaps, enable the Administration to accomplish its goal of rolling back the New Deal." Bush II followed the pattern with tax cuts overwhelmingly benefiting the very rich, and "the biggest surge in federal spending in twenty years,"[19] largely military, hence indirectly high-tech industry.

Government deficits require "fiscal discipline," which translates into cutbacks for services for the general population. The adminis-

tration's own economists estimate the bills that the government
will be unable to pay at $44 trillion. Their study was to be
included in the annual budget report published in February 2003
but was removed, perhaps because it forecast that closing the gap
would require a huge tax increase and Bush was trying to ram
through another tax reduction, again benefiting mainly the rich.
"President Bush is working overtime to deepen our fiscal trap,"
economists Laurence Kotlikoff and Jeffrey Sachs observe, reporting
the enormous anticipated fiscal gap. Among the results, they contend, will be "massive cuts in future Social Security and Medicare
benefits." White House spokesperson Ari Fleischer agreed with the
$44 trillion estimate and implicitly conceded the accuracy of the
analysis as well: "There is no question that Social Security and
Medicare are going to present [future] generations with a crushing
debt burden unless policymakers work seriously to reform those
programs"—which does not mean funding them by progressive
taxation. The problem is deepened by the serious financial crisis of
states and cities.[20]

The editors of the staid *Financial Times* are only "stating the
obvious," economist Paul Krugman comments, when they write that
the "more extreme Republicans" with their hands on the controls
seem to want a fiscal train wreck that "offers the tantalizing prospect
of forcing [cuts on social programs] through the back door." Slated
for demolition, Krugman contends, are Medicaid, Medicare, and
Social Security, but the same may be true for the whole range of
programs of the past century that were developed to protect the
population from the ravages of private power.[21]

Eliminating social programs has goals that go well beyond concentration of wealth and power. Social Security, public schools, and
other such deviations from the "right way" that US military power
is to impose on the world, as frankly declared, are based on evil
doctrines, among them the pernicious belief that we should care, as
a community, whether the disabled widow on the other side of town
can make it through the day, or the child next door should have a
chance for a decent future. These evil doctrines derive from the prin-

ciple of sympathy that was taken to be the core of human nature
by Adam Smith and David Hume, a principle that must be driven
from the mind. Privatization has other benefits. If working people
depend on the stock market for their pensions, health care, and other
means of survival, they have a stake in undermining their own interests: opposing wage increases, health and safety regulations, and
other measures that might cut into profits that flow to the benefac-
tors on whom they must rely, in a manner reminiscent of feudalism.

After a surge of presidential popularity following 9-11, polls
revealed increasing discontent with the social and economic policies
of the administration. If there was to be any hope of maintaining
political power, the Bush forces were virtually compelled to adopt
what Anatol Lieven calls "the classic modern strategy of an endangered right-wing oligarchy, which is to divert mass discontent into
nationalism,"[22] a strategy which is second nature to them in any
event, having worked so well during their first twelve years in office.

The strategy was outlined by Karl Rove, the chief political adviser: Republicans must "go to the country on the issue of national
security" in November 2002, because voters "trust the Republican
Party" for "protecting America." Similarly, he explained, Bush will
have to be portrayed as a wartime leader for the 2004 presidential
campaign. "As long as domestic issues were dominating news coverage and political battles over the summer, Bush and his Republicans lost ground," the chief international analyst for UPI pointed
out. But the "imminent threat" of Iraq was conjured up just in time,
in September 2002. Recognizing its vulnerability on domestic issues,
"the administration is campaigning to sustain and increase its power
on a policy of international adventurism, new radical preemptive
military strategies, and a hunger for a politically convenient and
perfectly timed confrontation with Iraq."[23]

For the midterm electoral campaign, the tactic worked—just.
Even though voters "believe that Republicans are more concerned
about large corporations than about ordinary Americans," they trust
the Republicans on national security.[24]

In September, the National Security Strategy was announced.

Manufactured fear provided enough of a popular base for the invasion of Iraq, instituting the new norm of aggressive war at will, and afforded the administration enough of a hold on political power so that it could proceed with a harsh and unpopular domestic agenda. Again, the script of the first tenure in power is being followed closely, though now with greater fervor, fewer external constraints, and considerably greater threats to peace.

INSIGNIFICANT RISKS

The war with Iraq was undertaken with the recognition that it might well lead to proliferation of WMD and terror, risks considered insignificant compared with the prospect of gaining control over Iraq, firmly establishing the norm of preventive war, and strengthening the hold on domestic power.

Evidence as to how seriously real security threats ranked on the priority list was provided immediately after the announcement of the imperial grand strategy on September 17, 2002. The administration at once publicly "abandoned an international effort to strengthen the Biological Weapons Convention against germ warfare," advising allies that further discussions would have to be delayed for four years.[25] As noted, in mid-October it was learned that during an earlier episode of playing with fire, the world was brought ominously close to nuclear war. Ten days later, on October 23, the UN Disarmament Committee adopted two crucial resolutions. The first called for stronger measures to prevent the militarization of space and thereby to "avert a grave danger for international peace and security." The second reaffirmed the 1925 Geneva Protocol "prohibiting the use of poisonous gases and bacteriological methods of warfare." Both passed unanimously, with two abstentions: the US and Israel. US abstention amounts to a veto: typically, a double veto, banning the events from reporting and history. In the mainstream media, there was no mention of these failed attempts by the rest of the world to prevent serious threats to survival.

The meager press coverage of the startling revelations at the Havana retrospective in October 2002 had little to say about the highly topical issues of international terrorism and forceful regime change, or about the Iraq connection, which was very much in the minds of the participants. On their way to Havana, they had surely read the letter sent by CIA director George Tenet to the Senate Intelligence Committee chair, Senator Bob Graham, reporting that although there was little likelihood that Saddam would initiate a terrorist operation with conventional weapons or any chemical or biological weapons he might have, the probability would rise to "pretty high" in the event of US attack. The FBI also reported concerns "that a war with Iraq could trigger new domestic terrorism risks," as did the head of Homeland Security. The leading international military-intelligence journal and allied intelligence agencies drew the same conclusions, adding the further observation that a US attack could "globalize anti-American and anti-Western sentiment. . . . Attacking Iraq would intensify Islamic terrorism, not reduce it": "a war in Iraq threatens to fuel unrest and create new terrorist threats, European security and police officials are warning their governments," recruiting new young people "to the ever-growing anti-US stand."[26]

Concurring, Richard Betts, a specialist on surprise attack and nuclear blackmail, wrote that in the event of a US invasion "Saddam will have no reason to withhold his best parting shot—which could be the use of [WMD] inside the United States"—that is, activating networks already in place. "The odds may be low," he observed: "perhaps as low" as what took place on 9-11.[27] Those who have any concern for the safety and security of the people of the United States and other likely targets would not, of course, dismiss the odds as negligible.

Mainstream experts agreed that an attack by the most powerful military force in history against a defenseless enemy might well stimulate the quest for revenge or deterrence. Prominent international relations scholars have pointed out that potential targets of US adventurism "know that the United States can be held at bay only by deterrence," primarily by WMD (Kenneth Waltz). In this way,

"American policies stimulate the vertical proliferation of nuclear weapons and promote their spreading from one country to another." The same policies stimulate terrorism: "Unsurprisingly, . . . weak states and disaffected people . . . lash out at the United States as the agent or symbol of their suffering," and if no efforts are made to address their grievances, they are likely to react with the means available to them, including terror. US intelligence added that the "deepening economic stagnation" caused by Washington's version of globalization was likely to have similar effects.[28]

These warnings were not new. It had been recognized for some time that the industrial powers were likely to lose their virtual monopoly of violence, retaining only an enormous preponderance. Well before 9-11, technical studies had concluded that "a well-planned operation to smuggle WMD into the United States would have at least a 90 percent probability of success." This has become "America's Achilles' Heel," a study with that title concluded, reviewing the many options available to terrorists. The Council on Foreign Relations Task Force study adds others. The imminence of the danger was evident after the 1993 attempt to blow up the World Trade Center, which, with better planning, might have killed tens of thousands of people, the WTC building engineers reported.[29]

It was also anticipated that an attack on Iraq might stimulate proliferation in more direct ways. Terrorism specialist Daniel Benjamin (no dove) observed that an invasion might cause "the greatest proliferation disaster in history." Saddam Hussein had proven himself to be a brutal tyrant, but a rational one. If he had chemical and biological weapons, they were kept under tight control and "subjected to a proper chain of command." He would surely not put them in the hands of the Osama bin Ladens of the world, a terrible threat to Saddam himself. But under attack, Iraqi society might collapse, and with it the controls over WMD, which might be offered to the huge "market for unconventional weapons"—a "nightmare scenario" from every point of view. Postwar investigation reveals that Benjamin's concerns may have been realized with the looting of nuclear sites.[30]

This prewar establishment critique had a number of important features. First, it echoed concerns in the same circles about the posture of a "rogue superpower" that much of the world regards as the greatest threat to world peace and "the single greatest external threat to their societies." Second, it encompassed an unusually broad spectrum of voices: the comments cited above come from US and world intelligence agencies; the world's leading military journal; the January 2003 issues of the two major national foreign policy journals; an unusual publication of the American Academy of Arts and Sciences; some of the most respected specialists on international affairs, terrorism, and strategic analysis; and even the "wizards of Davos" who dominate the world's economy. Whatever one thinks of their judgments, it would not be easy to find a historical precedent for such a critique of a planned war, just as there was no precedent at all for popular opposition to a war prior to its being officially launched.

Third, though this critique originated in the establishment, it was ignored. The administration made no effort to counter it, indeed hardly seemed to notice it, which makes sense. From a propaganda point of view, the most powerful state in history needs no justification or serious argument for its actions: declaration of noble intent should suffice. Just as the UN is informed that it can be "relevant" and authorize what we are going to do or suffer the consequences, so the world should be put on notice that the hegemonic power bears no burden of proof for its resort to violence, or any other action. It would be a derogation of authority to acknowledge, let alone refute, "critical noises" (to borrow McGeorge Bundy's derisive phrase). The critics are right that the superpower stance might lead to self-destruction, but such concerns have commonly not been a high priority of leaders.

In the present case, the administration was surely aware, even without warnings from respected authorities, that its planned war against Iraq and other related actions were likely to increase the risks of proliferation of WMD and terror against the US and its allies. But evidently it assigns low priority to such threats compared with other goals. Furthermore, though planners of course do not welcome the proliferation of WMD and terrorism, they know that they can exploit such developments for their own purposes, both global and domestic. Even the fear they elicit throughout the world is quite acceptable: they are not trying to be loved, but obeyed, and if this is achieved by fear, that is fine—another contribution to "maintaining credibility."

As for the goals, senior Middle East correspondent and analyst Youssef Ibrahim was no doubt oversimplifying when he identified them as "bolstering the president's popularity" for short-term political gain and "turning a 'friendly' Iraq into a private American oil pumping station."[31] But there is good reason to believe that his observations at least point in the right direction. Maintaining a hold on political power and enhancing US control of the world's primary energy sources are major steps toward the twin goals that have been declared with considerable clarity: to institutionalize a radical restructuring of domestic society that will roll back the progressive reforms of a century, and to establish an imperial grand strategy of permanent world domination. Compared with such ends, the risks may well seem insignificant.

THE WILD MEN IN THE WINGS

Establishment critics and the White House tended to focus on the same issues as the Security Council debates and the inspections: the Iraqi threat, WMD, and the subcategory of terror that enters the canon. None of the debates gave more than a passing nod to "democratization" or "liberation" or any other issues that lie beyond the potential threat to the US and its allies. There was little discussion, for example, of the possible effects of war on the population of Iraq, except among "the wild men in the wings," to borrow the term used by McGeorge Bundy to refer to those who felt that more was involved in the Vietnam War than military success and its cost to the invaders. As Washington marched resolutely to war against Iraq, the wild men and women were again looking beyond the narrow question of the costs to themselves.

With the Iraqi people at the edge of survival after a decade of destructive sanctions, international aid and medical agencies warned that a war might lead to a serious humanitarian catastrophe. Switzerland hosted a meeting of thirty countries to prepare for what might lie ahead. The US alone refused to attend. Participants, including the other four permanent Security Council members, "warned of devastating humanitarian consequences of a war." Former assistant secretary of defense Kenneth Bacon, head of the Washington-based Refugees International, predicted that "a war will generate huge flows of refugees and a public health crisis." Meanwhile, US plans for humanitarian relief in a postwar Iraq were criticized by international aid agencies as "short on detail, woefully lacking in money, and overly controlled by the military." UN officials complained, "There is a studied lack of interest [in Washington] in a warning call we are trying to deliver to the people planning for war, about what its consequences might be."[32]

Horrifying and brutal as Saddam Hussein's regime was, he nevertheless did direct oil profits to internal development. "A tyrant, at the head of a regime that has turned violence into an instrument of state," with a "hideous human rights record," he nevertheless "had hoisted half the country's population into the middle class, and Arabs the world over . . . came to study at Iraqi universities."[33] The 1991 war, involving the purposeful destruction of water, power, and sewage systems, took a terrible toll, and the sanctions regime imposed by the US and UK drove the country to the level of bare survival.[34] As one illustration, UNICEF's *2003 Report on the State of the World's Children* states that "Iraq's regression over the past decade is by far the most severe of the 193 countries surveyed," with the child death rate, "the best single indicator of child welfare," increasing from 50 to 133 per 1,000 live births, placing Iraq below every country outside Africa apart from Cambodia and Afghanistan. Two hawkish military analysts observe that "economic sanctions may well have been a necessary [sic] cause of the deaths of more people in Iraq than have been slain by all so-called weapons of mass destruction throughout history," in the hundreds of thousands according to conservative estimates.[35]

No Westerners know Iraq better than Denis Halliday and Hans von Sponeck, the respected UN diplomats who were the chief UN humanitarian coordinators, with an international staff of hundreds of investigators traveling daily through the country. Both resigned in protest at what Halliday described as the "genocidal" character of the US-UK sanctions regime. Both reject claims that food and medicine were being withheld by the authorities. Their successor, Tun Myat, backed their view, describing the Iraqi system "as the best distribution system that he had ever seen in his life, as a World Food Program official." The senior UN World Food Program official reported that the WFP had conducted more than a million inspections of the system and "uncovered no significant evidence of fraud or favoritism." He added that there was "no way we could create something else that would work half as well" as the Iraqi system, which is "the most efficient in the world," and that "the risk of a large-scale humanitarian crisis" would increase if anything happened to disrupt it.[36]

As Halliday, von Sponeck, and others had pointed out for years, the sanctions devastated the population while strengthening Saddam Hussein and his clique, also increasing the dependency of the Iraqi people on the tyrant for their survival. Von Sponeck, who resigned in 2000, reported that the US and UK "systematically tried to prevent [him and Halliday] from briefing the Security Council ... because they didn't want to hear what we had to say" about the savagery of the sanctions.[37] The US media apparently agree. Though the expert knowledge of the UN coordinators is without parallel, Americans have had to turn elsewhere to hear what they had to say, even at a moment of laserlike fixation on Iraq. Discussion of the effects of the sanctions has been minimal and apologetic, the usual procedure with regard to the crimes of one's own state.

Academic researcher Joy Gordon found that even the information that does reach the Security Council "is kept from public scrutiny," though she learned enough, as have others, to reveal a shameful record of deliberate cruelty and efforts pursued "aggressively throughout the last decade to purposefully minimize the humanitarian goods that enter the country ... in the face of enormous human suffering, including massive increases in child mortality and wide-

spread epidemics." The US blocked water tankers from reaching
Iraq on grounds so spurious that they were rejected by the UN arms
experts, "this during a time when the major cause of child deaths
was lack of access to clean drinking water, and when the country
was in the midst of a drought." Washington insisted that vaccines
for infant diseases be withheld until it was compelled to back down
in the face of vigorous protest by UNICEF and the World Health
Organization, supported by European biological-weapons experts,
who charged that the dual-use claims of the US were "flatly impossible."[38]

The International Red Cross, drawing on its own intimate famil-
iarity with the country, concluded in 1999 that after a decade of
sanctions, "the Iraqi economy lies in tatters" and "the 'oil-for-food'
programme, introduced by UN Resolution 986 in 1995, has not
halted the collapse of the health system and the deterioration of
water supplies, which together pose one of the gravest threats to the
health and well-being of the civilian population." Aid agencies "can
only hope to mitigate some of the worst effects of the sanctions [and]
cannot nearly cover the overwhelming needs of twenty-two million
people," the ICRC reported.[39]

Defenders of the sanctions regime argued that the appalling situation was Saddam's fault, because of his refusal to comply fully
with UN resolutions and his construction of palaces and monuments
to himself, and so on (funded by money diverted from smuggling
and other illegal operations, according to the testimony of UN
humanitarian coordinators and the World Food Program). The
argument, then, was that we had to punish Saddam for his crimes
by crushing his victims and strengthening their torturer. By similar
logic, if a criminal hijacks a school bus, we should blow it up and
murder the passengers, but rescue and reward the hijacker, justifying
the actions on grounds that it was his fault.[40]

"Studied lack of interest" in the likely consequences of war for
the population of the country to be invaded is conventional. The
same was true when, five days after 9-11, Washington demanded
that Pakistan eliminate "truck convoys that provide much of the

food and other supplies to Afghanistan's civilian population," and
caused the withdrawal of aid workers along with severe reduction
in food supplies, thereby leaving "millions of Afghans . . . at grave
risk of starvation"[41]—risk of what should properly have been
termed "silent genocide." Estimates of the numbers "at grave risk
of starvation" rose from 5 million before 9-11 to 7.5 million a
month later. The threat and then reality of bombing elicited sharp
protests from aid organizations and warnings of what might ensue,
which received only scattered and very partial attention, and little
reaction.

Perhaps it's worth repeating the obvious. One always hopes that
worst-case scenarios will not materialize, and every effort should
always be dedicated to that end. But exactly as in the case of Khrushchev's dispatch of missiles to Cuba, which could have led to
nuclear war but didn't, it is the range of likely possibilities that
determines the evaluation of policy choices that are made, at least
for those capable of entertaining elementary moral standards. Triv-
ially, that judgment remains true whatever the outcome, a truism
we understand well enough when applied to official enemies but find
much harder to apply to ourselves.

DEMOCRACY AND HUMAN RIGHTS

As noted, establishment critics restricted their comments regarding
the attack on Iraq to the administration arguments they took to be
seriously intended: disarmament, deterrence, and links to terrorism.
They scarcely made reference to liberation, democratization of the
Middle East, and other matters that would render irrelevant the
inspections and indeed everything that took place at the Security
Council or within governmental domains. The reason, perhaps, is
that they recognized that lofty rhetoric is the obligatory accompa-
niment of virtually any resort to force and therefore carries no information. The rhetoric is doubly hard to take seriously in the light of
the display of contempt for democracy that accompanied it, not to
speak of the past record and current practices.

Critics are also aware that nothing has been heard from the present incumbents—with their alleged concern for Iraqi democracy—to indicate that they have any regrets for their previous support for Saddam Hussein (or others like him, still continuing) nor have they shown any signs of contrition for having helped him develop WMD when he really was a serious danger. Nor has the current leadership explained when, or why, they abandoned their 1991 view that "the best of all worlds" would be "an iron-fisted Iraqi junta without Saddam Hussein" that would rule as Saddam did but not make the error of judgment in August 1990 that ruined Saddam's record.[42]

At the time, the incumbents' British allies were in the opposition and therefore more free than the Thatcherites to speak out against Saddam's British-backed crimes. Their names are noteworthy by their absence from the parliamentary record of protests against these crimes, including Tony Blair, Jack Straw, Geoff Hoon, and other leading figures of New Labour. In December 2002, Jack Straw, then foreign minister, released a dossier of Saddam's crimes. It was drawn almost entirely from the period of firm US-UK support, a fact overlooked with the usual display of moral integrity. The timing and quality of the dossier raised many questions, but those aside, Straw failed to provide an explanation for his very recent conversion to skepticism about Saddam Hussein's good character and behavior. When Straw was home secretary in 2001, an Iraqi who fled to England after detention and torture requested asylum. Straw denied his request. The Home Office explained that Straw "is aware that Iraq, and in particular the Iraqi security forces, would only convict and sentence a person in the courts with the provision of proper jurisdiction," so that "you could expect to receive a fair trial under an independent and properly constituted judiciary." Straw's conversion must, then, have been rather similar to President Clinton's discovery, sometime between September 8 and 11, 1999, that Indonesia had done some unpleasant things in East Timor in the past twenty-five years when it enjoyed decisive support from the US and Britain.[43]

Attitudes toward democracy were revealed with unusual clarity during the mobilization for war in the fall of 2002, as it became necessary to deal somehow with the overwhelming popular opposition. Within the "coalition of the willing," the US public was at least partially controlled by the propaganda campaign unleashed in September. In Britain, the population was split roughly fifty-fifty on the war, but the government maintained the stance of "junior partner" it had accepted reluctantly after World War II and had kept to even in the face of the contemptuous dismissal of British concerns by US leaders at moments when the country's very survival was at stake.

Outside the two full members of the coalition, problems were more serious. In the two major European countries, Germany and France, the official government stands corresponded to the views of the large majority of their populations, which unequivocally opposed the war. That led to bitter condemnation by Washington and many commentators. Donald Rumsfeld dismissed the offending nations as just the "Old Europe," of no concern because of their reluctance to toe Washington's line. The "New Europe" is symbolized by Italy, whose prime minister, Silvio Berlusconi, was visiting the White House. It was, evidently, unproblematic that public opinion in Italy was overwhelmingly opposed to the war.

The governments of Old and New Europe were distinguished by a simple criterion: a government joined Old Europe in its iniquity if and only if it took the same position as the vast majority of its population and refused to follow orders from Washington. Recall that the self-appointed rulers of the world—Bush, Powell, and the rest—had declared forthrightly that they intended to carry out their war whether or not the UN or anyone else "catches up" and "becomes relevant." Old Europe, mired in irrelevance, did not catch up. Neither did New Europe, at least if people are part of their countries. Poll results available from Gallup International, as well as local sources for most of Europe, West and East, showed that support for a war carried out "unilaterally by America and its allies" did not rise above 11 percent in any country. Support for a war if mandated by the UN ranged from 13 percent (Spain) to 51 percent (Netherlands).

Particularly interesting are the eight countries whose leaders declared themselves to be the New Europe, to much acclaim for their courage and integrity. Their declaration took the form of a statement calling on the Security Council to ensure "full compliance with its resolutions," without specifying the means. Their announcement threatened "to isolate the Germans and French," the press reported triumphantly, though the positions of New and Old Europe were in fact scarcely different. To ensure that Germany and France would be "isolated," they were not invited to sign the bold pronouncement of New Europe—apparently for fear that they would do so, it was later quietly indicated.[44]

The standard interpretation is that the exciting and promising New Europe stood behind Washington, thus demonstrating that "many Europeans supported the United States' view, even if France and Germany did not."[45] Who were these "many Europeans"? Checking polls, we find that in New Europe, opposition to "the United States' view" was for the most part even higher than in France and Germany, particularly in Italy and Spain, which were singled out for praise for their leadership of New Europe.

Happily for Washington, former communist countries too joined New Europe. Within them, support for the "United States' view," as defined by Powell—namely, war by the "coalition of the willing" without UN authorization—ranged from 4 percent (Macedonia) to 11 percent (Romania). Support for a war even with a UN mandate was also very low. Latvia's former foreign minister explained that we have to "salute and shout, 'Yes sir.' . . . We have to please America no matter what the cost."[46]

In brief, in journals that regard democracy as a significant value, headlines would have read that Old Europe in fact included the vast majority of Europeans, East and West, while New Europe consisted of a few leaders who chose to line up (ambiguously) with Washington, disregarding the overwhelming opinion of their own populations. But actual reporting was mostly scattered and oblique, depicting opposition to the war as a marketing problem for Washington.

Toward the liberal end of the spectrum, Richard Holbrooke stressed the "very important point [that] if you add up the population of [the eight countries of the original New Europe], it was larger than the population of those countries not signing the letter." True enough, though something is omitted: the populations were overwhelmingly opposed to the war, mostly even more so than in those countries dismissed as Old Europe.[47] At the other extreme of the spectrum, the editors of the *Wall Street Journal* applauded the statement of the eight original signers for "exposing as fraudulent the conventional wisdom that France and Germany speak for all of Europe, and that all of Europe is now anti-American." The eight honorable New European leaders showed that "the views of the Continent's pro-American majority weren't being heard," apart from the editorial pages of the *Journal,* now vindicated. The editors blasted the media to their "left"—a rather substantial segment—which "peddled as true" the ridiculous idea that France and Germany spoke for Europe, when they were clearly a pitiful minority, and peddled these lies "because they served the political purposes of those, both in Europe and America, who oppose President Bush on Iraq." This conclusion does hold if we exclude Europeans from Europe, rejecting the radical left doctrine that people have some kind of role in democratic societies.[48]

Back among the liberals, Thomas Friedman suggested that France should be driven off the Security Council and replaced by India, which is "just so much more serious than France these days. . . . France, as they say in kindergarten, does not play well with others," and therefore doesn't "line up against Saddam," but is "caught up with its need to differentiate itself from America" in an effort to be "unique." To translate, the French government acted in accord with popular opinion, which was opposed to Washington's war plans. Therefore France was "in kindergarten," though the population of New Europe must still have been in nursery school, judging by polls. India, on the other hand, is "serious," now that it is governed by a proto-fascist party that is handing the country's resources to foreign multinationals while preaching an ultra-nationalist line for domestic purposes, and had just been implicated in a horrendous massacre of Muslims in Gujarat. And as Friedman has reported enthusiastically elsewhere, India has a wonderful software industry and sectors of great wealth—uninterestingly, also hundreds of millions of people living under some of the worst conditions in the world, where the plight of women is not very different from life under the Taliban. All of this is of no concern as long as India is "serious," just as life under the Taliban was of no concern as long as they were considered cooperative.[49]

Others preferred the Kagan-Boot stand: Berlusconi, Aznar, and the other Churchillian figures who joined Washington demonstrated "unparalleled political courage" by keeping to their understanding of Right and Wrong instead of sheepishly succumbing to the "paranoid, conspiratorial anti-Americanism" of the vast majority of Europeans, who are "driven by avarice" and therefore unable to comprehend the "strain of idealism [that] makes America tick." True, those leaders made no discernible effort to enlighten the misguided populations whose views they disregarded while courageously lining up behind the most powerful military force in history. But perhaps they are not really duplicates of Churchill and FDR standing up to Hitler; rather of President Bush, whose "moral rectitude" derives from his "evangelical zeal," as proven by the fact that his PR agents tell us so.[50]

There are many other illustrations. When Gerhard Schroeder dared to take the position of the overwhelming majority of German voters in the 2002 election, he was bitterly condemned for his shocking failure of leadership, one illustration of a serious problem—"the government lives in fear of its voters"—that Germany must overcome if it wants to be accepted in the civilized world.[51]

The case of Turkey is particularly revealing. Like others throughout the region, Turks despised Saddam Hussein but did not fear him. They also strongly opposed the war: about 90 percent in January 2003, when efforts were peaking to ensure that political leaders, if not their populations, would join Washington's enterprise. The government acted in accord with the will of the people. That shows that the elected government lacks "democratic credentials," we learned on the day the polls were released, in a commentary by former ambassador to Turkey Morton Abramowitz, now a distinguished senior statesman and commentator. Ten years ago, he explained, "most of Turkey, like today, was against any involvement in a war with Iraq." But there was "one notable exception": President Turgut Ozal, a true democrat who "overrode his countrymen's pronounced preference to stay out of the Gulf war." Sadly, however, the current leadership is now "following the people when it comes to participating in another Iraq war," rather than succumbing to intense pressures from Washington. "Regrettably," Abramowitz sighed, "for the US there is no true democrat around," as there was ten years ago.[52]

Demonstrating still more clearly the lack of democratic credentials of the governing party, its unofficial leader, Recep Tayyip Erdogan, not only criticized Washington's rush to war but took a step into truly forbidden territory, criticizing "countries—the US included—that built up their own weapons of mass destruction while trying to force others to get rid of theirs."[53]

As US pressures mounted, Turkey's democracy began to improve. While popular opinion apparently turned even more strongly against the war, the government finally yielded to severe US economic and other coercion, and agreed to comply with Washington's demands over "overwhelming" popular opposition. A "Western diplomat"— probably from the US Embassy—told the press that he was "encouraged" by the decision, and found it a "very positive thing." Turkey correspondent Amberin Zaman added that

> A war against Iraq remains deeply unpopular among the Turkish population. That is why Thursday's parliamentary session was closed to the public and balloting was secret. Headlines were stinging in their criticism of Turkey's ruling Justice and Development Party on Friday. The front page of the respected daily *Radikal* said "the parliament ran away from the people."

With near unanimity, Turks opposed Washington's orders, but it was understood that the leadership must obey, and Turkey joined New Europe.[54]

Or so it appeared. In the end, the Turks proceeded to teach a lesson in democracy to the West. Parliament finally refused to allow US troops to be deployed fully in Turkey. To formulate the outcome within the conventional framework:

> The ground war has been hampered because Turkey did not accept its role as host of the northern front forces, again for political reasons. Its government was too weak in the face of antiwar feeling.[55]

The presuppositions are clear. Strong governments disregard their populations and "accept the role" assigned to them by the global ruler; weak governments succumb to the will of 95 percent of their population.

The crucial point was expressed clearly by Pentagon planner Paul Wolfowitz. He too berated the Turkish government for its misbehavior, but went on to condemn the military, who "did not play the strong leadership role that we would have expected" but betrayed weakness in permitting the government to honor near-unanimous public opinion. Turkey, he argued, had therefore to step up and say, "We made a mistake. . . . Let's figure out how we can be as helpful as possible to the Americans." Wolfowitz's stand is particularly instructive because he is presented as the leading visionary in the crusade to democratize the Middle East.[56]

The pronouncements about the Old and New Europe, and the hysteria that often accompanied them, provide some informative lessons about prevailing attitudes toward democracy among political and intellectual elites. Dislike of democracy is nothing new. For obvious reasons, it is a traditional stance of those who have a share in power and privilege. But it is rarely so starkly illuminated. That may help explain why establishment critics scarcely refer to the democratization rhetoric that accompanies the political leadership's dramatic display of contempt for democracy, evidently widely shared, to judge by commentary.

Knowledgeable commentators have pointed to the "uncomfortable dualism" in Bush's foreign policy, with "Bush the neo-Reaganite" making "ringing calls for a vigorous new democracy campaign in the Middle East," while policy imperatives tempt "Washington to put aside its democratic scruples and seek closer ties with autocracies"— as in the past, with remarkable consistency. Reviewing this "dualism" and the continuing support for brutal and repressive regimes, Thomas Carothers expressed his hope that Bush would shift to "the true spirit of President Ronald Reagan's foreign policy" with its "attempts to spread democracy."[57]

These hopes are particularly interesting because of their source. Carothers has done some of the most careful work elucidating the "true spirit" of Reaganite dedication to democracy. He combines the standpoint of a scholar with that of an insider, having been a participant in the Reagan State Department's Democracy Enhancement projects in Latin America. He regards these programs as "sincere [but a] failure." Where Washington's influence was least, in the southern cone of Latin America, there was progress toward democracy, which the Reagan administration sought to impede but finally accepted. Where Washington's influence was greatest, success was least. The reason, Carothers explains, is that the Reaganite yearning for democracy was restricted to "limited, top-down forms of democratic change that did not risk upsetting the traditional structures of power with which the United States has long been allied." Washington sought to maintain "the basic order of . . . quite undemocratic societies" and to avoid "populist-based change." Carothers recognizes that there is a liberal critique of the Reaganite approach, but he rejects it because of its "perennial weak spot": it offers no alternative. The option of allowing the population a meaningful voice in running their own affairs is not an alternative, not even to be dismissed. Carothers also does not discuss the dedicated efforts during those years to undermine the threat of more meaningful democracy where it arose.[58]

The targeted populations are well aware of the nature of the democracy that is being brought to them. It has been regularly observed that the extension of formal democracy in Latin America has been accompanied by increasing disillusionment about democracy. One reason, pointed out some years ago by Argentine political scientist Atilio Boron, is that the new wave of democratization in Latin America has coincided with neoliberal economic reforms, which undermine effective democracy.[59] The postwar Bretton Woods system was based on capital controls and relatively fixed currencies, not only in the expectation of economic benefit, as proved to be the case, but also to allow governments space to carry out highly popular social democratic policies. It was understood that the kind of financial liberalization that opened the neoliberal era in the 1970s reduces the options for democratic choice, transferring decisions to the hands of a "virtual Senate" of investors and lenders.[60] Governments now face a " 'dual constituency conundrum,' " which pits the interests of voters against foreign currency traders and hedge fund managers 'who conduct a moment-to-moment referendum' on the economic and financial policies of developing and developed nations alike," and the competition is highly unequal.

John Maynard Keynes warned seventy years ago "that nothing less than the democratic experiment in self-government was endangered by the threat of global financial market forces." The secretary-general of the Organization of American States, a strong advocate of neoliberal globalization, opened the annual session by warning that free movement of capital, "the most undesirable feature of globalisation"—in fact, its core feature—is the "greatest obstacle" to democratic governance, just as Keynes had warned.[61] The fears go back to Adam Smith. His sole use of the phrase "invisible hand" in *Wealth of Nations* is in a discussion of the harmful consequences of foreign investment, which England need not fear, he believed, because an "invisible hand" will induce investors to keep their capital at home.

The same is true of other parts of the neoliberal package: privatization, for example, reduces the arena of potential democratic choice, dramatically in the case of liberalization of "services," which has evoked enormous popular opposition. Even in narrow economic terms, the privatization programs were imposed with little if any solid empirical evidence or theoretical grounding.[62]

Disillusionment with formal democracy has been evident in the

US as well, increasing through the neoliberal period. There was much clamor about the "stolen election" of November 2000, and surprise that the public did not seem to care very much. Likely reasons are suggested by public opinion studies, which reveal that on the eve of the election, three-quarters of the population regarded it as a game played by large contributors, party leaders, and the PR industry, which crafted candidates to say "almost anything to get themselves elected." On almost all issues, citizens could not identify the stands of the candidates—as intended. Issues on which the public differs from elite opinion are generally off the agenda. Voters were directed to "personal qualities," not "issues." Among voters, heavily skewed toward the wealthy, those who recognize their class interests to be at stake tend to vote to protect those interests: for the more reactionary of the two business parties. But the general public splits its vote in other ways, sometimes, as in 2000, leading to a statistical tie. Among working people, noneconomic issues such as gun ownership and "religiosity" were leading factors, so that people often voted against their own primary interests—apparently assuming that they had little choice. In 2000, feelings of "powerlessness" reached the highest level recorded, over 50 percent.[63]

What remains of democracy is largely the right to choose among commodities. Business leaders have long explained the need to impose on the population a "philosophy of futility" and "lack of purpose in life," to "concentrate human attention on the more superficial things that comprise much of fashionable consumption."[64] Deluged by such propaganda from infancy, people may then accept their meaningless and subordinate lives and forget ridiculous ideas about managing their own affairs. They may abandon their fate to corporate managers and the PR industry and, in the political realm, to the self-described "intelligent minorities" who serve and administer power.

From this perspective, conventional in elite opinion, the November 2000 elections did not reveal a flaw of US democracy, but rather its triumph. And generalizing, it is fair to hail the triumph of democracy throughout the hemisphere, and elsewhere, even though the populations do not see it that way.

LIBERATION FROM TYRANNY: CONSTRUCTIVE
SOLUTIONS

The implausibility of the belief that Washington is suddenly concerned with democracy and human rights in Iraq, or elsewhere,
should not prevent the "wild men in the wings" from persisting in
their commitment to these ends and, to the extent possible, exerting
influence in that direction.

In the case of Iraq, there was always good reason to take seriously
the conclusions of the most knowledgeable observers that a "constructive solution" to regime change in Iraq "would be to lift the
economic sanctions that have impoverished society, decimated the
Iraqi middle class and eliminated any possibility for the emergence
of alternative leadership," while "twelve years of sanctions have
only strengthened the current regime" (Hans von Sponeck). Furthermore, the sanctions compelled the population to depend for survival on the reigning tyranny, reducing even more the likelihood of
a constructive solution. "We have sustained [the regime and] denied
the opportunities for change," Denis Halliday added: "I believe if
the Iraqis had their economy, had their lives back, and had their
way of life restored, *they* would take care of the form of governance
that they want, that they believe is suitable to their country."[65]

Were these illusions? The historical record hardly suggests so.
Again, consider the fate of the miserable tyrants supported by the
current incumbents until the very end of their bloody rule, all overthrown by internal revolt. The case of Ceauşescu, only one of many,
is particularly instructive because of the nature of the internal tyrannies.

As priorities shifted in 2002, it was claimed that those who
shared responsibility for twenty years of torture of Iraqis were entitled to resort to violence to bring about democracy. Even their consistent record of support for savagery and tyranny and their hostility
to democracy, demonstrated with unusual passion at that very
moment, provided no reason to question the proclaimed intentions.
But suspending disbelief, violence can be considered only if constructive solutions have clearly failed. Since such solutions were not even

permitted in the case of Iraq, it can hardly be maintained that the stage of last resort had been reached. That conclusion holds whatever one's subjective judgments may be about the likelihood of success, all basically irrelevant. To paraphrase Lara Marlowe, if this is to be the model for the hegemonic superpower, heaven help us all.

Since the Reagan-Bush I years (in fact before), Washington had supported Saddam Hussein in varying ways. After he stepped out of line in August 1990, policies and pretexts varied, but one element remained constant: the people of Iraq must not control their country. To repeat, the tyrant was permitted to suppress the 1991 uprising because, we were informed, Washington sought a military junta that would rule the country with an "iron fist," and if no alternative is available, Saddam would have to do. The rebels failed because "very few people outside Iraq wanted them to win"—meaning Washington and its local allies, who held the "strikingly unanimous view" that "whatever the sins of the Iraqi leader, he offered the West and the region a better hope for his country's stability than did those who have suffered his repression." It was impressive to see how uniformly all of this was suppressed in the shocked commentary and reporting on the exposure of the mass graves of the victims of Saddam's US-authorized paroxysm of terror, offered as justification for the recent war on "moral grounds" now that we have seen "the mass graves and the true extent of Saddam's genocidal evil," all known at once in 1991 but ignored because of the imperative of "stability."[66]

The uprising would have left the country in the hands of Iraqis who might have been independent of Washington. The sanctions of the following years undercut the possibility of the kind of popular revolt that had overthrown other monsters who were also strongly supported by the current incumbents. The US sought to instigate coups by groups it controlled, but a popular rebellion would not have left the US in charge. At the Azores summit in March 2003, Bush reiterated that stand, declaring that the US would invade even if Saddam and his cohorts were to leave the country.

The question of who should rule Iraq remains a prime issue of contention. Leading figures of the US-backed opposition demanded at once that the UN play a vital role in postwar Iraq and rejected US control of reconstruction or of the post-Saddam government. They strongly opposed "US hegemony over Iraq." Even Washington's chosen figures vigorously protested the plans to sideline them in favor of a US occupation. There were also indications that the Shi'ite majority might support an Islamic Republic if given a voice, hardly to the taste of Washington and its plans for the region.

There seems little reason to doubt that US policymakers will attempt to follow the consistent practice elsewhere: formal democracy is fine, but only if it obeys orders, like New Europe, or the "limited top-down" democracies in Latin America run by "the traditional structures of power with which the United States has long been allied" (Carothers). Brent Scowcroft, national security adviser for Bush I, spoke for the moderates when he observed that if there is an election in Iraq and "the radicals win. . . . We're surely not going to let them take over."[67] Thus if the Shi'ite majority has a significant voice in post-Saddam Iraq and joins others in the region in trying to improve relations with Iran, they will be "radicals" and treated accordingly. One can only expect the same if secular democrats win who prove to be "radicals," unless we decide that history is bunk.

The basic lines of US thinking were illustrated in the organization chart of the "Civil Administration of Postwar Iraq." There are sixteen boxes, each containing a name in boldface and a designation of the person's responsibility, from presidential envoy Paul Bremer at the top (answering to the Pentagon), down through the chart. Seven are generals, most of the rest government officials, none Iraqis. At the very bottom, there is a seventeenth box, about one third the size of the others, with no names, no boldface, and no functions: it reads "Iraqi ministry advisers."[68]

Some puzzled notice has been taken of the change in US policy with regard to postwar control in Iraq. Elsewhere, Washington has been happy to transfer responsibility and costs to others, but in Iraq, it has insisted on running the show itself. There is no inconsistency. "Iraq is not East Timor, Kosovo and Afghanistan," Condoleezza

Rice rightly stressed.[69] She did not spell out the distinction. Perhaps it is too transparent: Iraq is a major prize; the others are considered basket cases. Therefore Washington must be in charge, not the UN, not the Iraqi people.

Putting aside the crucial question of who will be in charge, those concerned with the tragedy of Iraq had three basic goals: (1) overthrowing the tyranny, (2) ending the sanctions that were targeting the people, not the rulers, and (3) preserving some semblance of world order. There can be no disagreement among decent people on the first two goals: achieving them is an occasion for rejoicing, particularly for those who protested US support for Saddam before his invasion of Kuwait and again immediately afterward, and opposed the sanctions regime that followed; they can therefore applaud the outcome without hypocrisy. The second goal could surely have been achieved, and possibly the first as well, without undermining the third. The Bush administration openly declared its intention to dismantle what remained of the system of world order and to control the world by force, with Iraq serving as the "petri dish," as the *New York Times* called it, for establishing the new "norms." It was that declared intention that elicited fear and often hatred throughout the world, and despair among those who are not content to "live in infamy"[70] and are concerned about the likely consequences of choosing to do so. That is of course a choice, one that is very largely in the hands of the American people.

Chapter 6

Dilemmas of Dominance

Enthusiasm about the New Europe of the former Soviet empire is not solely based on the fact that its leadership is willing to "salute and shout, 'Yes sir.' " More fundamental reasons were articulated as the European Union considered extension of membership to these countries. The US strongly supported this move. The countries of the East are "Europe's real modernizers," political commentator David Ignatius explained. "They can blow apart the bureaucratism and welfare-state culture that still hobble much of Europe" and "let free markets function the way they should"[1]—as in the US, where the economy relies heavily on the state sector, and the current incumbents broke postwar records in protectionism during their first tenure in office.

Since "the freedom-loving, technology-adapting people of the East are paid a small fraction of what workers in the West earn," Ignatius continues, they can drive all of Europe toward "the realities of modern capitalism": the American model, apparently ideal by definition. The model has per capita growth rates approximately equal to Europe's and unemployment at about the same level, along with the highest rates of inequality and poverty, the highest workloads, and some of the weakest benefits and support systems in the advanced industrial world. The median male wage in 2000 was still below the 1979 level after the late-nineties boomlet, though productivity was 45 percent higher, one sign of the sharp shift toward benefits for capital that is being accelerated more radically under Bush II.

The potential contributions of Eastern Europe to undermining quality of life for the majority in the West was recognized immediately after the fall of the Berlin Wall. The business press was exultant about the "green shoots in Communism's ruins," where "rising unemployment and pauperization of large sections of the industrial working class" meant that people were willing "to work longer hours than their pampered colleagues" in the West, at 40 percent of the wages and with few benefits. Further "green shoots" include enough repression to keep working people in line and attractive state subsidies for Western investors. These market reforms would enable Europe to "hammer away at high wages and corporate taxes, short working hours, labor immobility, and luxurious social programs." Europe would be able to follow the American pattern, where the decline of real wages in the Reagan years to the lowest level among the advanced industrial societies (apart from Britain) was "a welcome development of transcendent importance." With Communism's ruins playing something like the role of Mexico, the advantages can now be brought to Western Europe as well, driving it toward the US-British model.[2]

Communism's ruins have many advantages over the regions that have been under unbroken Western domination for centuries. Those on the eastern side of the 500-year-old fault line dividing East and West (not quite that of the Cold War, but similar) enjoyed much higher standards of health and education after the East exited from its status as the West's original "third world," and they even have the right skin color. With the return of something like traditional relationships, the East can now provide other benefits, including a huge flood of easily exploited labor. The Ukraine is now reported to be replacing Southern Europe as the source of cheap labor in the West, depriving the collapsing Ukrainian economy of its most productive workers. Like their counterparts from Central America, Ukrainian emigrants send back enormous remittances, thus helping to keep what remains of the society alive. Working and living conditions are so awful that death rates are high, and perhaps 100,000 Ukrainian women are held in sexual slavery. Not an unfamiliar story.[3]

It is clear enough why the "de facto world government" described in the business press should welcome Eastern Europe's "market reforms," but for US elites they have a further significance. Like independent social and economic development in the third world, Western Europe's social-market system could be a "virus that might infect others," hence a form of "successful defiance" that must be dispatched to oblivion. The European welfare state systems could have a dangerous impact on American public opinion, as revealed by the continued popularity in the US of a universal tax-based health care system, despite constant denigration in the media and the exclusion of the option from the electoral agenda on grounds that it is "politically impossible" no matter what the public may think about it.

The "realities of modern capitalism" illustrated in the regions long subject to Western control have been brought to much of Eastern Europe as its economies have been "Latin-Americanized." The reasons are debated, but the essential facts of the social and economic collapse are not. The demographic consequences, while uncertain in scale, provide one index. The UN Development Program estimates ten million excess male deaths during the 1990s, approximately the toll of Stalin's purge sixty years earlier, if these figures are near accurate. "Russia appears to be the first country to experience such a sharp decrease in births versus deaths, for reasons other than war, famine or disease," David Powell writes. The demographic crisis is in part attributed to the crumbling of Russia's health care system under market reforms. The general collapse has been so severe that even the monstrous Stalin is remembered with some appreciation: more than half of Russians "believe Stalin's role in Russian history was positive, while only a third disagreed," polls indicated in early 2003.[4] The plans of the US overseers of Iraq seem rather similar to those that were applied in Russia, and that have led to dismal outcomes elsewhere with fair consistency.

On European unification, Washington's attitudes have always been complex. Like its predecessors, the Kennedy administration pressed for European unity, but with some concern that Europe might go its own way. The respected senior diplomat David Bruce was a leading advocate for European unification in the Kennedy years, but—typically—saw "dangers" if Europe "struck off on its own, seeking to play a role independent of the United States."[5]

The guiding principles were well expressed by Henry Kissinger in his "Year of Europe" address in 1973. The world system, he advised, should be based on the recognition that "the United States has global interests and responsibilities" while its allies have only "regional interests." The US must be "concerned more with the overall framework of order than with the management of every regional enterprise."[6] Europe must not pursue its own independent course, based on its Franco-German industrial and financial heartland—another reason for concern about "Old Europe," quite apart from the reluctance of its governments to follow Washington's commands with regard to the Iraq war.

The principles remain in force despite changing circumstances. Quite apart from their potential contributions to undermining the social-market systems of Western Europe, Eastern European countries are expected to be a "Trojan horse" for US interests, undermining any drift toward an independent role in the world.

By 1973, US global dominance had declined from its post–World War II peak. One measure is US control of the world's wealth, which is estimated to have shrunk from roughly 50 percent to half of that as the world economy moved to a "tripolar" order, with three major power centers: North America, Europe, and Japan-based Asia. These structures have since been modified further, particularly with the rise of the East Asian "tigers" and the entry of China into the global system as a major player. The basic concerns about the prospect of an independent Europe extend to Asia as well, in new ways.

Long before World War II, the US was by far the greatest economic power in the world but not a leading actor in global management. The war changed that. Rival powers were either devastated or severely weakened, while the US gained enormously. Industrial production almost quadrupled under the semi-command economy. By 1945 the US had not only overwhelming economic dominance but also a position of incomparable security: it controlled the hemisphere, the surrounding oceans, and most of the territory bordering them. US planners moved quickly to organize the global system, following plans that had already been developed to satisfy the "requirement[s] of the United States in a world in which it proposed to hold unquestioned power" while limiting the sovereignty of those who might pose a challenge.[7]

The new global order was to be subordinated to the needs of the US economy and subject to US political control as much as possible. Imperial controls, especially the British, were to be dismantled while Washington extended its own regional systems in Latin America and the Pacific on the principle, explained by Abe Fortas, that "what was good for us was good for the world." This altruistic concern was not appreciated by the British Foreign Office. Officials recognized that Washington, guided by "the economic imperialism of American business interests, [is] attempting to elbow us out," but could do little about it. The minister of state at the Foreign Office commented to his cabinet colleagues that Americans believe "that the United States stands for something in the world—something of which the world has need, something which the world is going to like, something, in the final analysis, which the world is going to take, whether it likes it or not."[8] He was articulating the real-world version of Wilsonian idealism, the version that conforms to the historical record.

US planning at the time was sophisticated and thorough. The highest priority was to reconstruct the industrial world along lines that would satisfy the requirements of the business interests that dominate policy formation: in particular, to absorb US manufacturing surpluses, overcome the "dollar gap," and offer opportunities for investment. The outcomes were appreciated by the domestic beneficiaries. Reagan's Commerce Department observed that the Marshall Plan "set the stage for large amounts of private U.S. direct investment in Europe," laying the groundwork for multinational corporations (MNCs). *Business Week* described MNCs in 1975 as "the economic expression" of the "political framework" established by postwar policymakers in which "American business prospered and expanded on overseas orders . . . fueled initially by the dollars of the Marshall Plan" and protected from "negative developments" by "the umbrella of American power."[9]

Other parts of the world were assigned their "functions" by State Department planners. Thus Southeast Asia was to provide resources and raw materials to the former imperial masters, crucially Britain but also Japan, which was to be granted "some sort of empire toward the south," in the phrase of George Kennan, head of the State Department's Policy Planning Staff.[10] Some areas were of little interest to the planners, notably Africa, which Kennan advised should be handed over to Europeans to "exploit" for their reconstruction. A different postwar Europe-Africa relationship comes to mind in the light of history but does not seem to have been considered.

The Middle East, in contrast, was to be taken over by the United States. In 1945, State Department officials described Saudi Arabian energy resources as "a stupendous source of strategic power, and one of the greatest material prizes in world history"; the Gulf region generally was considered "probably the richest economic prize in the field of foreign investment." Eisenhower later described it as the "most strategically important area of the world." Britain agreed. Its planners described the resources of the region in 1947 as "a vital prize for any power interested in world influence or domination."[11] France was expelled from the Middle East by legalistic maneuvers, and Britain declined over time to junior partner.

Kennan, who was farsighted, recognized that by controlling Japan's supplies of energy, primarily in the Middle East at the time, the US would achieve some "veto power" over Japan's potential military and industrial policy, though Japanese prospects were generally disparaged at the time. The issue has been the source of continued conflict since, with regard to Europe as well, as both Europe and Japan have sought a degree of energy independence.

Meanwhile Asia was changing. A prestigious task force, reporting in 2003, described Northeast Asia as "the epicenter of international commerce and technological innovation. . . . the fastest-growing economic region in the world for much of the past two decades," by now accounting "for nearly 30 percent of global GDP, far ahead of the United States," and also holding about half of global foreign exchange reserves. These economies also "account for nearly half of global inbound foreign direct investment" and are becoming an increasing source of outbound FDI, flowing within East Asia and to Europe and North America, which now trade more with Northeast Asia than with each other.[12]

The region is, furthermore, an integrated one. Eastern Russia is rich in natural resources, for which the industrial centers of Northeast Asia are the natural market. Integration would be enhanced by economic unification of the two Koreas with gas pipelines passing through North Korea and extension of the trans-Siberian railroad on the same course.

North Korea was the most dangerous and ugly member of the "axis of evil," but lowest on the target list. Like Iran, but unlike Iraq, it failed the first of the criteria for a legitimate target: it was not defenseless. Presumably, the Pentagon is working on ways to knock out the North Korean deterrent, massed artillery aimed at Seoul and US forces, which are being withdrawn out of artillery range, arousing concerns in Korea about US intentions. Considered in isolation, North Korea also fails the second criterion for a target; it is one of the poorest and most miserable countries in the world. But as part of the Northeast Asia complex, it gains importance for the reasons indicated by the task force. Hence it is not an unlikely target of attack, if the technical problem of countering its deterrent can be overcome.

The task force recommends that Washington seek a diplomatic solution to the current crisis. It should continue the process, begun haltingly and unevenly under Clinton, aimed at "normalizing United States economic and political relations with North Korea, guaranteeing the security of a non-nuclear North Korea, promoting the reconciliation of North and South Korea, and drawing North Korea into economic engagement with its neighbors." Such interactions could accelerate economic reforms already under way in North Korea, leading in time "to a diffusion of economic power that would loosen totalitarian political controls and moderate human rights abuses." These policies would conform to the regional consensus, including the North Korean dictatorship, it appears. The alternative—confrontation in the manner of Bush-Rumsfeld-Cheney grand strategy—is "the road to perdition," the task force argues.

The recommended alternative poses certain problems, however. As the task force describes, Northeast Asia is a rapidly developing and integrated region, which might go off on an independent course, just as continental Europe might. That raises the problem Kissinger outlined. In 1998 the National Bureau of Asian Research warned that "pipelines that promote greater regional integration in Northeast Asia might exclude U.S. involvement except in a marginal way" and could accelerate a process of evolution "into regional blocs."[13] These pipelines "could enhance regional stability and provide a cheap alternative to oil imported from the Middle East," Selig Harrison adds, but "the United States seems uneasily wary of pipeline networks in Northeast Asia." The US is aware that the countries of the region "want to reduce what they find to be an increasingly uncomfortable reliance on the US"; or from another point of view, the "veto power" the US exercises by virtue of its control of Middle East oil and the sea-lanes for tanker traffic. The threat of potential independence may prove an impediment to diplomatic settlement. For partially related reasons, China is regarded as a prime potential enemy by Washington hawks, and much military planning is geared to that contingency. Recent efforts to strengthen India-US strategic relations are partly motivated by the same concerns, along with Washington's concerns about its control over the world's largest energy reserves in the Middle East.

Washington's approach to North Korea resembles its stance on Iran and pre-invasion Iraq. In all three cases, neighboring countries had been pursuing efforts to overcome hostility and move toward integration, also attempting to lend support to reformist tendencies, or at least help lay the basis for them, and those efforts continue with regard to Iran and North Korea. The US somewhat hesitantly followed a similar approach toward North Korea during the Clinton years, with partial success, but apart from that, Washington has preferred confrontation. While the reasons for that preference are not identical in the three cases, there are common threads, which become clearer in the context of the grand strategy.

In the early postwar years, US planners sought to fashion East and Southeast Asia into a Japan-centered system within the "overall framework of order" maintained by the US. The basic framework was outlined in the San Francisco Peace Treaty (SFPT) of 1951, which formally ended the war in Asia.[14] Apart from the three French colonies in Indochina, the only Asian countries that accepted the SFPT were Pakistan and Ceylon, both recently freed from British rule and remote from the Asian war. India refused to attend the San Francisco conference because of the terms of the treaty, among them the US insistence on retaining Okinawa as a military base, as it still does, over strong protests from Okinawans, whose voices barely register in the US.

Truman was outraged by India's disobedience. His reaction, no less elegant than the current reaction to the disobedience of Old Europe and Turkey, was that India must have "consulted Uncle Joe and Mousie Dung of China." The white man got a name, not just a vulgar epithet. Partly that may be ordinary racism, or perhaps it is because Truman genuinely liked and admired "Old Joe," who reminded him of the Missouri boss who had launched his political career. In the late 1940s, Truman found Old Joe to be a "decent fellow," though "a prisoner of the Politburo" who "can't do what he wants to." Mousie Dung, however, was a yellow devil.

These distinctions extended wartime propaganda. Nazis were evil but merited a certain respect: in the stereotype, at least, they were blond, blue-eyed, orderly, far more appealing than the Frogs, whom Truman particularly disliked, not to speak of the Wops. And they were a wholly different species from the Japs, who were vermin to be crushed, at least once they became enemies; before that, the US was ambivalent about Japanese depredations in Asia, as long as US business interests were protected.

The primary victims of Japanese fascism and its predecessors—

China and the Japanese colonies of Korea and Formosa (Taiwan)—
did not attend the San Francisco Peace Conference and were
accorded no serious concern. Koreans and Chinese received no reparations from Japan; nor did the Philippines, which also did not
attend the conference. Secretary of State Dulles condemned Filipinos
for the "emotional prejudices" that kept them from grasping why
they would have no relief for the torture they had endured. Initially,
Japan was to pay reparations, but only to the US and other colonial
powers, despite the fact that the war was a Japanese war of aggression in Asia through the 1930s and only became a US-led Western
war with Japan after Pearl Harbor. Japan was also to reimburse the
US for the costs of the occupation. For its Asian victims, Japan was
to pay "compensation" in the form of export of Japanese manufacturing products using Southeast Asian resources, a central part of
the arrangements that, in effect, reconstructed something like the
"New Order in Asia" that Japan had attempted to construct by
conquest, but was now gaining under US domination, so that it was
unproblematic.

Some Asian victims of Japanese fascism—forced laborers and
prisoners of war—brought suit against Japanese corporations with
subsidiaries in the US, the legal successors of those responsible for
the crimes. On the eve of the fiftieth anniversary of the SFPT, their
suit was dismissed by a California judge, on grounds that their
claims were barred by the terms of the SFPT. Relying on an amicus
brief filed by the State Department in support of the accused Japanese corporations, the court ruled that the SFPT had "served to
sustain U.S. security interests in Asia and to support peace and stability in the region." Asia historian John Price described this judgment as "one of the more abysmal moments of denial," pointing
out that at least ten million people had been killed in wars in the
region while Asia was enjoying "peace and stability."

In May 2003, John Ashcroft's Justice Department updated the
stand of Clinton's State Department, submitting an amicus brief in
support of the energy giant UNOCAL that would "roll back twenty
years of judicial rulings for victims of human rights abuse," Human

Rights Watch warned. The Justice Department brief goes far beyond defense of the energy corporation against charges of brutal treatment of Burmese workers, slave laborers in effect. It calls for a "radical reinterpretation" of the Alien Tort Claims Act (ATCA), which "permits victims of serious violations of international law abroad to seek civil damages in U.S. courts against their alleged abusers who are found in the United States." The Bush administration is the first to call for reversing court decisions upholding the ATCA. It is "a craven attempt to protect human rights abusers at the expense of victims," HRW executive director Kenneth Roth observes[15]— particularly when the abusers are energy corporations, a cynic might add.

The tripolar order that was taking shape from the early 1970s has since become more firm, and with it, the concern of US planners that not only Europe but also Asia might seek a more independent course. From a longer historical perspective, that would not be too surprising. In the eighteenth century, China and India were major commercial and industrial centers. East Asia was far ahead of Europe in public health and probably sophistication of market systems. Life expectancy in Japan may have been higher than in Europe. England was trying to catch up in textiles and other manufactures, borrowing from India in ways that are now called piracy and are banned in the international trade agreements imposed by the rich states under a cynical pretense of "free trade"; the US relied heavily on the same mechanisms, as have other states that have developed. As late as the mid-nineteenth century, British observers claimed that Indian iron was as good as or better than British iron, and much cheaper. Colonization and forced liberalization converted India to a British dependency. It only resumed its growth and ended murderous famines after independence. China was not subjugated until the second British opium war 150 years ago, and also only resumed development after independence. Japan was the only part of Asia to resist colonization successfully, and the only one to develop, along with its colonies. It is not, then, a great surprise that Asia is returning to a position of considerable wealth and power after regaining sovereignty.

These long-term historical processes, however, extend the problems of sustaining the "overall framework of order" in which others must respect their proper place. The problems are not restricted to "successful defiance" in the third world, a major theme of the Cold War years, but reach the industrial heartlands themselves. Violence is a powerful instrument of control, as history demonstrates. But the dilemmas of dominance are not slight.

Chapter 7

Cauldron of Animosities

Let us return to Michael Krepon's belief that the final days of 2002 might be "the most dangerous time since the 1962 Cuban missile crisis." His primary concern was the "unstable nuclear-proliferation belt stretching from Pyongyang to Baghdad," including "Iran, Iraq, North Korea, and the Indian subcontinent."[1] Similar concerns, widely held, were heightened by Bush administration initiatives of 2002–3 that were seriously increasing international tensions and threats.

There is a far more fearsome nuclear power nearby, rarely featured in public discussion in the US because it is an appendage of US power. That convention is not observed within the unstable belt itself, or even within the US Strategic Command (STRATCOM), which is responsible for the nuclear arsenal. General Lee Butler, commander in chief of STRATCOM in 1992–94, observed that "it is dangerous in the extreme that in the cauldron of animosities that we call the Middle East, one nation has armed itself, ostensibly, with stockpiles of nuclear weapons, perhaps numbering in the hundreds, and that inspires other nations to do so." Israel's WMD are of concern to the world's second leading nuclear power as well.[2]

Similar concerns were expressed, more obliquely, in Security Council Resolution 687, which was selectively invoked by the Bush and Blair administrations in their efforts to provide a quasi-legal basis for their invasion of Iraq. Neither that nor any other resolution grants such authorization, but 687 did call for elimination of Iraqi WMD and delivery systems—as a step toward "the goal of establishing in the Middle East a zone free from weapons of mass destruction and all missiles for their delivery" (Article 14). US intelligence and other sources assume that Israel has several hundred nuclear weapons and has been developing chemical and biological weapons.

Article 14 is commonly ignored in US commentary, but not elsewhere. Iraq, for example, called on the Security Council to apply Article 14. Its motives do not obviate the importance of the issue. General Butler's concerns are not trivial. Undoubtedly, Israeli military power will continue to "inspire other nations" to develop WMD, including quite possibly even Iraq, if it is granted a modicum of independence.

The issue addressed by Article 14 had arisen before, on the eve of the first Gulf war. After invading Kuwait in August 1990, Iraq made a number of proposals for withdrawal within the context of a broader regional settlement. These were leaked to the press by US government officials who found them "serious" and "negotiable." How serious they were we cannot judge: the US "immediately dismissed" them, according to the only journalist in the country who reported the matter carefully, Knut Royce of *Newsday*. It is of some interest that in the final polls before the bombing, two thirds of the American public favored a conference on the Israel-Arab conflict if it would lead to Iraqi withdrawal.[3] Doubtless those figures would have been higher if the public had known that Iraq had just made a similar proposal, dismissed by Washington. A devastating war and even more destructive aftermath might have been prevented, hundreds of thousands of lives saved, and perhaps a basis laid for the overthrow of Saddam's tyranny. It is possible that steps might have been taken toward elimination of WMD and delivery systems in the region and beyond, perhaps even extending to the great powers, for thirty years in violation of their commitment under the Nuclear Nonproliferation Treaty to take good-faith steps toward eliminating nuclear weapons, matters of no slight significance.

Well beyond WMD, Israel's military capacities are regarded in the region as "dangerous in the extreme." Though a very small country, Israel has chosen to become, in effect, an offshore US military and technology base and as such has been able to develop highly advanced military forces. The core of the economy is a military-linked high-tech industrial system, with close ties to the US economy. Not surprisingly, Israel is coming to resemble its patron in other ways as well. A parliamentary (Knesset) investigation found that "Israel is now rated second in the Western world, after the United States, in terms of social gaps in income, property, capital, education and spending, as well as in the extent of poverty." Its formerly quite successful social welfare system has eroded, and social-cultural values have changed significantly as well.[4]

Like its patron, Israel has military forces that are off the spectrum of societies comparable in other dimensions. The head of research and development for the Israel Defense Forces (IDF) described its air and armored forces as larger and technologically more advanced than those of any NATO power apart from the US.[5] Its conventional military forces are used to attack its neighbors and to control and subjugate the population in the territories it occupies, in ways not easily overlooked in the region or by people elsewhere who are concerned with human rights.

Israel also has a close military alliance with the other major regional military power, Turkey. The US-Turkey-Israel alliance is sometimes called "the axis of evil," in the Middle East.[6] The term is understandable. There is always plenty of evil to go around, and this axis at least has the merit of existing, unlike the one concocted by George Bush's speechwriters, which consists of two states that had been at war for twenty years and a third that was presumably thrown in because it is non-Muslim and universally reviled.

US academic specialist Robert Olson reports that 12 percent of Israel's offensive aircraft are to be "permanently stationed in Turkey" and have been "flying reconnaissance flights along Iran's border," signaling to Iran "that it would soon be challenged elsewhere by Turkey and its Israeli and American allies." He suggests that these operations are part of a long-term effort to undermine and perhaps partition Iran, separating its northern Azeri regions (rather as Russia attempted to do in 1946, one of the early Cold War crises), thus turning the country into "an anemic geopolitical entity," barred from access to the Caspian Sea and Central Asia generally. Olson also discusses one of the usual background concerns: to expedite development of oil pipelines from the Caspian region to Turkey and the Mediterranean, cutting out Iran.[7]

The US-Turkey alliance might undergo some changes if the US is able to shift military bases from Eastern Turkey to Iraq, right in the heart of the world's richest energy reserves. US anger over Turkey's democratic deviation in 2002–3 could weaken US-Turkey military and intergovernmental relations, but that seems doubtful.

The existing tripartite alliance extends to parts of Central Asia and recently to India as well. Since its government came under the control of the Hindu right in 1998, India has shifted its international stance considerably, moving toward a closer military relationship with both the US and its Israeli client. Indian political analyst Praful Bidwai writes that the ruling Hindu nationalist "fascination with Zionism is rooted in Islamophobia (and anti-Arabism) and hyper-nationalism. Its ideology is Sharon's machismo and ferocious jingoism. It sees Hindus and Jews (plus Christians) as forming a 'strategic alliance' against Islam and Confucianism." Addressing the American Jewish Committee in Washington, India's national security adviser, Brajesh Mishra, called for development of a US-Israel-India "triad" that will have "the political will and moral authority to take bold decisions" in combating terror. According to Bidwai, "the growing Indo-Israel political-military contacts" are supplemented by coordination of the influential Hindu nationalist and Israeli lobbies in the US.[8]

India and Israel are both significant military powers, with nuclear weapons and delivery systems, and the emerging alliance system is another factor contributing to WMD proliferation, terror, and disorder in the unstable belt and beyond.

US-ISRAEL RELATIONS: ORIGINS AND MATURATION

It does not take much insight into world affairs to predict that the cauldron of animosities in the Middle East will continue to boil. Internal conflicts have been exacerbated as the industrial world shifted toward an oil-based economy from World War I, and the incomparable petroleum resources of the Middle East were discovered. After World War II, a high priority of US policy was to ensure its control over a region of such great material wealth and strategic significance.

In its day in the sun, Britain had controlled the region by delegating authority to clients, with British force in the background. In the terminology of the Foreign Office, local management was to be left to an "Arab façade" of weak compliant rulers, while Britain's "absorption" of these virtual colonies would be "veiled by constitutional fictions," a device considered more cost-effective than direct rule. With variations, the device is familiar elsewhere.

The population did not passively submit. Fortunately for imperial planners, air power was becoming available to control civilian populations, though some, like Winston Churchill, were enamored of the possibilities of using poison gas to subdue "recalcitrant Arabs" (mainly Kurds and Afghans). In the interwar years, there were attempts to ban or limit war, but Britain made sure these would not interfere with imperial rule, setting a precedent for its successor in world control. Specifically, Britain undermined attempts to restrict the use of air power against civilians. The reasons were expressed succinctly by the distinguished statesman Lloyd George, who praised the British government for "reserving the right to bomb niggers."[9]

Fundamental moral principles tend to have a long life. This one is no exception.

The US took over the British framework but added another layer of control: peripheral states, preferably non-Arab, that could serve as "local cops on the beat," in the terminology of the Nixon administration. Police headquarters would of course remain in Washington, with a branch office in London. Turkey was a leading member of the club from the outset, joined by Iran in 1953, when a US-UK military coup restored the shah, overthrowing a conservative parliamentary government that was seeking to control its own resources.

The US has been concerned more with control than access. After World War II, North America was the world's major oil producer, though this position was not expected to last long. Later, a major exporter to the US was Venezuela. Current projections of US intelligence are that the US will continue to rely primarily on Atlantic Basin resources—those in the Western Hemisphere and West Africa—which are more stable and reliable than those of the Middle East.[10] But as throughout the postwar period, that does not remove the perceived need to retain control.

Control over the great material prize of the Gulf ensures that US-UK energy corporations will be the main beneficiaries of enormous profits. The wealth recycles to the US and British economies in many other ways as well, including military hardware (hence high-tech industry generally), construction projects, and treasury securities. The recognized "stupendous strategic power" of the region translates into a lever of world domination. All of this was understood clearly by those who planned the postwar world, and retains its force. US intelligence expects Gulf energy resources to become even more significant in the years ahead,[11] hence also the drive to maintain control, whether the US itself relies heavily on these resources or not.

The global system of military bases from the Pacific to the Azores was designed in considerable measure for operations in the Gulf region. US counterinsurgency and subversion in Greece and Italy in the 1940s were in part motivated by concern over the free flow of Middle East oil to the West. By now the basing system extends to the former Soviet satellites Bulgaria and Romania. Since the Carter years, the major US intervention forces have been aimed at the Gulf. Until recently, the only fully reliable military base nearby was the British-held island of Diego Garcia, from which the inhabitants were expelled. The US still refuses them the right of return, overruling decisions of the British courts;[12] the issue is unknown in the US, much like the case of Okinawa. The Afghan war left the US with military bases in Afghanistan and Central Asia, helping to position

US corporations more favorably in the current phase of the "great game" to control Central Asian resources, and also to extend the encirclement of the far more important Persian Gulf. It had long been anticipated that one of Washington's goals in Iraq was to obtain military bases right in the heart of the oil-producing regions, as reported at the war's end.[13]

Other likely goals also moved into the public domain at the war's end. "The two things that were never openly discussed, that never became part of the national conversation, were oil and money," Bob Herbert commented: "Those crucial topics were left to the major behind-the-scenes operators, many of whom are now cashing in."[14]

US relations with Israel largely developed within this general context.[15] In 1948 the Joint Chiefs of Staff were impressed with Israel's military prowess, describing Israel as second only to Turkey in military power in the region. They suggested that Israel might offer the US means "to gain strategic advantage in the Middle East" to offset Britain's declining role. Ten years later, these considerations gained some concrete significance.

The year 1958 was highly significant in world affairs. The Eisenhower administration identified three major crises: Indonesia, North Africa, and the Middle East. All involved oil producers and Islamic political forces, which were then secular.

Eisenhower and Secretary of State Dulles stressed that there was no Russian involvement in any of these crises. The problem was the familiar devil: "radical nationalism." In North Africa, the concern was the Algerian struggle for independence, which the US wanted quickly settled. In Indonesia, the culprit was Sukarno, who was one of the leaders of the despised nonaligned movement and was also allowing too much democracy: a popular-based party of poor peasants was gaining influence. In the Middle East, the villain was Nasser, described as a "new Hitler" by panicked US and British leaders. He too was a pillar of the nonaligned movement, and his influence, it was feared, might tempt others to pursue an independent course. Those fears appeared to be realized in 1958 when a coup in Iraq, assumed to be Nasserite in origin, overthrew the British-backed government. Consequences reverberate to the present.

The Iraqi coup led to intense US-UK discussions. Policymakers were concerned that Kuwait might seek independence and that even Saudi Arabia might succumb to the disease. The British economy was heavily reliant on profits from Kuwaiti oil production and investment. Britain decided to grant Kuwait nominal independence, though "we must also accept the need, if things go wrong, ruthlessly to intervene, whoever it is has caused the trouble," Foreign Secretary Selwyn Lloyd explained. The US adopted the same stand on forceful intervention with regard to the bigger prizes, Saudi Arabia and the other Gulf emirates. Eisenhower sent military forces to Lebanon to block a perceived nationalist threat there and to ensure control over pipelines. He reiterated his concern over the "most strategically important area of the world" and emphasized that loss of control "would be far worse than the loss of China"—regarded as the worst postwar catastrophe—"because of the strategic position and resources of the Middle East."[16]

Another country of critical importance that might, it was feared, fall under Nasserite influence was Jordan, then the regional base for British military power. Israel assisted in assuring British control. Washington planners recognized that Israel was the only regional power that had taken risks for the sake of "relieving the situation in the area." A memorandum for the National Security Council advised that "if we choose to combat radical Arab nationalism and to hold Persian Gulf oil by force if necessary, a logical corollary would be to support Israel as the only strong pro-West power left in the Near East,"[17] along with the peripheral powers, Turkey and Iran. At the same time, in 1958, Israel-Turkey relations were established with a visit to Turkey by Prime Minister David Ben-Gurion. By 2000, Efraim Inbar writes, Israel's relations to Turkey were "second only to the closeness of Israel-US ties."[18]

In 1967 the US-Israeli alliance was firmly in place. Israel destroyed Nasser, thus protecting the "façade" in the Arabian peninsula and also striking a powerful blow against the nonaligned movement. That was considered a major contribution to US power. There was also a significant effect within the US ideological domain, an important topic that I will have to put aside.[19]

Recall the three major crises of 1958. The threat of independent Arab nationalism in the Middle East was overcome by the 1967 war. The North African crisis ended with Algerian independence.[20] The crisis in Indonesia was resolved by a huge massacre, mainly of landless peasants, which the CIA described as one of the great mass murders of the twentieth century, comparable to those of Hitler, Stalin, and Mao. This "staggering mass slaughter," as the *New York Times* called it, was greeted with unrestrained euphoria in the West. It eliminated the mass-based political party of the poor and opened the doors wide to Western investors. As in the Middle East, another pillar of the nonaligned movement was demolished. Somewhat similar processes were under way in Latin America and, to a more limited extent, in India, the last major stronghold of nonalignment. Throughout, the US role was significant, sometimes crucially so. The US is a global power, like England before it. It is often misleading to focus on one region of the world, forgetting that global planning is in Washington.

Keeping nevertheless to the Middle East, in 1970 Israel performed another service by deterring possible Syrian intervention to protect Palestinians who were being massacred in Jordan. US aid to Israel quadrupled. US intelligence, along with such influential figures concerned with the Middle East as Senator Henry Jackson, described the tacit alliance of Israel-Iran-Saudi Arabia as a solid basis for US power in the region, with Turkey taken for granted.

In 1979 the shah fell and the Israel-Turkey alliance became even more important as a regional base. The alliance welcomed a new member, replacing the shah: Saddam Hussein's Iraq, which the Reagan administration removed from the official list of terrorist states in 1982 so that the US could freely provide the tyrant with aid.

Israel's choices over the past thirty years have reduced its options considerably; on its present course, it has virtually no alternative to serving as a US base in the region and complying with US demands. The options were starkly illuminated in 1971, when President Anwar Sadat of Egypt offered Israel a full peace treaty in return for Israeli withdrawal from Egyptian territory. Sadat offered nothing to the Palestinians and omitted reference to the other occupied territories. In his memoirs, Yitzhak Rabin, then ambassador to the US, refers to the "famous" offer as a "milestone" on the path to peace, though it contained "bad news" as well: the condition that Israel withdraw from Egyptian territory, in accord with official US policy and the basic diplomatic document, Security Council Resolution 242 of November 1967.

Israel had a fateful choice: it could accept peace and integration into the region or insist on confrontation, hence inevitable dependency on the US. It chose the latter course, not on grounds of security but because of a commitment to expansion. That is clear in Israeli sources. General Haim Bar-Lev, a leading figure in the governing Labor Party, expressed the common understanding when he wrote in a Labor Party journal that "we can have peace, but I think if we continue to hold out we can obtain more." The "more" that was of primary interest at the time was the northeastern Sinai, from which the inhabitants were brutally expelled into the desert to make way for the establishment of the all-Jewish city of Yamit. In 1972, General Ezer Weizman, later president, added that a political settlement without expansion would mean that Israel could not "exist according to the scale, spirit, and quality she now embodies."

The crucial question was how Washington would react. After internal debate, the government abandoned its official policy in favor of Kissinger's principle of "stalemate": no diplomacy, only force. It should be recalled that this was a period of extreme triumphalism, later greatly regretted in Israel. The US and Israel took it for granted after 1967 that Arabs could pose no military threat. The Egyptian peace offer is not "famous" in the US: rather, unknown, a common fate of events that do not conform to doctrinal requirements.

Sadat still hoped to gain US acquiescence, by expelling his Russian advisers and other moves. He also warned that "Yamit means war." He was not taken seriously. In 1973 he did launch a war, which was a near disaster for Israel and also led to a nuclear alert in the US. At that point, Kissinger realized that Egypt could not simply be dismissed, and launched his "shuttle diplomacy," which led finally to the Camp David settlement of 1978–79. At Camp

David the US and Israel accepted Sadat's 1971 offer, but on terms much less favorable from their point of view: by then the fate of the Palestinians had become an issue, and Sadat joined most of the rest of the world in insisting on their rights.

These events are hailed as a US diplomatic triumph. Jimmy Carter won the Nobel Peace Prize primarily for the culminating achievement. The entire process was, in reality, a diplomatic catastrophe. The US-Israel rejection of diplomacy led to a terrible war, great suffering, and a superpower confrontation that could have gotten out of hand. But one of the prerogatives of power is the ability to write history with confidence that there will be little challenge. The disaster therefore enters history as a grand triumph of the US-run "peace process."

Israel recognized at once that with the Arab deterrent removed, it could intensify its expansion into the occupied territories and attack its northern neighbor, as it proceeded to do in 1978 and 1982, continuing to occupy parts of Lebanon for almost twenty years. The 1982 invasion and its immediate aftermath left some 20,000 dead; according to Lebanese sources, the toll in the following years was about 25,000. The topic is of little concern in the West, on the principle that crimes for which we are responsible require no inquiry, let alone punishment or reparations.

After many bombings and other provocations failed to elicit a pretext for the planned 1982 invasion, Israel finally seized upon the attempted assassination of its ambassador in London by the terrorist group headed by Abu Nidal, who had been condemned to death by the PLO and had been at war with it for years. Resort to this pretext was acceptable to articulate American opinion, which also had no problem with Israel's immediate response: an attack on the Sabra-Shatila Palestinian refugee camps in Beirut, where 200 people were killed, according to a reliable American observer.[21] UN attempts to halt the aggression were blocked by immediate US vetoes. So matters continued through eighteen bloody years of Israeli atrocities in Lebanon, rarely with even a thin pretext of self-defense.[22]

Chief of Staff Rafael ("Raful") Eitan echoed the common

understanding in Israel when he at once declared the 1982 invasion to be a success because it weakened the "political status" of the PLO and set back its struggle for a Palestinian state. Leading US intellectuals also welcomed the "political *defeat*" of the PLO, clearly recognizing that to be the goal of the war while anointing it a "just war" (Michael Walzer).[23] Most public commentary and media, however, preferred tales about unprovoked rocket attacks on innocent Israelis and similar fabrications, though by now the truth is sometimes recognized. *New York Times* correspondent James Bennet writes that the goal of the 1982 invasion "was to install a friendly regime and destroy Mr. Arafat's Palestinian Liberation Organization. That, the theory went, would help persuade Palestinians to accept Israeli rule in the West Bank and Gaza Strip."[24] To my knowledge, this is the first report in the American mainstream of what was well known in Israel and has been published in marginalized dissident circles in the US for twenty years. It is also a textbook illustration of massive international terrorism, if not the more severe crime of aggression, tracing right back to Washington, which provided the requisite economic, military, and diplomatic support. Without such authorization and aid, Israel can do very little. There are many illusions about this in the Arab countries and elsewhere. Particularly for the victims, it is not wise to live with illusions.

On the diplomatic front, by the mid-1970s US-Israeli isolation increased as the Palestinian issue entered the international agenda. In 1976 the US vetoed a resolution calling for a Palestinian state alongside Israel, incorporating the basic wording of UN Resolution 242 from 1967. From then to the present the US has blocked the possibility of a diplomatic settlement in the terms accepted by virtually the entire world: a two-state settlement on the international border, with "minor and mutual adjustments"; that was the principle of official, though not actual, US policy until the Clinton administration formally abandoned the framework of international diplomacy, declaring UN resolutions "obsolete and anachronistic." It is noteworthy that the US stand is also opposed by most of the

US population: a large majority support the "Saudi Plan," proposed in early 2002 and accepted by the Arab League, which offered full recognition and integration of Israel into the region in exchange for withdrawal to the 1967 borders, yet another version of the long-standing international consensus that the US has blocked. Large majorities also believe that the US should equalize aid to Israel and the Palestinians under a negotiated settlement, and should cut aid to either party that refuses to negotiate: meaning, at the time of the poll, that it should cut aid to Israel. But few understand what any of this implies, and almost nothing is reported about it.[25]

After the first Gulf war, Washington felt that it was in a position to impose its own preferred solution. Although never fully elaborated, the 1991 version was to be more forthcoming than the administration position announced in December 1989, which endorsed without qualifications the Israeli coalition government (Shamir-Peres) plan stipulating that there can be no "additional Palestinian state" (Jordan already being "a Palestinian state," in their conception) and that the fate of the territories will be determined "in accordance with the basic guidelines of the [Israeli] government." Washington convened the Madrid conference, with Russian participation to offer a fig leaf of internationalism.

But a problem arose at the conference. The Palestinian delegation was headed by Haydar 'Abd al-Shafi, a conservative nationalist known for his integrity and one of the most respected Palestinian figures. The delegation refused to agree to continued Israeli settlement programs in the occupied territories, thus deadlocking the negotiations, because the US and Israel refused to agree to this condition, even to consider it seriously. Recognizing that his public support was collapsing within the territories and the Palestinian diaspora, Yasir Arafat undercut the Palestinian delegation by secret negotiations with Israel, leading to the "Oslo process," initiated officially with much pomp in September 1993 at the White House. The wording of the Oslo agreements made it clear that they were a mandate for continued Israeli settlement programs, as the Israeli leadership (Yitzhak Rabin and Shimon Peres) took no pains to conceal.

For that reason, 'Abd al-Shafi refused to have anything to do with the official peace process.[26]

So matters proceeded through the 1990s, as Israeli settlement and integration of the territories proceeded steadily, with full US support. In 2000, the final year of Clinton's term (and Israeli Prime Minister Ehud Barak's), settlement reached its highest peak since 1992, striking further blows at the possibility of a resolution of the conflict by peaceful diplomatic means.

CAMP DAVID II AND BEYOND: TOWARD A "PERMANENT NEOCOLONIAL DEPENDENCY"

US-Israeli rejectionism runs through the Camp David negotiations of 2000. The conventional image is that Clinton and Barak made a "magnanimous" offer of unparalleled "generosity," but the treacherous Palestinians turned it down, preferring violence. There is a simple way to evaluate these claims: present a map of the territorial settlement proposed. No map has been found in US media or journals, apart from scholarly sources and the dissident literature. A look at the maps reveals that the Clinton-Barak offer virtually divided the West Bank into three cantons, effectively separated from one another by two salients consisting of expansive Jewish settlement and infrastructure developments. The three cantons have only limited access to East Jerusalem—the center of Palestinian commercial, cultural, and political life. And all are separated from Gaza.

Admittedly, this would have been an improvement over the status quo, with Palestinians in the West Bank confined to more than 200 cantons, some a few square kilometers, and the situation in the Gaza Strip was in many ways worse.

Shortly before joining the Barak government and becoming the chief negotiator at Camp David, Shlomo Ben-Ami, considered a dove in the Israeli spectrum, published an academic study in which he outlined the goal of the Oslo "peace process": to establish a "neocolonial dependency" for the Palestinians, which will be "permanent."[27] That is essentially what was offered at Camp David.

In Israel, maps did appear in the mainstream press, and the proposals are commonly described as modeled on South Africa's Bantustans of forty years ago. Respected commentators report that the South African model was considered very seriously in high military and political echelons in the 1970s and 1980s, and is the model today.[28] Israel also considered South Africa a valued ally, as did the US, through the Reagan years.

After the failure of Camp David 2000, negotiations continued. They led to high-level (but unofficial) meetings at Taba, Egypt, in January 2001. These appeared to be making considerable progress, though the major territorial problems remained, in less extreme forms. There is a careful record of the Taba negotiations in a report by the European Union observer Miguel Moratinos, approved by both sides.[29] The basic differences were narrowed but not entirely bridged. For the West Bank, there was agreement in principle on the long-standing international consensus honoring the internationally recognized border, with "minor and mutual adjustments," now not so minor because of the US-backed Israeli settlement and infrastructure programs that, as noted, rapidly expanded as the Oslo process proceeded on its largely predictable course. Palestinian negotiators at Taba agreed to include within Israel the post-Oslo settlements established around the vastly expanded Jerusalem, but called for a one-to-one territorial swap—with the support of some Israeli hawks, who welcome the opportunity to transfer Israeli Arabs out of the country, thus relieving the much-feared "demographic problem": too many non-Jews in a Jewish state. But the Israeli negotiators insisted on a two-to-one, or larger, swap in their favor, with Palestinians offered a worthless area adjacent to the Sinai Desert. The primary territorial issue remained the status of the Israeli town of Ma'aleh Adumim to the east of Jerusalem, and the infrastructure linking it to the expanded areas to be annexed to Israel, developed mostly in the 1990s with the clear intent of virtually bisecting the West Bank. These issues remained unresolved, along with some others, but there is good reason to accept Akiva Eldar's conclusion that progress was real and promising, even if not formal.

The negotiations were called off by Barak prior to the Israeli elections, and in the face of escalating violence were never resumed, so we cannot know where they might have led.

The basic issues were reviewed by Hussein Agha and Robert Malley, two well-informed commentators, in *Foreign Affairs*.[30] They observed, accurately, that "the outlines of a solution have basically been understood for some time now": a territorial divide on the international border, with a one-to-one land swap. They write that "the way to get [to the solution] has eluded all sides from the start," but while accurate, the statement is misleading. The way has been blocked for twenty-five years by the United States, and Israel continues to reject it even at the dovish extreme of the mainstream political spectrum, as the Moratinos report again documents.

During the Bush II–Sharon years, the prospects for a diplomatic solution have declined further. Israel has expanded its settlement programs, with continued US backing. The Israeli human rights organization B'Tselem was finally able to obtain official maps indicating Israeli territorial intentions.[31] Israeli settlements now control 42 percent of the West Bank. The boundaries of Ma'aleh Adumim, for example, reach from the area of Greater Jerusalem almost to the isolated Palestinian town of Jericho, a salient that largely isolates the southern region of the West Bank. Another salient to the north also remains, partially separating the northern from the central sectors. The result is a harsh version of the three-canton arrangement for the West Bank, all virtually separated from a small part of East Jerusalem, and of course from Gaza, however its fate is determined.

The situation in 2003 is described in the primary US scholarly source on the settlements by its editor, Geoffrey Aronson, after a visit to the southern area.[32] "In virtually every Israeli settlement, colonization efforts are proceeding apace," leading to "revolutionary changes in patterns of transportation and access" aimed at "consolidating Israel's ability to secure a permanent hold over these lands," integrated within the much-expanded Israel. "In contrast, the dynamic for Palestinians is just the opposite—an ever-increasing network of barricades, obstacles, patrol roads, and prohibitions that isolate them from settlements, from each other, and from places of work, compromising their ability to lead normal lives and impoverishing an entire national community."

As for Bush administration plans in mid-2003, there are two sources, rhetoric and action. At the rhetorical level, one reads of Bush's "vision" of a Palestinian state, and the US-inspired "road map." In the real world, the Bush administration repeatedly blocked public release of the road map of the "quartet" (EU, UN, Russia, US), much to the annoyance of the other members. The vision was left vague, and remained so after the road map was finally released, accompanied by Bush's modest announcement that "the road map represents a starting point toward achieving the vision of two states. . . . that I set out in June 24, 2002"; namely, a pale and indistinct version of the "vision" that had been common coin for over a quarter-century, but blocked by the US.[33]

The first steps on the road map are explicit: Palestinians must immediately terminate resistance to the occupation, including attacks on Israeli soldiers in the occupied territories, and Israel must declare its commitment to "the two-state vision . . . expressed by President Bush," its nature unclear. "As comprehensive security performance moves forward, I.D.F. withdraws progressively from areas occupied since Sept. 28, 2000, and the two sides restore the status quo that existed" at that time. Satisfactory performance will be determined by Israel and Washington. The "status quo" that is to be restored leaves Palestinians confined to hundreds of cantons, surrounded by the settlements and infrastructure constructed by the US-backed Israeli military occupation. The future of these settlements remains unclear. Israel "immediately dismantles settlement outposts erected since March 2001," something on which all but the ultra-right in Israel agree, and at some time left unspecified Israel "freezes all settlement activity (including natural growth of settlements)." Until that time, the settlements can continue to expand. If the time for "freezing" ever comes, the Bantustan-style arrangements instituted through the 1990s in the context of the US-Israel "peace process," continued under the road map, will presumably be well established.

Later still there is to be "implementation of prior agreements, to enhance maximum territorial contiguity [for the Palestinian state], including further action on settlements." The "further action" remains unspecified. There are no prior agreements that yield meaningful "territorial contiguity." The only serious proposals that have been made are not on the agenda. Whatever Bush's "two-state vision" may be, it is apparently not the two-state vision supported by virtually the entire world that the US has blocked since the mid-1970s, nor the Saudi plan ratified by the Arab League and supported by a majority of the American population, nor the solution whose outlines "have basically been understood for some time now" described by Agha and Malley. There is no hint of any of these ideas.[34]

Furthermore, although there is immediate (and violent) enforcement of the road map's conditions on the Palestinians, there is no enforcement of conditions on the US-funded Israeli settlement and development programs. There is a rich record about all of this, and no reason to expect any significant change.

Though the political road map remains vague with regard to Israel's responsibilities, other demands are quite specific. The huge US subsidy to Israel is, for the first time, conditioned on Israel's performance: not on its implementation of the terms of the road map but on an economic plan that "will slash public sector jobs and wages and lower taxes," measures that have been "dubbed an 'economic road map.' " The plan is described by Israel's leading newspaper as a "new theory, . . . according to which the US openly intervenes in forcing a neo-liberal order in Israel"—a theory that is welcome to the Israeli business sector but led immediately to a strike of 700,000 workers.[35]

Also quite specific are operations to create "facts on the ground" while talk proceeds, in the traditional manner. Notable among them is the construction of the "separation wall" that incorporates parts of the West Bank within Israel. The justification offered for the barrier is security: for Israelis, not Palestinians, whose security problems are far more grave. A barrier with a land swap would provide no

less security. The most security would be given by a wall a few miles
inside Israel, to allow the IDF to patrol fully on both sides. But such
proposals would not incorporate Palestinian land within Israel, and
would disrupt the lives of Israelis rather than Palestinians, and are
therefore unthinkable. World Bank–sponsored reports conclude that
the wall will leave almost 100,000 Palestinians on the Israeli side,
along with "some of the richest agricultural land in the West Bank."
The wall also places a good part of the vitally important West Bank
aquifer under Israeli control. One West Bank town, Qalqilya, is
already virtually surrounded by the wall, cut off from its lands, 30
percent of its water supplies, and whatever territories will be
assigned someday to the "viable" Palestinian state with "territorial
contiguity." More than half of Qalqilya's agricultural lands were
reported to have been confiscated, to be annexed to Israel, with the
munificent offer of onetime compensation equal to the market price
of one year's harvest.[36]

Immediately after Colin Powell went to Israel to meet with Prime
Minister Sharon and discuss the road map, Sharon informed the press
that as the wall proceeded south of Qalqilya, it would sweep well to
the east to enclose the Israeli settlements of Ariel and Emmanuel,
thereby partially separating the northern Palestinian enclave from the
central one by a salient of Israeli settlements and infrastructure, as in
the Clinton-Barak Camp David plan. There can be little doubt that
the second and more important of the Clinton-Barak extensions of
Israeli territory, dividing the central enclave from the southern one,
will also be incorporated, de facto, within Israel, in some manner.
There is also little reason to doubt that Israeli communities that
remain outside the wall will retain their current status as, effectively,
parts of Israel, linked to it by large-scale infrastructure, protected by
the IDF, and free to expand within their allotted territory until some
order to the contrary comes from above.

The very well-informed Harvard University scholar Sara Roy, relying on internal sources, writes that the World Bank "estimates that
some 232,000 people living in 72 communities will be affected" by
the first, northern phase of the wall's construction, "with 140,000

living on the eastern side of the wall but, in effect, encircled within its winding path"; and that completion "could isolate as many as 250,000-300,000 Palestinians while annexing "as much as 10% of the West Bank to Israel." She suggests further that "the wall's design [may be] aimed at carving out and encircling the 42% (or less) of the West Bank that Sharon has said he is prepared to cede to a Palestinian state." If so, Sharon may have in mind something like the plan he proposed in 1992, now recognizing that the political spectrum has shifted so far toward the extremist-nationalist pole that what seemed audacious then may be portrayed as a dramatic concession today.[37]

"The facts on the ground," Israeli journalist Amira Hass comments, "are determining—and will continue to determine—the area where the road map will be applied, the area where the entity known as the 'Palestinian state' will be established":

> A visit to the [places] where the Public Works Commission, the Defense Ministry, Housing Ministry and the IDF bulldozers are busy at work, makes it possible to see why it's easy for Prime Minister Ariel Sharon to talk about a "Palestinian state." . . . The massive construction in Jerusalem and its environs, from Bethlehem to Ramallah, and the Dead Sea to Modi'in, has already ruled out any Palestinian urban, industrial or cultural development worthy of the name in the area of East Jerusalem. The southern enclave of the West Bank, from Hebron to Bethlehem, will be cut off from the central enclave of the Ramallah area by an ocean of manicured Israeli settlements, tunnel roads and highways. The northern enclave, from Jenin to Nablus, will be cut off from the center by the massive settlement bloc of Ariel-Eli-Shiloh.[38]

As for the "settlement freeze," when Sharon persuaded his extremist cabinet to accept the road map he explained that "there is no restriction here, and you can build for your children and grandchildren, and I hope for your great-grandchildren as well."[39]

At the rhetorical level, the road map appears to offer more to the Palestinians than the Oslo process: it uses such terms as "Palestinian state," "end to the occupation," "freeze on all settlement activity," etc., all phrases missing from the Oslo protocols. But the appearance is deceptive. Apart from extremist elements, Israel and its sponsor have no intention of taking over territories beyond useful and desirable limits or of having Israel administer the bulk of the Palestinian population. Construction of "facts on the ground" has proceeded sufficiently to allow the free use of terms that might previously have impeded plans that have been implemented for the past decade and are now being established more firmly.

Apart from the rhetoric about "visions," there is a more significant source of information: actions. Keeping just to a few illustrations, in December 2000 the Bush administration caused some consternation abroad when it vetoed a Security Council resolution, advanced by the European Union, calling for implementation of Washington's Mitchell Plan and efforts to reduce violence by the dispatch of international monitors, to which Israel strongly objects: their presence is likely to reduce Palestinian violence but would also impede Israeli repression and terror.

Ten days before the veto, Washington boycotted a conference in Geneva of the High Contracting Parties of the Geneva Conventions called to review the situation in the occupied territories. The boycott yielded the usual "double veto": the decisions are blocked, and the events are barely reported and erased from history. The conference reaffirmed the applicability of the Fourth Geneva Convention to the occupied territories, so that many US-Israeli actions there are war crimes under US law. The conference again condemned US-funded Israeli settlements and the practice of "wilful killing, torture, unlawful deportation, wilful depriving of the rights of fair and regular trial, extensive destruction and appropriation of property . . . carried out unlawfully and wantonly."[40]

The Fourth Geneva Convention, instituted to criminalize formally the crimes of the Nazis in occupied Europe, is a core principle of international humanitarian law. Its applicability to the Israeli-occupied territories has repeatedly been affirmed, among other occasions, by UN ambassador George Bush (September 1971) and by Security Council resolutions. These include Resolution 465 (1980), adopted unanimously, which condemned US-backed Israeli practices as "flagrant violations" of the convention, and Resolution 1322 (October 2000), 14–0 (US abstaining), which called on Israel "to abide scrupulously by its responsibilities under the Fourth Geneva Convention." As High Contracting Parties, the US and the European powers are obligated by solemn treaty to apprehend and prosecute those responsible for such crimes, including their own leadership. By continuing to reject that duty, they are "enhancing terror"—to borrow Bush II's words condemning Palestinians. The US stance has shifted over the years from endorsement of the applicability of the conventions to the occupied territories, to abstention during the Clinton years, and finally to undermining them under Bush II.

The Bush administration signaled its tacit endorsement of violent repression in the occupied territories in other ways as well. Thus, while Ariel Sharon was conducting his brutal offensive in the West Bank in April 2002, Colin Powell was sent to "bring peace." He meandered through the Mediterranean, arriving in Israel just as the defenders of Jenin were running out of food and ammunition; one may presume that State Department intelligence was able to work out that calculation. A Pentagon official stated the obvious: "Powell's itinerary, he said, was designed 'to give Sharon some more time.'" A State Department official added that "the Israelis are not listening so much to what we say, but are watching what we do. . . . And what we're doing is giving them more time to withdraw"[41]— when they finished their work: leveling the refugee camp at Jenin, smashing much of the old city of Nablus, and destroying the institutional and cultural infrastructure of Palestinian life in Ramallah with the viciousness that has been IDF practice for many years.

In December 2002, the UN General Assembly reiterated the near-universal opposition to Israel's effective annexation of Jerusalem, in defiance of Security Council resolutions going back to 1968 (passed with US support). For the first time, the US voted against the resolution, formally reversing the long-standing official US position on the status of Jerusalem. The US was joined by Israel, several Pacific island dependencies, and Costa Rica. If intended seriously, this reversal virtually eliminates the possibility of a political settlement. The Bush administration also continued to sustain violence by voting against a resolution calling for international efforts "to halt the deteriorating situation between Israel and the Palestinians, reverse all measures taken on the ground since the latest violence began in September 2000, and push for a peace agreement" (passed 160–4, the US joined by Israel, Micronesia, and the Marshall Islands). Following the conventional pattern, none of this seems to have been reported in the US.[42]

Bush also declared the archterrorist Sharon a "man of peace" and demanded that Arafat be replaced by a prime minister who will meet US-Israeli demands, though "unlike Mr. Arafat [he] does not have a popular following."[43] All of this provides further illustration of the president's "vision of democracy."

In February 2003, Bush delivered what the *New York Times* called "his first significant remarks about the Israeli-Palestinian conflict in eight months," in a speech to the far-right American Enterprise Institute. The speech was mostly vacuous, but it did indeed contain one significant remark. Bush declared obliquely that Israel could continue its programs of settlement and development in the occupied territories. The form of his endorsement was the statement that "as progress is made toward peace, settlement activity in the occupied territories must end," implying that it can continue until the US determines (unilaterally, as always) that progress has been made.[44] Again, Bush's sole "significant remark" reverses official government policy. Previously the settlement programs had been considered illegal, or at least "unhelpful." Now they are implicitly authorized. In defense of the administration, one may argue that official doctrine has been brought into conformity with near-invariant practice.

Prevailing values are often expressed implicitly, as on the first anniversary of 9-11, when the president took the occasion to provide $200 million in supplemental funding for the rich country of Israel while rejecting $130 million for emergency supplemental aid to Afghanistan.[45] And not only in the US. Thus former UK foreign secretary Douglas (Lord) Hurd wrote that "two unsolved problems torment the Middle East: the danger from Saddam Hussein and the insecurity of Israel."[46] The insecurity of Palestinians in the thirty-sixth year of military occupation is not an "unsolved problem"; in fact, it remains unmentioned.

The steps that undermine the prospects for a peaceful diplomatic settlement are continually justified as a response to Palestinian terror, which did indeed escalate, including terrible crimes against Israeli civilians during the al-Aqsa Intifada that broke out at the end of September 2000. The Intifada also brought into the open significant changes that had been taking place within Israel. The authority of the Israeli military by then reached such levels that military correspondent Ben Kaspit described the country as "not a state with an army, but an army with a state."[47]

Kaspit's analysis is basically confirmed, and deepened historically, by another prominent military correspondent, Reuven Pedatzur, reviewing Israel's "culture of power" and "consistent choice of the military option" over peaceful means, since its founding. In his discussion of a book by military historian Motti Golani, Pedatzur writes that Golani is, "of course, correct" in his "bald denial of the sacrosanct Israeli ethos according to which Israel has always aspired to peace, whereas its neighbors have consistently refused to tread the path of peace, choosing the path of war instead." The facts are sharply different, both agree. One prime reason is "the institutionalization of power and its total transfer to the responsibility of the political and military establishments." The military command intervenes in "political-diplomatic debate," sometimes by threat of force, effectively formulating policy to an extent unknown in any other democratic society. Guided by this "military culture," "Israel's political-military leadership uses fear-mongering tactics in security issues, . . . generat[ing] anxiety in order to mobilize Israeli society and to deflect the public's gaze from domestic problems, such as a deteriorating economic situation or a growing unemployment rate." The "formula"—familiar enough elsewhere, including the US—was established by Israel's founding father David Ben-Gurion in the earliest days of the state, and "fear-mongering . . . would be used in the following decades," to the present. Author and reviewer join other Israeli commentators in warning of the "serious danger" of the "formation of a consensus . . . according to which, in Israel's situation, democratic considerations are a luxury," with "signs of fascism."[48]

Kaspit's observations were motivated by the utter contempt shown by the military command for the orders of the civilian government in the early months of the Intifada, a stance that is particularly noteworthy since the prime minister was a former chief of staff and other civilian officials were also from the upper military echelons. Like other powerful military forces facing largely defenseless opponents, the IDF instantly resorted to extreme violence. When the head of military intelligence requested an inquiry into "how many bullets the IDF fired from the start of the hostilities," he and other generals were shocked to learn that in the first few days of the Intifada the IDF fired a million bullets and other projectiles—"a bullet for each child," one officer of the high command commented with disgust. Military sources confirmed a report that in one incident, a single shot, fired in the air to illustrate the reality to a European observer, evoked two solid hours of intense fire from Israeli troops and tanks.

According to IDF accounting, the ratio of Palestinian to Israeli dead was almost twenty to one in the first month of the Intifada (seventy-five Palestinians, four Israelis), in areas under military occupation, with resistance scarcely going beyond stone throwing. The army's force of huge, US-provided bulldozers was also called into action to destroy dwellings, fields, olive groves, and forests with utter abandon, following policies that have made Israel "synonymous with bulldozer," one correspondent wrote with dismay, reversing founding ideals about "making the desert bloom."[49]

From the outset Israel used US military helicopters to attack civilian targets, killing and wounding dozens of people. Clinton responded instantly with the largest deal in a decade for military helicopters; there were no constraints on use, the Pentagon informed journalists. The facts, well known at once, were unreported in the US.

Israel was breaking no new ground. US forces in the Gulf War in 1991 enjoyed such overwhelming military superiority that troops could enter Iraq behind plows mounted on tanks and earthmovers, which bulldozed live Iraqi soldiers into trenches in the desert, an "unprecedented tactic," Patrick Sloyan reported. "Not a single American was killed during the attack that made an Iraqi body count impossible." The victims were mostly Shi'ite and Kurdish peasant conscripts, it appears, hapless victims of Saddam Hussein hiding in holes in the sand or fleeing for their lives. The report elicited little interest or comment.[50]

Such slaughters are not only routine when there is an overwhelming disparity of force, but are often lauded by the perpetrators. To select an illustration concerning the non-Muslim member of the "axis of evil," it is unlikely that North Koreans have forgotten the "object lesson in air power to all the Communists in the world and especially to the Communists in North Korea" that was delivered in May 1953, a month before the armistice, and reported enthusiastically in a US Air Force study. There were no targets left in the flattened country, so US bombers were dispatched to destroy irrigation dams "furnishing 75 percent of the controlled rice supply for North Korea's rice production." "The Westerner can little conceive the awesome meaning which the loss of this staple commodity has for the Asian—starvation and slow death," the official account continues, recounting the kinds of crimes that led to death sentences at Nuremberg.[51] One may wonder whether such memories are in the background as the desperate North Korean leadership plays "nuclear chicken."

It is important to be aware of how routine these practices are, hence how likely they are to recur unless inhibited from within the powerful states. We can observe with horror the ruins of Grozny; and if historical memory is allowed, can recall the devastation left by US saturation bombing in Indochina. Revenge knows few limits when the privileged and powerful are subjected to the kind of terror they regularly mete out to their victims. To take an example from earlier years, when British citizens were murdered in the course of a rebellion in occupied India 150 years ago (the "Indian mutiny," in imperial parlance), Britain's reaction was ferocious. It was "a ghastly and horrible picture showing man at his worst," Nehru wrote from his prison cell during World War II, citing British and Indian sources (the latter banned under the Raj). A current scholarly history records the "common practice" of "wanton attacks on passive villagers and unarmed Indians, even faithful domestic servants," brutal murder of captured "mutineers," "entire villages put to the torch for the 'crime' of proximity" to the site of real or alleged Indian atrocities, as a "terrible racial ferocity . . . erupted and inspired British vengeance." Another describes how "tens of thousands of soldiers and village guerrillas were hanged, shot, or blown from guns," leading to a significant drop in population in several regions. The tone is illustrated by the advice in May 1857 by John Nicholson—"the hero of Delhi," an "upright man," and "professed Christian," according to his contemporary admirers: "Let us propose a bill for the flaying alive, impalement or burning of the murderers of the women and children at Delhi. The idea of simply hanging the perpetrators of such atrocities is maddening." The atrocities to which he referred included those revealed in "detailed but imaginary accounts" of other righteous Christians, who carried out unspeakable atrocities in revenge.[52]

To illustrate the impact of the sobering lessons of World War II, in Kenya in the 1950s some 150,000 people died in the course of Britain's repression of a colonial revolt, a campaign conducted with hideous terror and atrocities but, as always, guided by the highest ideals. The British governor had explained to the people of Kenya in 1946 that Britain controls their land and resources "as of right, the product of historical events which reflect the greatest glory of our fathers and grandfathers." If "the greater part of the wealth of the country is at present in our hands," that is because "this land we have made is our land by right—by right of achievement," and Africans will simply have to learn to live in "a world which we have made, under the humanitarian impulses of the late nineteenth and the twentieth century."[53]

History is replete with precedents for what we see before our eyes, day after day, though the stakes grow more awesome along with the means of destruction available.

Israeli commanders rely not only on the standard military doctrine of those who have overwhelming force at their command but also on their own experience. When they ordered massive violence to "crush" Palestinians with cruel "collective punishment" in October 2000, they probably did not anticipate that the tactics would arouse the victims to "bloody revenge."[54] That did not happen when Prime Minister Rabin sent his troops to crush the population of the territories by breaking bones, beatings, torture, and humiliation during the first Intifada a decade earlier. Then the tactics largely worked, as they had in the past.[55]

In December 1982, after an outburst of settler and IDF terror and atrocities in the territories that shocked even Israeli hawks, a prominent Israeli academic specialist on military affairs warned of the dangers to Israeli society when three-quarters of a million young people who have served in the IDF "know that the task of the army is not only to defend the state in the battlefield against a foreign army, but to demolish the rights of innocent people just because they are Araboushim living in territories that God promised to us." The essential principle had been formulated in the early years of the occupation by Moshe Dayan: Israel should tell the Palestinians in the territories that "we have no solution, you shall continue to live like dogs, and whoever wishes may leave, and we will see where this process leads."[56] But the Palestinians remained "samidin," who endured but scarcely retaliated.

The second Intifada was different. This time the orders to crush Palestinians relentlessly and teach them "not to raise their heads" escalated the cycle of violence, spilling into Israel itself, which had lost the substantial immunity to retaliation from within the territories that had prevailed for more than three decades of military occupation. Echoing the concerns of twenty years earlier, an editorial in Israel's leading daily concluded that:

> Two-and-a-half years of intense fighting against Palestinian terrorism have turned the Israel Defense Forces into an obdurate and callous army, focused on its mission out of an indifference

to the consequences of its actions. The IDF, which brought up
generations of soldiers on the myth of purity of arms and educated its commanders with the idea of the moral, deliberating
soldier, who takes tough decisions, while thinking of humane
considerations, is turning into a killing machine whose effi-
ciency is awe-inspiring, yet shocking.[57]

As the official ratio of Palestinians to Israelis killed moved from
twenty-to-one to close to three-to-one, attitudes in the US changed
from inattention to atrocities or support for them to extreme outrage: at the atrocities directed at innocent US clients. These were
indeed outrageous. The selective vision, however, speaks for itself,
not least because of its deep roots in the culture and history of con-
querors.

Chapter 8

Terrorism and Justice: Some Useful Truisms

On a highly controversial topic like the one we turn to now, perhaps it is a good idea to begin with a few simple truths.

The first is that actions are evaluated in terms of the range of likely consequences. A second is the principle of universality; we apply to ourselves the same standards we apply to others, if not more stringent ones. Apart from being the merest truisms, these principles are also the foundation of just war theory, at least any version of it that deserves to be taken seriously. The truisms raise an empirical question: Are they accepted? Investigation will reveal, I believe, that they are rejected almost without exception.

The first truism may merit a word of elaboration. The actual consequences of an action may be highly significant, but they do not bear on the moral evaluation of the action. No one celebrates Khrushchev's success in placing nuclear missiles in Cuba because it did not lead to nuclear war, or condemns the fear-mongers who warned of the threat. Nor do we applaud North Korea's Dear Leader for developing nuclear weapons and providing missile technology to Pakistan, or denounce those who warn of possible consequences because they haven't taken place. An apologist for state violence who took such positions would be regarded as a moral monster or lunatic. That's obvious, until it comes time to apply the same criteria to ourselves. Then the stance of the lunatic and moral monster is taken to be highly honorable, indeed obligatory, and adherence to the truisms is condemned with horror.

Let us, nevertheless, accept the truisms for what they are: truisms. And then think about a few crucial current cases to which they apply.

TRUISMS AND TERROR

Take 9-11. It is widely argued that the terrorist attacks changed everything dramatically as the world entered a new and frightening "age of terror"—the title of a collection of academic essays by Yale University scholars and others.[1] It is also widely held that the term *terror* is very hard to define.

We might ask why the concept of terror should be considered particularly obscure. There are official US government definitions that fall well within the range of clarity of other usages that are regarded as unproblematic. A US Army manual defined *terrorism* as "the calculated use of violence or threat of violence to attain goals that are political, religious, or ideological in nature . . . through intimidation, coercion, or instilling fear." The official US Code gave a more elaborate definition, essentially along the same lines. The British government's definition is similar: "Terrorism is the use, or threat, of action which is violent, damaging or disrupting, and is intended to influence the government or intimidate the public and is for the purpose of advancing a political, religious, or ideological cause."[2] These definitions seem fairly clear. They are close enough to ordinary usage, and are considered appropriate when discussing the terrorism of enemies.

The official US definitions are the ones I have been using in writing about the topic since the Reagan administration came into office in 1981, declaring that a war on terror would be a centerpiece of its foreign policy. The reliance on these definitions is particularly appropriate for our purposes because they were formulated when the first war on terror was declared. But almost no one uses them, and they have been rescinded, replaced by nothing sensible. The reasons do not seem obscure: the official definitions of *terrorism* are virtually the same as the definitions of *counterterror* (sometimes called "low-intensity conflict," or "counterinsurgency"). But counterterror is official US policy, and it plainly will not do to say that the US is officially committed to terrorism.[3]

The US is by no means alone in this practice. It is traditional for states to call their own terrorism "counterterror," even the worst mass murderers: the Nazis, for example. In occupied Europe they claimed to be defending the population and legitimate governments from the partisans, terrorists supported from abroad. That was not entirely false; even the most egregious propaganda rarely is. The partisans were undoubtedly directed from London, and they did engage in terror. The US military had some appreciation of the Nazi perspective: its counterinsurgency doctrine was modeled on Nazi manuals, which were analyzed sympathetically, with the assistance of Wehrmacht officers.[4]

It is this common practice that allows for the conventional thesis that terror is a weapon of the weak. That is true, by definition, if *terror* is restricted to their terrorism. If the doctrinal requirement is lifted, however, we find that, like most weapons, terror is primarily a weapon of the powerful.

Another problem with the official definitions of *terror* is that it follows from them that the US is a leading terrorist state. That much is hardly controversial, at least among those who believe that we should pay some attention to such institutions as the International Court of Justice or the UN Security Council, or mainstream scholarship, as the examples of Nicaragua and Cuba unequivocally reveal. But that conclusion won't do either. So we are left with no sensible definition of *terrorism*—unless we decide to break ranks and use the official definitions that have been abandoned because of their unacceptable consequences.

The official definitions do not answer every question precisely. They do not, for example, draw a sharp boundary between *international terrorism* and *aggression,* or between *terror* and *resistance.* These issues have arisen in interesting ways, which have direct bearing on the redeclared war on terror and on today's headlines.

Take the distinction between *terror* and *resistance.* One question that arises is the legitimacy of actions to realize "the right to self-determination, freedom, and independence, as derived from the Charter of the United Nations, of people forcibly deprived of that right . . . particularly peoples under colonial and racist regimes and foreign occupation." Do such actions fall under *terror* or *resistance*? The quoted words are from the most forceful denunciation of the crime of terrorism by the UN General Assembly, which stated further that "nothing in the present resolution could in any way prejudice the right" so defined. The resolution was adopted in December 1987, just as officially recognized international terrorism reached its peak. It is obviously important. The vote was 153 to 2 (with a single abstention, Honduras), hence even more important.[5]

The two countries that voted against the resolution were the usual ones. Their reason, they explained at the UN session, was the paragraph just quoted. The phrase "colonial and racist regimes" was understood to refer to their ally, apartheid South Africa. Evidently the US and Israel could not condone resistance to the apartheid regime, particularly when it was led by Mandela's African National Congress, one of the world's "more notorious terrorist groups," as Washington determined at the time. The other phrase, "foreign occupation," was understood to refer to Israel's military occupation, then in its twentieth year. Evidently, resistance could not be condoned in that case either.

The US and Israel were alone in the world in denying that such actions can be legitimate resistance, and declaring them to be terrorism. The US-Israeli stand extends beyond the occupied territories. Thus the US and Israel regard Hezbollah, for example, as one of the leading terrorist organizations in the world, not because of its terrorist acts (which are real) but because it was formed to resist the Israeli occupation of southern Lebanon, and succeeded in driving out the invaders after two decades of defiance of Security Council orders to withdraw. The US even goes so far as to call people "terrorists" if they resist direct US aggression: the South Vietnamese, for example; or recently, the Iraqis.[6]

The public knows nothing about the major UN condemnation of

what Reagan called the "evil scourge of terrorism" and its fate, by virtue of the usual double veto. To learn about such matters one has to wander into forbidden territory: the historical and documentary record, or marginalized critical literature.

Despite the unclarities, and the sharp divide between the US–Israel and the world, the official US definitions of *terror* seem fairly adequate to the purposes at hand.

Let us turn to the belief that 9-11 signaled a sharp change in the course of history. That seems questionable. Nonetheless, something dramatically new and different did happen on that terrible day. The target was not Cuba, or Nicaragua, or Lebanon, or Chechnya, or one of the other traditional victims of international terrorism, but a state with enormous power to shape the future. For the first time, an attack on the rich and powerful countries succeeded on a scale that is, regrettably, not unfamiliar in their traditional domains. Alongside horror at the crime against humanity and sympathy for the victims, commentators outside the ranks of Western privilege often responded to the 9-11 atrocities with a "welcome to the club," particularly in Latin America, where it is not so easy to forget the plague of violence and repression that swept through the region from the early 1960s, or its roots.

The plague can in part be traced to a decision by the Kennedy administration in 1962 to change the mission of the Latin American military, effectively, from "hemispheric defense" to "internal security." The effect was a shift from toleration "of the rapacity and cruelty of the Latin American military" to "direct complicity" in their crimes, to support for "the methods of Heinrich Himmler's extermination squads," in the words of Charles Maechling, who led US counterinsurgency and internal defense planning from 1961 to 1966.[7] The perception of the victims is similar. To take one case of unusual current significance, the highly respected president of the Colombian Permanent Committee for Human Rights, Alfredo Vásquez Carrizosa, writes that the Kennedy administration "took great pains to transform our regular armies into counterinsurgency brigades, accepting the new strategy of the death squads," ushering in "what is known in Latin America as the National Security Doctrine . . . not defense against an external enemy, but a way to make the military establishment the masters of the game [with] the right to combat the internal enemy . . . : it is the right to fight and to exterminate social workers, trade unionists, men and women who are not supportive of the establishment, and who are assumed to be communist extremists. And this could mean anyone, including human rights activists such as myself."[8]

The "great pains" to which he refers coincided with the fateful 1962 decision. In that year, Kennedy sent a Special Forces mission to Colombia, led by General William Yarborough. Yarborough advised "paramilitary, sabotage and/or terrorist activities against known communist proponents," to be "employed now . . . [i]f we have such an apparatus" in place—"we" because there is no need to prevaricate in secret communications.[9] In counterinsurgency doctrine, the phrase "known communist proponents" extends to the categories of "assumed communist extremists" that Vásquez Carrizosa enumerates, a fact well known to Latin Americans, just as they know that the primary victims are the poor and oppressed who are daring to raise their heads.

The National Security Doctrine reached Central America in the 1980s. El Salvador became the leading recipient of US military aid as state terror reached its awful peak. When Congress hampered direct military aid and training by imposing human rights conditions, as in Guatemala after massive government atrocities, surrogates undertook the task.

The victims do not easily forget, though among the powerful, these crimes are subject to the standard "ritual avoidance" of unacceptable facts. Hardly a day passes without examples. Thus, a front-page story in the national press warns that the threat of Al Qaeda is increasing, as it is turning from targets that are "well protected . . . to so-called soft targets."[10] The story should at once recall Washington's official instructions to its proxy forces to attack "soft targets" in Nicaragua immediately after it was ordered by the highest international authorities to terminate its terrorist war, and the reaction to these orders.

Whether attacking "soft targets" is right or wrong, terrorism or a noble cause, depends on who is the agent. The practice is routine, and unproblematic once moral truisms have been deemed irrelevant and unwanted facts efficiently "disappeared."

THE ART OF "DISAPPEARING" UNWANTED FACTS

One contributor to the Yale volume (Charles Hill) observed that 9-11 opened the second "war on terror," the first having been declared by the Reagan administration twenty years earlier, a rare recognition of reality. And "we won" the first war, Hill reports triumphantly, though the terrorist monster was only wounded, not slain.[11] How "we won" is someone else's department: the Jesuit intellectuals in Central America, the School of the Americas, truth commissions, serious scholarship, activist and solidarity literature, and the memories of the survivors.

We can learn a good deal about the current war on terror by inquiring into the first phase, and how it is now portrayed. One leading academic specialist describes the 1980s as the decade of "state terrorism," of "persistent state involvement, or 'sponsorship,' of terrorism, especially by Libya and Iran." The US merely responded with "a 'proactive' stance toward terrorism." Others recommend the methods by which "we won": the operations for which the US was condemned by the World Court and Security Council (absent the veto) are a model for "Nicaragua-like support for the Taliban's adversaries." A prominent historian of the subject, David Rapoport, finds deep roots for the terrorism of Osama bin Laden: in South Vietnam, where "the effectiveness of Vietcong terror against the American Goliath armed with modern technology kindled hopes that the Western heartland was vulnerable too."[12]

The villainy of the terrorists attacking us everywhere is awesome indeed.

Keeping to convention, these analyses portray the US as a benign victim, defending itself from the terror of others: the Vietnamese (in South Vietnam), the Nicaraguans (in Nicaragua), Libyans and Iranians (if they ever suffered a slight at US hands, it passes unnoticed), and other anti-American forces worldwide. If not everyone in the world shares that perception of history, then they too are "anti-American" and can be safely dismissed.

As discussed earlier, the plague of US-backed state terror that spread through Latin America in the 1960s peaked in Central America in the 1980s, as Reagan's "war on terror" took its deadly toll. Central America was one prime focus of that onslaught. The other was the Mideast/Mediterranean region. Here, too, the contrast between what actually happened and what is portrayed is dramatic and revealing. In this region, the worst single atrocity during the 1980s was the Israeli invasion of Lebanon in 1982, which, like the murderous and destructive Rabin-Peres invasions of 1993 and 1996, had little pretense of self-defense. In the light of crucial Reagan-Clinton support, these operations add to Washington's record of state-supported international terrorism.

The US was directly involved in many other acts of terror in the region, including the three candidates for the prize of most extreme terrorist atrocity of 1985, when terrorism in that region was selected by editors as the lead story of the year: (1) the car bomb outside a mosque in Beirut that killed 80 people (mostly women and girls) and wounded 250 others, timed to explode as people were leaving and traced back to the CIA and British intelligence; (2) Shimon Peres's bombing of Tunis, killing 75 people, Palestinians and Tunisians, expedited by the US and praised by Secretary of State Shultz, then unanimously condemned by the UN Security Council as an "act of armed aggression" (US abstaining); and (3) Peres's "Iron Fist" operations directed against what the Israeli high command called "terrorist villagers" in occupied Lebanon, reaching new depths of "calculated brutality and arbitrary murder" in the words of a Western diplomat familiar with the area, amply supported by direct coverage, total casualties unknown in accord with the usual conventions.

All these atrocities fall within the category of state-supported international terrorism, if not the more severe war crime of aggression. This accounting excludes many other atrocities, such as the regular kidnappings and killings on the high seas by Israeli naval forces attacking ships in transit between Cyprus and northern Lebanon, with many of those captured brought to Israel and kept in prison without charge as hostages, and numerous other crimes that are not crimes because they were backed by Washington.[13]

In journalism and scholarship on terrorism, 1985 is recognized to be the peak year of Middle East terrorism, but not because of these events; rather, because of two terrorist atrocities in which a single person was murdered, in each case an American.[14]

In the worst of the two terrorist atrocities that passed through the doctrinal filters, a crippled American Jew, Leon Klinghoffer, was brutally murdered during the hijacking of the *Achille Lauro* cruise ship in October 1985 by a Palestinian terrorist group led by Abu Abbas. The murder "seemed to set a standard for remorselessness among terrorists," *New York Times* correspondent John Burns wrote. Burns described Abu Abbas as the "has-been monster" who may "finally have to face a day of reckoning with American Justice" for his role in the crime. One of the heralded achievements of the invasion of Iraq was the capture of Abu Abbas a few months later.[15]

The Klinghoffer murder remains the most vivid and lasting symbol of the ineradicable evil of Arab terrorism and the unanswerable proof that there can be no negotiating with these vermin. The atrocity was very real, and is in no way mitigated by the terrorists' plea that the hijacking was in retaliation for the far more murderous US-backed Israeli terrorist attack on Tunis a week earlier. But the bombing of Tunis does not enter the canon of terrorism because it is subject to the wrong-agent fallacy. It remained unmentioned when Abu Abbas was captured. There would of course be no difficulty in apprehending the "monsters" Shimon Peres and George Shultz, who are far from "has beens," and bringing them to "a day of reckoning with American justice." But that is beyond unthinkable.

Also efficiently "disappeared" are recent events that bear more than a superficial similarity to the Klinghoffer murder. The reaction was silence when British reporters found "the flattened remains of a wheelchair" in the remnants of the Jenin refugee camp after Sharon's spring 2002 offensive. "It had been utterly crushed, ironed flat as if in a cartoon," they reported: "In the middle of the debris lay a broken white flag." A crippled Palestinian, Kemal Zughayer, "was shot dead as he tried to wheel himself up the road. The Israeli tanks must have driven over the body, because when [a friend] found it, one leg and both arms were missing, and the face, he said, had been ripped in two."[16] If even reported in the US, this would have been dismissed as an inadvertent error in the course of justified retaliation. Kemal Zughayer does not deserve to enter the annals of terrorism along with Leon Klinghoffer. His murder was not under the command of a "monster" but a "man of peace," who enjoys a soulful relation with the "man of vision" in the White House.

The basic dynamic at work was outlined twenty years ago by one of Israel's most eminent writers and commentators, Boaz Evron, after an upsurge of settler-IDF violence that caused much consternation in Israel. Evron wrote a sardonic account of how to deal with the lower orders—the "Araboushim" in Israeli slang. Israel should "keep them on a short leash," he wrote, so that they recognize "that the whip is held over their head." As long as not too many people are being visibly killed, then Western humanists will "accept it all peacefully" and even ask, "What is so terrible?"[17]

The guardians of journalistic integrity in the US understand the lesson without Evron's advice. The most prestigious media watchdog, the *Columbia Journalism Review,* gave its cherished "laurel" to the US media for their coverage of Sharon's spring 2002 offensive in Jenin, Nablus, Ramallah, and elsewhere, in the thirty-fifth year of Israel's occupation of the West Bank and Gaza. The recipients earned the laurel, according to the *Review,* for ensuring that scrutiny of the offensive would focus on one cardinal question: Was there a purposeful massacre of hundreds of civilians in the Jenin refugee camp?[18] If not, then civilized people can "accept it all peacefully."

We might try a thought experiment. Suppose that Syria had occupied Israel for thirty-five years, employing the means and measures of Israel's occupation, and then proceeded further to duplicate

Sharon's 2002 offensive: rampaging through Jewish towns, leveling large areas with bulldozers and tanks, keeping the population under siege for weeks without food or water or access to medical care, destroying cultural centers and the institutions of government and archaeological treasures, making it crystal clear to the Yids in every possible way that "the whip is held over their head"—but not slaughtering hundreds of them at once. According to the standards of the "laurel," only an anti-Arab racist would object—and discovery of the scattered parts of a murdered Jewish cripple in a wheelchair crushed by a Syrian tank would merit no notice, let alone stern "American Justice."

Reviewing "the Jenin story," the *Review* berated the British press for "embracing Israel's guilt as established fact" and ridiculed the UN for "preparing an investigation by a team whose political sympathies ensured that its conclusions would be challenged," certainly by the independent thinkers of the *Review*. "Amid all this confounding din," the editors asked, "what was the world to believe?"

Fortunately, all was not lost: "Enter the independent U.S. news media, on a fact-finding mission of their own," which refuted the anti-Israel slanders and revealed that there was "no deliberate, cold-blooded murder of hundreds" at Jenin—in fact, reaching exactly the same conclusions as the disreputable British media (and others), which, however, did not adopt the framework of US-Israeli propaganda as rigidly as the editors of the *Review* demand, and scrutinized the Israeli invasion beyond that single question.

The "independent U.S. media" did not merit the insulting praise of their cheerleader. Careful readers could learn about the crimes that had taken place, though not in the shocking detail presented in the Israeli and European press. And they were carefully protected from the complicity of their own government, in routine fashion.

When the "wrong agents" are implicated in state-supported international terrorism, we sometimes discover that terrorist atrocities are not fully effaced, but rather praised. An instructive case is the country that replaced El Salvador as the leading recipient of US military aid and training: Turkey, where "state terror" was practiced on a massive scale through the Clinton years, relying on US support.[19] I borrow the term *state terror* from the Turkish state minister for human rights, referring to the vast atrocities against Kurds in 1994, and from sociologist Ismail Besikci, returned to prison after publishing his book *State Terror in the Near East,* having already served fifteen years for recording Turkish repression of Kurds. As elsewhere, unacceptable facts were "disappeared," but the events did not pass entirely unnoticed. The State Department's *Year 2000* report on Washington's "efforts to combat terrorism" singled out Turkey for its "positive experiences" in combating terror, along with Algeria and Spain, worthy colleagues. This praise was reported without comment in a front-page story in the *New York Times* by its specialist on terrorism. In a leading journal of international affairs, Ambassador Robert Pearson reports that the US "could have no better friend and ally than Turkey" in its efforts "to eliminate terrorism" worldwide, thanks to the "capabilities of [Turkey's] armed forces" demonstrated in their "anti-terror campaign" in the Kurdish southeast.[20] As noted, the voluntary US censorship of Turkish state terror was eased slightly in early 2003 during Turkey's democratic deviation, though the decisive role of the United States remained well concealed.[21]

The considerations just reviewed, a small sample, suggest one simple way to reduce the threat of terror: stop participating in it. That would be a significant contribution to a general "war on terror." Nevertheless, it would not address the category of terror that passes through the doctrinal filters: *their* terror against *us* and our clients, an extremely serious matter, no doubt. Let us put that issue aside for a moment and consider a related domain in which attention to truisms may have some value.

TRUISMS AND JUST WAR THEORY

The theory of just war has enjoyed a revival in the context of the "new era of humanitarian intervention" and international terrorism. Consider the strongest case put forth: the bombing of Afghanistan, a paradigm example of just war, according to the Western consensus. The respected moral-political philosopher Jean Bethke Elshtain summarizes received opinion fairly accurately when she writes that "nearly everyone, with the exception of absolute pacifists and those who seem to think we should let ourselves be slaughtered with impunity because so many people out there 'hate' us, agrees" that the bombing of Afghanistan was clearly a just war.[22] To mention just one additional example, *New York Times* columnist Bill Keller, now executive editor, remarks that when "America dispatched soldiers in the cause of 'regime change' " in Afghanistan, "the opposition was mostly limited to the people who are reflexively against the American use of power," either timid supporters or "isolationists, the doctrinaire left and the soft-headed types Christopher Hitchens described as people who, 'discovering a viper in the bed of their child, would place the first call to People for the Ethical Treatment of Animals.' "[23]

These are empirical statements, so despite the near-unanimity of the declarations, we are entitled to ask whether they are true. Let's ignore the fact that "regime change" was not "the cause" of war in Afghanistan but rather an afterthought late in the game. Were there opponents of the bombing who were not either absolute pacifists or absolute lunatics?

It turns out that there were, and the opponents formed an interesting collection. To begin with, they apparently included the great majority of the population of the world when the bombing was announced. So we discover from an international Gallup poll in late September 2001. The lead question was this: "Once the identity of the terrorists is known, should the American government launch a military attack on the country or countries where the terrorists are based or should the American government seek to extradite the terrorists to stand trial?" Whether such diplomatic means could have succeeded is known only to ideological extremists on both sides; tentative explorations of extradition by the Taliban were instantly rebuffed by Washington, which also refused to provide evidence for its accusations.

World opinion strongly favored diplomatic-judicial measures over military action. In Europe, support for military action ranged from 8 percent in Greece to 29 percent in France. Support was least in Latin America, the region that has the most experience with US intervention: it ranged from 2 percent in Mexico to 11 percent in Colombia and Venezuela. The sole exception was Panama, where only 80 percent preferred peaceful means, 16 percent military attack. Support for strikes that included civilian targets was much less. Even in the two countries polled that supported the use of military force, India and Israel (where the reasons were parochial), considerable majorities opposed such attacks. There was, then, overwhelming opposition to Washington's actual policies, which not only included civilian targets but even turned major urban concentrations into "ghost towns" from the first moment, the press reported.

The Gallup poll was not reported in the US, though it was elsewhere, including Latin America.[24]

Notice that even this very limited support for the bombing was based on a crucial presupposition: that those responsible for 9-11 were known. But they were not, as the government quietly informed us eight months after the bombing. In June 2002, FBI director Robert Mueller testified before a Senate committee, delivering what the press described as some of "his most detailed public comments on the origins of the attacks" of 9-11.[25] Mueller informed the Senate that "investigators *believe* the idea of the Sept. 11 attacks on the World Trade Center and Pentagon came from al Qaeda leaders in Afghanistan," though the plotting and financing may trace to Germany and the United Arab Emirates. "We *think* the masterminds of it were in Afghanistan, high in the al Qaeda leadership," Mueller said. If the indirect responsibility of Afghanistan could only be surmised in June 2002, it evidently could not have been *known* eight months before, when President Bush ordered the bombing of Afghanistan.

According to the FBI, then, the bombing was a war crime, an act of aggression, based on mere supposition. It also follows directly that there was virtually no detectable world support for the policies actually undertaken, since even the minimal support recorded by polls was based on a presupposition that Washington and London knew to be false.

Perhaps the former director of Human Rights Watch Africa, now a professor of law at Emory University, spoke for many others around the world when he addressed the International Council on Human Rights Policy in Geneva in January 2002, saying that "I am unable to appreciate any moral, political or legal difference between this *jihad* by the United States against those it deems to be its enemies and the *jihad* by Islamic groups against those they deem to be their enemies."[26]

What about Afghan opinion? Information is scanty but not entirely lacking. In late October 2001, after three weeks of intense bombing, 1,000 Afghan leaders gathered in Peshawar, some exiles, some coming from within Afghanistan, all committed to overthrowing the Taliban regime. It was "a rare display of unity among tribal elders, Islamic scholars, fractious politicians, and former guerrilla commanders," the press reported. They had many disagreements but unanimously "urged the US to stop the air raids" and appealed to the international media to call for an end to the "bombing of innocent people." They urged that other means be adopted to overthrow the hated Taliban regime, a goal they believed could be achieved without further death and destruction.

A similar message was conveyed by Afghan opposition leader Abdul Haq, who was highly regarded in Washington and by Afghan President Hamid Karzai. Just before he entered Afghanistan without US support, and was then captured and killed, Haq condemned the bombing then under way and criticized the US for refusing to back his efforts and those of others "to create a revolt within the Taliban." The bombing was "a big setback for these efforts," he said: The US "is trying to show its muscle, score a victory and scare everyone in the world. They don't care about the suffering of the Afghans or how many people we will lose." The prominent Afghan women's organization RAWA, which received some belated recognition when it became ideologically serviceable to express concern about the fate of women in Afghanistan, also bitterly condemned the bombing.[27]

Among other opponents of the bombing were the major aid and relief agencies, deeply concerned over the likely effect on the population, agreeing with academic specialists that the bombing posed a "grave risk" of starvation for millions of people.[28]

In short, the lunatic fringe was not insubstantial.

Let us turn now to the most elementary principle of just war theory, universality. Those who cannot accept this principle should have the decency to keep silent about matters of right and wrong, or just war.

If we can rise to this level, some obvious questions arise: for example, have Cuba and Nicaragua been entitled to set off bombs in Washington, New York, and Miami in self-defense against ongoing terrorist attack? Particularly so when the perpetrators are well known and act with complete impunity, sometimes in brazen defiance of the highest international authorities, so that the cases are far clearer than Afghanistan? If not, why not? Certainly one cannot appeal to the scale of crimes to justify such a stand; the merest look at the factual record bars that move.

If these questions are not answered, just war pronouncements cannot be taken seriously. I have yet to discover a single case where the questions are even raised. That leads to some conclusions that may not be particularly attractive but that might merit attention and self-examination—and serious concern about the long-term implications of the apparent inability to accept the principle of universality that underlies these failures.

Although the critical questions are not answered, or in fact even raised, related issues occasionally do come up, and in a manner that gives some useful insight into the prevailing moral and intellectual culture. The Latin American correspondent of the New York Times informs us that Latin American intellectuals have "reflexively accorded . . . anti-American leaders immunity to the moral standards applied to other leaders." His evidence is a statement by Latin American intellectuals warning against a post-Iraq invasion of Cuba.

He believes a "psychological explanation" may be necessary to account for their failure to adopt "universal moral standards."[29] No psychological explanation seems necessary, however, when he and his associates "reflexively accord" their leaders "immunity to the moral standards" they apply to others: specifically, the moral standards that would call for severe punishment for anyone else who dared to carry out terrorist wars comparable to those that their leaders have conducted against Cuba and Nicaragua.

Consider how Elshtain's argument on Afghanistan fares within her own framework. She formulates four criteria for just war. First, force is justified if it "protects the innocent from certain harm"; her sole example is when a country has "certain knowledge that genocide will commence on a certain date" and the victims have no means of self-defense. Second, the war "must be openly declared or otherwise authorized by a legitimate authority." Third, it "must begin with the right intentions." Fourth, it "must be a last resort after other possibilities for the redress and defense of the values at stake have been explored."

The first condition is inapplicable to Afghanistan. The second and third are meaningless: an open declaration of war by an aggressor confers no support whatsoever for a claim of just war; the worst criminals claim "right intentions," and there are always acolytes to endorse the claims. The fourth obviously does not apply in Afghanistan. Therefore her paradigm case collapses entirely, under her own criteria.

That aside, whatever one thinks of Elshtain's belief that the bombing of Afghanistan met her conditions, these conditions hold with far greater clarity for many of the victims of US state-supported international terrorism. On her own grounds, then, these victims should be granted the right to wage a just war against the US by bombing and terror, as long as it is openly declared and accompanied by a pronouncement of "right intentions." The reduction to absurdity, however, presupposes that we adopt the principle of universality, unmentioned in her historical/philosophical study and tacitly rejected in the standard fashion.

Let's bring in some further relevant facts. The official motive for the bombing of Afghanistan was to force the Taliban to hand over people that the US suspected of involvement in the crimes of 9-11; the US refused, however, to provide any evidence. At the time when Taliban reluctance to comply was the lead story of the day, arousing much fury, Haiti *renewed* its request for extradition of Emmanuel Constant, leader of the paramilitary forces that had primary responsibility for the brutal murder of thousands of Haitians during the early 1990s, when the military junta was supported, not so tacitly, by the first Bush and Clinton administrations. The request apparently did not even merit a response, or more than the barest report. Constant had been sentenced in absentia in Haiti; it is widely assumed that the US is concerned that if he testifies, he may reveal contacts between the state terrorists and Washington.[30] Does Haiti therefore have the right to set off bombs in Washington? Or to try to kidnap or kill Constant in New York, where he lives, killing bystanders in approved Israeli style? If not, why not? Why is the question not even raised in this case, or in that of other murderous state terrorists who enjoy safe haven in the US? And if the question is considered too absurd even to consider (as it is, by elementary moral standards), where does that leave the consensus on the resort to violence by one's own leaders?

Referring to 9-11, some argue that the evil of terrorism is "absolute" and merits a "reciprocally absolute doctrine" in response: ferocious military assault in accord with the Bush doctrine that "*If you harbor terrorists, you're a terrorist; if you aid and abet terrorists, you're a terrorist—and you will be treated like one.*"[31]

It would be hard to find anyone who accepts the doctrine that massive bombing is a legitimate response to terrorist crimes. No sane person would agree that bombing Washington would be legitimate in accord with the "reciprocally absolute doctrine" on response to terrorist atrocities, or a justified and properly "calibrated" response to them. If there is some reason why this observation is inappropriate, it has yet to be articulated, even contemplated, as far as I have been able to discover.

Consider some of the legal arguments that have been presented to justify the US-UK bombing of Afghanistan. Christopher Greenwood argues that the US has the right of "self-defense" against "those who caused or threatened . . . death and destruction," appealing to the World Court ruling in the Nicaragua case. The paragraph he cites applies far more clearly to the US war against Nicaragua than to the Taliban or Al Qaeda, so if it is taken to justify intensive US bombardment and ground attack in Afghanistan, then Nicaragua should have been entitled to carry out much more severe attacks against the US. Another distinguished professor of international law, Thomas Franck, supports the US-UK war on grounds that "a state is responsible for the consequences of permitting its territory to be used to injure another state"; the principle is surely applicable to the US in the case of Nicaragua, Cuba, and many other examples.[32]

Needless to say, in no such case would an appeal to the right of "self-defense" against continuing acts of "death and destruction" be remotely tolerable: *acts,* not merely threats.

The same holds for more nuanced proposals for an appropriate response to terrorist atrocities. Military historian Michael Howard proposes "a police operation conducted under the auspices of the United Nations . . . against a criminal conspiracy whose members should be hunted down and brought before an international court, where they would receive a fair trial and, if found guilty, be awarded an appropriate sentence." Reasonable enough, though the idea that such measures be applied to the US or Britain is unthinkable.[33]

Two Oxford scholars propose a principle of "proportionality": "The magnitude of response will be determined by the magnitude with which the aggression interfered with key values in the society attacked"; in the case of 9-11, "freedom to pursue self-betterment in a plural society through market economics." That value was viciously attacked on 9-11 by "aggressors . . . with a moral orthodoxy divergent from the West." Since "Afghanistan constitutes a state that sided with the aggressor," and refused US demands to turn over suspects, "the United States and its allies, according to the principle of magnitude of interference, could justifiably and morally resort to force against the Taliban government."[34]

If the moral orthodoxy of the West accommodates the principle of universality, it follows that Cuba and Nicaragua (in fact, many others) can "justifiably and morally resort to" far greater force against the US government. Uncontroversially, the US terrorist attacks and other illegal actions against Cuba and Nicaragua "interfered with key values in the society attacked," far more dramatically than in the case of 9-11, and were intended to do so. Furthermore, since Britain "sided with the aggressor," Oxford too should be subject to attack, at least by Nicaragua.

We are entitled to ask why the conclusion cannot even be contemplated (quite properly, of course) and what that implies about the elite intellectual culture.

The conclusions with regard to the principle of universality extend far beyond these cases, including even such minor escapades (by US-UK standards) as Clinton's missile attack on the al-Shifa pharmaceutical plant in Sudan in 1998, which led to "several tens of thousands" of deaths, according to the only reputable estimates we have, estimates consistent with the immediate assessment of Human Rights Watch and later reports of knowledgeable observers.[35] A crime of even a fraction of the scale would elicit fury if the target were the US, Israel, or some other worthy victim, and retaliation of a kind that one hesitates to imagine, which would furthermore be acclaimed as a paradigm example of just war. The principle of proportionality entails that Sudan had every right to carry out massive terror in retaliation, even more so if we adopt the more extreme view that Clinton's missile attack had "appalling consequences for the economy and society" of Sudan,[36] so that the atrocity was much worse than the crimes of 9-11, which were appalling enough but did not have such consequences.

Almost all of the limited commentary on the Sudan bombing keeps to the question of whether the plant was believed to produce chemical weapons. True or false, that has no bearing at all on the crime; specifically, on "the magnitude with which the aggression interfered with key values in the society attacked." Many point out that the resulting deaths were unintended, so that the perpetrators, and those who disregard the consequences of the attack, are not culpable. The argument again illustrates, dramatically, the standard rejection of the principle of universality. We would never accept this stand for a moment with regard to others: many of the atrocities we (rightly) denounce are unintended, though that is considered irrelevant—when the perpetrator is someone other than ourselves. But a much harsher conclusion follows, immediately and unequivocally. The claim that the actions were not criminal can be sustained only on the assumption that the fate of the victims was of no concern to the perpetrators. We cannot seriously doubt that the likely human consequences were understood by US planners; the CIA knew as well as Human Rights Watch and many others that they were destroying the country's major source of pharmaceuticals and veterinary medicines, and what the likely effects would be. And the same conclusions could have been drawn at once, and surely can be now, by anyone who thinks that the effects of our violence on poor Africans might merit some concern. The acts can be excused, then, only on the Hegelian doctrine that Africans are "mere things," whose lives have "no value." Observing the attitudes and practice that prevail, those outside the ranks of Western privilege may draw their own conclusions about the "moral orthodoxy of the West."

CONFRONTING TERROR

Let us now restrict the term *terror*—improperly, but in accord with near-universal convention—to the subcategory that passes through the doctrinal filters.

The wars contemplated as part of the redeclared "war on terror" are to go on for a long time. "There's no telling how many wars it will take to secure freedom in the homeland," the president announced.[37] That's fair enough. Potential threats are virtually limitless everywhere, even at home, as the anthrax attack and the failed investigations of it illustrate.

Not only is the "war on terror," as conceived, likely to go on for a long time, but it also did not suddenly become a crucial issue on

9-11. The terrorist attacks of that day were not entirely unexpected, yet another reason to question the widely held belief that 9-11 signaled a sharp change in the course of history. Even readers of newspaper headlines, and surely government planners, were well aware years earlier that atrocities of the 9-11 variety might occur. After all, in 1993, one almost *did* occur. Organizations presumably related to those responsible for 9-11 came perilously close to blowing up the World Trade Center and killing perhaps tens of thousands of people. It was also known, at once, that they had far more ambitious plans that were barely aborted in time. Even with the hideous consummation of these plans on 9-11, risk assessments did not significantly change.

Prospects of major terrorist atrocities were publicly discussed well before 9-11. And there could have been little doubt of the nature of the radical Islamist terrorist organizations since at least 1981, when elements that formed part of the core of Al Qaeda in later years assassinated President Sadat of Egypt; or a few years later, when groups that may have been loosely related drove US forces out of Beirut, killing hundreds of troops and many civilians in separate attacks. Furthermore, the thinking of those involved in these and other similar actions was reasonably well understood, certainly by the US intelligence agencies that had helped to recruit, train, and arm them from 1980 and continued to work with them even as they were attacking the United States. The Dutch government inquiry into the Srebrenica massacre revealed that while radical Islamists were attempting to blow up the World Trade Center, others from the CIA-formed networks were being flown by the US from Afghanistan to Bosnia, along with Iranian-backed Hezbollah fighters and a substantial supply of arms. They were being brought to support the US side in the Balkan wars, while Israel (along with Ukraine and Greece) was arming the Serbs (possibly with US-supplied arms).[38]

The atrocities of 9-11 serve as a dramatic reminder of what has long been understood: the rich and powerful no longer are assured the near monopoly of violence that has largely prevailed throughout history; and with modern technology, the prospects are horrendous indeed. Though terrorism is rightly feared everywhere and is indeed an intolerable "return to barbarism," it is not surprising that perceptions about its nature differ rather sharply at opposite ends of the guns, a fact that is ignored at their peril by those whom history has accustomed to immunity while they perpetrate terrible crimes, quite apart from the moral cowardice so starkly revealed.

There are broad tendencies in global affairs that are expected to enhance the threat of this category of terror. Some are discussed by the US National Intelligence Council (NIC) in its projections for the coming years.[39] The NIC expects the official version of globalization to continue on course: "Its evolution will be rocky, marked by chronic financial volatility and a widening economic divide." Financial volatility very likely means slower growth, extending the pattern of neoliberal globalization (for those who follow the rules) and harming mostly the poor. The NIC goes on to predict that as this form of globalization proceeds, "deepening economic stagnation, political instability, and cultural alienation [will] foster ethnic, ideological and religious extremism, along with the violence that often accompanies it," much of it directed against the United States. "Unsurprisingly," Kenneth Waltz observes, the weak and disaffected "lash out at the United States as the agent or symbol of their suffering."[40] The same assumptions are made by military planners, a matter to which we return.

Those concerned to reduce the threat of terror will attend carefully to such factors as these, and also to specific actions and long-term policies that exacerbate them. They will also distinguish carefully between the terrorist networks themselves and the larger community that provides a reservoir from which radical terrorist cells can sometimes draw. That community includes the poor and oppressed, who are of no concern to the terrorist groups and suffer from their crimes, as well as wealthy and secular elements, who are bitter about US policies and quietly express support for bin Laden, whom they detest and fear, as "the conscience of Islam," because at least he reacts to these policies, even if in horrifying and disastrous ways.[41]

The distinction is elementary. Among those who wish to mitigate terrorist threats, it is understood that "unless the social, political, and economic conditions that spawned Al Qaeda and other associated groups are addressed, the United States and its allies in Western Europe and elsewhere will continue to be targeted by Islamist terrorists." Accordingly, "the US should, for its own self-protection, expand efforts to reduce the pathology of hatred before it mutates into even greater danger," seeking to "moderate . . . conditions that breed violence and terrorism." The "key to strategically weakening al-Qaeda is to erode its fledgling support base—to wean away its supporters and potential supporters." Washington planner Paul Wolfowitz adds that it is crucial to eliminate policies that have been "a huge recruiting device for al Qaeda."[42]

Nothing can appease those "who believe a 'clash of civilisations' with the west will restore Islam as a world power," the editors of the *Financial Times* write. But to "crush them . . . successfully they must be separated from their widening constituency." They add: "Put another way, while only might can destroy al-Qaeda, its expanding support base can be eroded only by policies Arabs and Muslims see as just." Even destruction of Al Qaeda will do little if "the underlying conditions that facilitated the group's emergence and popularity—political oppression and economic marginalization— will persist." Correspondingly, continuation of Washington's backing for "sordid governments" can only "bolster al-Qaeda's claims that the US supports the oppression of Muslims and props up brutal governments."[43] That is quite aside from specific policies regarding Palestine and Iraq and others, which have converted "a generation of Arabs wooed by the United States and persuaded by its principles [to] among the most vociferous critics of America's world view, [including] affluent businessmen with ties to the West, U.S.-educated intellectuals and liberal activists."[44]

Terrorist networks can be severely weakened. That happened to Al Qaeda after 9-11, thanks to the kind of police work Michael Howard recommended: notably in Germany, Pakistan, and Indonesia. But their "support base" has to be approached in radically different ways: by considering grievances and, if they are legitimate, addressing them in a serious way, as should be done irrespective of any threat. "Delicate social and political problems cannot be bombed or 'missiled' out of existence," two political scientists point out: "By dropping bombs and firing missiles, the United States only spreads these festering problems. Violence can be likened to a virus; the more you bombard it, the more it spreads."[45]

The *Financial Times* editors are right to say that the terrorist atrocity in Jiddah, which occasioned their comments, was "not unexpected." And more generally, that "it had long been obvious" that the "network inspired by Osama bin Laden would use the upheaval of the Iraq war to relaunch attacks against western targets and drum up support for its jihad."

It was widely predicted by intelligence services and analysts in the mainstream that the invasion of Iraq would be likely to inspire terrorism. It is therefore "not unexpected [that] since the United States invaded Iraq in March, [US] officials said, the [Al Qaeda] network has experienced a spike in recruitment," and "there is an increase in radical fundamentalism all over the world." A UN report indicated that recruitment for Al Qaeda accelerated in thirty to forty countries as the US "began building up for the Iraq invasion."[46] An intelligence report by a European ally warns that the invasion "could have a cataclysmic effect on the mobilization for Al Qaeda."[47] "That the conflict in Iraq led to a rise in recruitment for radical groups is now so clear that even US officials admit it," a close observer of Al Qaeda and terrorism writes: "This is a huge setback in the 'war on terror.' " The war has, in fact, created a new "terrorist haven": Iraq itself.[48]

With regard to the terrorist networks themselves, scholarship is virtually unanimous in taking them at their word, which has matched their deeds from the days when they were organized by the CIA and its associates. Their goal, in their terms, is to drive the infidels from Muslim lands, to overthrow the corrupt and brutal governments imposed and sustained by the infidels, and to institute an extremist version of Islam. They despise the Russians with passion but ceased their terrorist attacks against Russia based in Afghanistan when Russia withdrew, though these continue from

Chechnya. And as bin Laden announced in 1998, "the call to wage war against America was made [when it sent] tens of thousands of its troops to the land of the two Holy Mosques over and above . . . its support of the oppressive, corrupt and tyrannical regime that is in control. These are the reasons for the singling out of America as a target."[49] But their goals may well become more ambitious, and their recruiting base more expansive as well, if the enthusiasts for a "clash of civilizations" prefer to try to " 'missile' delicate social and political problems out of existence" rather than address the problems and thus infringe on power and privilege.

The bombing in Jiddah after the Iraq war fits the pattern of earlier actions. The target was the civilian compound of Vinnell Corp., a subsidiary of Northrop Grumman, which provides retired US military officers "to train the elite armed forces that protect the royal family," not from foreign invasion. A Vinnell training facility had been bombed in 1995. The bombing "makes the point that you are going after aspects of the military presence in Saudi Arabia," a British risk analyst observed: the military "contractors who play a very important supporting role."[50]

Michael Ignatieff, who advocates a US imperial role in the Middle East, reflects a broad consensus in writing that the "larger challenge" for the US, and "the chief danger in the whole Iraqi gamble," is "to enforce a peace on the Palestinians and Israelis." The US-enforced peace "must, as a minimum, give the Palestinians a viable, contiguous state" and rebuild "their shattered infrastructure." To leave "the Palestinians to face Israeli tanks and helicopter gunships is a virtual guarantee of unending Islamic wrath against the United States."[51]

Ignatieff writes that "Americans have played imperial guarantor" since the 1940s, but he does not explain what the US has "guaranteed" since it assumed the mantle. He also overlooks the fact that Israeli gunships are US gunships with Israeli pilots, and that the tanks would not be able to do their work without US largesse. Also unexamined is why the US should be expected to reverse so dramatically the policy of unilateral rejectionism tracing back over thirty years. Putting these and other not inconsequential matters aside, his perception has considerable plausibility.

Those who have an interest in mitigating rather than "enhancing terror" (to borrow again the president's words) might do well to attend to the advice of those with the most experience in confronting it. None have more experience than Israel's General Security Service (Shabak), responsible for "counterterror" in the occupied territories. The head of Shabak from 1996 to 2000, Ami Ayalon, observed that "those who want victory" against terror without addressing under-lying grievances "want an unending war"—much as President Bush proclaimed. The former head of Israeli military intelligence (1991–1995), Uri Sagie, draws similar conclusions. As the Lebanon inva-sion and other military actions illustrate, he wrote, Israel will get nowhere by following the slogan "We will teach you what is good for you [by our superior force]. We must see things from the per-spective of the other side. . . . Those who hope for mutual survival with the Arabs must accept a minimum of respect for Arab society." The alternative is unending war.[52]

Ayalon and Sagie are speaking of Israel-Palestine, where the "solution to the problem of terrorism is to offer an honorable solu-tion to the Palestinians respecting their right to self-determination." So Yehoshaphat Harkabi—former head of Israel military intelligence and a leading Arabist—observed twenty years ago, at a time when Israel still retained its substantial immunity from retali-ation from within the occupied territories.[53]

The observations generalize in familiar ways: Northern Ireland, to mention one case, is far from a paradise but vastly improved over the days when Britain ignored legitimate grievances in favor of force.

The specific policies that inflamed the potential "support base" for Islamic terrorism were Israel-Palestine and the murderous US-UK sanctions regime in Iraq. But long before, there were more fun-damental issues. Again, it makes little sense to ignore these, at least for those who hope to reduce the likelihood of further terrorist crimes or to answer George W. Bush's plaintive question, "Why do they hate us?"

The question is wrongly put: they do not hate *us,* but rather the policies of our government, something quite different. If the question is properly formulated, answers to it are not hard to find. In the critical year 1958, President Eisenhower and his staff discussed what he called the "campaign of hatred against us" in the Arab world, "not by the governments but by the people." The basic reason, the National Security Council advised, was the perception that the US supports corrupt and brutal governments and is "opposing political or economic progress" in order "to protect its interest in Near East oil."[54]

The *Wall Street Journal* and others found much the same when they investigated attitudes of westernized "Moneyed Muslims" after 9-11: bankers, professionals, managers of multinationals, and so on. They strongly support US policies in general but are bitter about US support for corrupt and repressive regimes that undermine democracy and development, and the more specific and recent issues concerning Israel-Palestine and Iraq sanctions.[55]

These are attitudes of people who like Americans and admire much about the United States, including its freedoms. What they hate are official policies that deny them the freedoms to which they too aspire. Attitudes in the slums and villages are probably similar, but harsher. Unlike the "moneyed Muslims," the mass of the population have never agreed that the wealth of the region should be drained to the West and local collaborators, rather than serving domestic needs.

Many commentators prefer more comforting answers: anger in the Muslim world is rooted in resentment of our freedom and democracy; in their own cultural failings tracing back many centuries; in their alleged inability to take part in the form of "globalization" in which they, in fact, happily participate; and other such deficiencies. More comforting, perhaps, but not too wise.

Little has changed since 9-11. Washington's increased support for the dictatorships of Central Asia is only one illustration, arousing deep hostility among democratic forces. Ahmed Rashid reports that in Pakistan as well "there is growing anger that U.S. support is allowing [Musharraf's] military regime to delay the promise of democracy." A well-known Egyptian academic traces hostility toward the US to its support for "every possible anti-democratic government in the Arab-Islamic world. . . .When we hear American officials speaking of freedom, democracy and such values, they make terms like these sound obscene." An Egyptian writer added that "living in a country with an atrocious human rights record that also happens to be strategically vital to US interests is an illuminating lesson in moral hypocrisy and political double standards." Terrorism, he said, is "a reaction to the injustice in the region's domestic politics, inflicted in large part by the US." The director of the terrorism program at the Council of Foreign Relations agreed that "backing repressive regimes like Egypt and Saudi Arabia is certainly a leading cause of anti-Americanism in the Arab world," but warned that "in both cases the likely alternatives are even nastier."[56]

There is a long and illuminating history of the problems in supporting democratic forms while ensuring that they will lead to preferred outcomes, not just in the Middle East. And it doesn't win many friends.

Opinion surveys in early 2003 reveal that from Morocco to the Gulf Emirates, "a huge majority . . . said that, if given the choice, they would like their Islamic clergy to play roles bigger than the subservient ones currently prescribed by most Arab governments." Almost 95 percent dismissed the idea that the US is committed to "a more democratic Arab or Muslim world," believing instead that the war in Iraq was waged to ensure "control of Arab oil and the subjugation of the Palestinians to Israel's will"; and "overwhelming margins" expect terrorism to increase as a consequence of the invasion. Throughout the Arab and Muslim worlds, as far as Indonesia, Islamic fundamentalism is on the rise, appealing not only to the poor but increasingly to more privileged and educated sectors as well, while "America's natural friends, who could provide liberal alternatives," share the "deep mistrust of U.S. intentions and policies."[57] Attitudes remain rooted in the same perceptions as half a century ago, for substantial reasons.

"George Bush is despised even by those who used to admire the US," Jonathan Steele reports from Jordan: "anger with Britain and America has grown" and "Blair's promises of action to solve the Palestinian-Israeli conflict are not taken seriously." Even the most Western-oriented Jordanians believe that the war "set [democracy] back across the Middle East" and placed "advocates of modernisation and secular values . . . on the defensive," and "few doubt that yet more violence will emerge."[58]

A prominent Egyptian intellectual for whom the US "was a 'dream', a paragon of liberal values to be emulated by Arabs and Muslims," and who "has devoted decades of his life to modernizing Islamic life and promoting understanding between Muslims and non-Muslims," regards the Bush administration as "narrow-minded, pathological, obstinate and simplistic." It is to blame for the fact that "to most people in this area, the United States is the source of evil on planet earth," he says. "Similar opinions can also be heard these days from wealthy Arab businessmen, university professors, senior government officials and Western-leaning political analysts"[59]— very much as before, but now with far greater intensity and despair.

If the voice of the people is allowed a hearing in the "New Middle East," it might turn out to be the voice of radical Islamists calling for *jihad,* or of secular nationalists whose perceptions of history, and current practice, are not quite those of Anglo-American elites.

What has been reviewed here is the barest sample of what we readily discover if we pay some attention to elementary fact and agree to apply to ourselves the standards we impose on others. More follows if we are willing to enter the moral arena in a serious way, going beyond the merest truisms and recognizing the obligation to help suffering people as best we can, a responsibility that naturally accrues to privilege. It is not pleasant to speculate about the likely consequences if concentrated power continues on its present course, protected from the scrutiny that would be second nature if we were to take seriously the legacy of freedom we enjoy.

Chapter 9

A Passing Nightmare?

After 9-11, the country was "peering into the abyss of the future."[1]
The awesome threat of terror, though clear enough since the attack
on the World Trade Center in 1993, was now too palpable to
ignore.

To be more precise, it was the public that was peering into the
abyss. Those at the center of power relentlessly pursue their own
agendas, understanding that they can exploit the fears and anguish
of the moment. They may even institute measures that deepen the
abyss and may march resolutely toward it, if that advances the goals
of power and privilege. They declare that it is unpatriotic and dis-
ruptive to question the workings of authority—but patriotic to institute harsh and regressive policies that benefit the wealthy, undermine
social programs that serve the needs of the great majority, and subordinate a frightened population to increased state control. "Literally before the dust had settled" over the World Trade Center ruins,
Paul Krugman reported, influential Republicans signaled that they
were "determined to use terrorism as an excuse to pursue a radical
right-wing agenda."[2] He and others have documented the relentless
pursuit of that agenda. A natural reaction of concentrated power to
any crisis, it was unusually ugly in this case.

Other states perceived the same opportunity. Russia eagerly

joined the "coalition against terror" expecting to receive authorization for its atrocities in Chechnya, and was not disappointed. China happily joined for similar reasons. Israel recognized that it would be able to crush Palestinians even more brutally, with even firmer US support. And so on, throughout much of the world.

The threat of international terrorism is surely severe. The horrendous events of 9-11 had perhaps the most devastating instant human toll on record, outside of war. The word *instant* should not be overlooked; the crime is not otherwise unusual in the annals of violence that falls short of war, as is understood very well by the traditional victims.

The threat of terrorism is, however, not the only abyss into which we peer. A much more grave threat to biology's only experiment with higher intelligence is posed by weapons of mass destruction. In an important 1995 document, the US Strategic Command (STRATCOM) described nuclear weapons as the most valuable in the arsenal, because "unlike chemical or biological weapons, the extreme destruction from a nuclear explosion is immediate, with few if any palliatives to reduce its effect." Furthermore, "nuclear weapons always cast a shadow over any crisis or conflict," hence must be visible, at the ready. The study advises that planners should not portray themselves "as too fully rational and cool-headed. . . . That the U.S. may become irrational and vindictive if its vital interests are attacked should be a part of the national persona we project." It is "beneficial" for our strategic posture if "some elements may appear to be potentially 'out of control.' " Clinton's STRATCOM was proposing a version of Nixon's famous "madman theory," which he and Kissinger applied in an October 1969 nuclear alert that they believed to be risk-free but that might have gotten out of control because of critical factors they ignored—yet another example of the unpredictable consequences of the threat or use of force, which in the current era can be very serious indeed.

The US must retain the right of first use of nuclear weapons, STRATCOM advised further, even against non-nuclear powers that have signed the 1970 Nuclear Non-Proliferation Treaty, and must continue to maintain its launch-on-warning posture for strategic nuclear missiles, on hair-trigger alert. It appears that the Clinton administration adopted these proposals.[3]

The US is unusual, perhaps unique, in the access it allows to high-level planning documents, an important achievement of American democracy. This one, like others, has been available for years but is scarcely known; not a democratic triumph.

Severe threats are not limited to the weapons of mass destruction in the hands of the powerful. Small nuclear weapons can be smuggled into any country with relative ease, along with other potentially very destructive varieties of WMD.[4] The most immediate threat, a Department of Energy task force advised, is that "there could be 40,000 nuclear weapons . . . in the former Soviet Union, poorly controlled and poorly stored." One of the first acts of the Bush administration was to cut back a small program to assist Russia in safeguarding and dismantling these weapons and providing alternative employment for nuclear scientists, a decision that increases the risks of accidental launch, and also leakage of "loose nukes," perhaps followed by nuclear scientists with no other way to employ their skills.[5]

Programs for missile defense are expected to enhance these threats. US intelligence predicts that any American deployment will impel China to develop new nuclear-armed missiles, expanding its arsenal tenfold, probably with multiple warheads (MIRV), "prompting India and Pakistan to respond with their own buildups," with a likely ripple effect to the Middle East. Intelligence officials also predict that "Russia and China both would increase proliferation, including 'selling countermeasures for sure' to such nations as North Korea, Iran, Iraq, and Syria." These and other analyses conclude further that Russia's "only rational response to the [National Missile Defense] system would be to maintain, and strengthen, the existing Russian nuclear force."[6]

The Bush administration announced that "it has no objections to [China's] plans to build up its small fleet of nuclear missiles," shifting policy in the hope of gaining Chinese acquiescence to the planned dismantling of core arms control agreements. For similar reasons, Clinton negotiators had encouraged Russia to adopt a launch-on-warning strategy, a proposal that nuclear experts regarded as "pretty bizarre" because we know that Russia's deteriorating warning systems are "full of holes" and prone to false alerts, increasing the "threat of Russian unauthorized, accidental, and erroneous launches." Chinese resumption of nuclear testing was also being quietly endorsed, it was reported. Strategic analysts pointed out that this change of policy would encourage China to aim more nuclear-armed missiles at the US and Japan, with the expected effect on Japanese and Taiwanese programs. At the same time, the press reported that the US would impose sanctions on China for allowing the transfer to Pakistan of "missile parts and technology that are essentially for weapons that can carry nuclear warheads."[7]

All "pretty bizarre," if security is a highly valued concern.

Missile defense and other military programs of the Bush administration are "inherently provocative" to Russia and China, John Steinbruner and Jeffrey Lewis point out. Like other strategic analysts, they describe the Strategic Offensive Reductions Treaty signed by Bush and Putin in May 2002 as mostly for show: it "will not meaningfully diminish the lethal potential of either nation's nuclear force." Nor will it establish a stable strategic balance: "the deteriorating Russian arsenal will become increasingly vulnerable to preemptive attack, particularly as the United States undertakes planned modernization of nuclear forces and the deployment of missile defenses"—probably driving Russia to react in turn, as later reports indicate. China also recognizes US programs to be a direct threat to its minimal deterrent force, and is likely to readjust priorities from economic development to defense. China was particularly alarmed, Steinbruner and Lewis write, by a 1998 long-range planning document of the US Space Command outlining a new concept of "global engagement," including "space-based strike capabilities" that would allow the US to attack any country and to "deny similar capability to any other countries," another Clinton-era precursor to the National Security Strategy of September 2002. The UN Conference on Disarmament has been deadlocked since 1998 by China's insistence on maintaining the use of space for peaceful means and Washington's refusal to agree, alienating many allies and creating conditions for confrontation.[8]

A May 2003 Rand Corporation study concludes that "the potential for an accidental or unauthorized nuclear missile launch in Russia or the United States has grown over the past decade despite warmer U.S.-Russian relations." Neglecting these risks "could produce possibly the greatest disaster in modern history, and possibly in world history," said former senator Sam Nunn, cochairman of the Nuclear Threat Initiative, which funded the report. The major threat derives from the thousands of nuclear warheads that each side maintains, with the US increasing its nuclear capabilities, which will drive Russia to heightened alert status and probable implementation of "a 'launch-on-warning' approach to warfare requiring rapid reaction" for launching some 3,000 warheads, sharply increasing the danger of nuclear destruction by accident. Nunn, too, dismisses the Bush-Putin treaty of 2002 as meaningless. Like the US, Russia responded to the treaty by rapidly increasing the scale and sophistication of its nuclear and other military systems, motivated in part by concerns about US plans.[9]

The extent of the problem of "grave proliferation risks" from stockpiles of nuclear, biological, and chemical weapons was also revealed in a study issued by a consortium of influential research centers. It concludes that "virtually none" of Russia's plutonium and "less than one-seventh" of its highly enriched uranium has been rendered unusable for nuclear weapons, and "the same is true for the United States." Moreover, " 'Thousands of weapons scientists and workers [in Russia] are still unemployed or underemployed,' the report says, and susceptible to lucrative offers of work from countries that could have secret germ weapons programs." There has been some progress under the Nunn-Lugar Cooperative Threat Reduction Program, but the tasks ahead remain daunting.[10]

As noted, the National Security Strategy of 2002 virtually ignored measures to alleviate the threat of military confrontation. No less disturbing, it invited potential adversaries to "continue to seek deter-

222   HEGEMONY OR SURVIVAL

rence through their own mass-casualty weapons and novel means to
deliver them," thus breeding proliferation and all that it entails.
Bush's budget proposals reflected the same priorities. Missile defense
alone received more funding than the entire State Department, and
four times as much as "programs to safeguard dangerous weapons
and materials in the former Soviet Union." Maintaining the US
nuclear arsenal and preparing for resumption of nuclear tests
received almost five times as much funding as initiatives to control
"loose nukes" and fissile materials.[11]

Even before the National Security Strategy was announced, Bush
had called for programs for offensive use of nuclear arms. His Pentagon planners described both nuclear and non-nuclear weapons as
"offensive strike systems" that can be a "key pillar of a 'new triad'
of offensive, defensive and military industrial resources," providing
new means to "defeat opponents decisively." Traditional policy "has
been turned upside down," Ivo Daalder of Brookings observes, as
nuclear weapons become "a tool of warfighting rather than deterrence," also eroding the distinction between conventional weapons
and WMD. Bush further proceeded "to lower the nuclear threshold
and break down the firewall separating nuclear weapons from everything else" as the US prepared for the invasion of Iraq, making the
world "infinitely more dangerous than it was two years ago, when
George W. Bush took the presidential oath of office," military analyst William Arkin wrote.[12]

In May 2003, Congress adopted the Bush administration programs, opening the door to "a new generation of nuclear weapons,
potentially touching off an arms race as other nations try to match
American capability."[13] The Senate Armed Services Committee
repealed a 1993 ban on research and development of low-yield
nuclear weapons. Though the technology is so advanced that others
are unlikely to follow suit directly, the change in policy is nevertheless "good news" to nuclear states in Asia, an Indian disarmament
expert comments unhappily, helping them "claim that they can
refine their weapons systems and the research also." Another adds
that "the policy of the US toward Iraq and North Korea only gives

more incentive for nations to get nuclear weapons. . . . If the US tests weapons, then China will test [and] there will be domestic pressure for India to test as well," then Pakistan: "You're opening a can of worms."[14] Defense analyst Harlan Ullman warned that a country that is specifically threatened, like Iran, "might hurry its nuclear weapons program after seeing the United States lead an assault on Iraq," providing the pretext for an invasion of Iran, in a self-fulfilling prophecy. Others expect that Pakistan, "feeling pushed into desperation by India and its significant superiority in conventional forces, would feel freer to use nuclear weapons in a first strike."[15]

Extension of the arms race to space has been a core program for some years; *race* is a misleading term, because the US is competing alone, for the moment. Militarization of space, including such programs as ballistic missile defense (BMD), increases the danger of destruction for the US, as for others. But that is nothing new: history provides many examples of policy choices that increase security threats, consciously. More ominous is the fact that the choices make some sense within prevailing value systems. Both topics merit some thought.

Consider a few crucial stages of the Cold War arms race. At mid-twentieth century, the main threat to US security—then only a potential threat—was Intercontinental Ballistic Missiles (ICBMs). Russia might have accepted a treaty banning these delivery systems, knowing that it was far behind. In his authoritative history of the arms race, McGeorge Bundy reports that he could find no record of any interest in pursuing this possibility.[16]

Recently released Russian archives yield some new understanding of these matters, though also leaving "unresolved mysteries," the bitterly anti-Communist Soviet scholar Adam Ulam observed. One such mystery is whether Stalin was serious in a March 1952 proposal that appeared to allow unification of Germany, as long as Germany did not join a military alliance directed against the Soviet Union—hardly an extreme condition a few years after Germany had, once again, virtually destroyed Russia. Washington "wasted little effort in flatly rejecting Moscow's initiative," Ulam commented, on grounds that "were embarrassingly unconvincing," leaving open "the basic question": "Was Stalin genuinely ready to sacrifice the newly created German Democratic Republic (GDR) on the altar of real democracy," with consequences for world peace that could have been enormous? Recent archival research surprised many scholars, Melvyn Leffler writes, by revealing that after Stalin's death, "[Lavrenti] Beria—the sinister, brutal head of the secret police—propos[ed] that the Kremlin offer the West a deal on the unification and neutralization of Germany," apparently agreeing "to sacrifice the East German communist regime to reduce East-West tensions" and improve internal political and economic conditions in Russia. That such opportunities existed, and were squandered in favor of securing German participation in NATO, was strongly argued by the noted political analyst James Warburg right at the time, but the suggestion was ignored or ridiculed.[17]

The archives do, however, shed light on other Soviet proposals that were quickly rejected in favor of a risk-filled military buildup. They reveal that after Stalin's death, Khrushchev called for mutual reduction of offensive military forces and, when these initiatives were ignored by the Eisenhower administration, implemented them unilaterally over the objections of his own military command, in order to concentrate on economic growth. He believed that the US was using the arms race to destroy the far weaker Soviet economy, hoping "by that means to obtain its goals even without war." Kennedy planners knew of Khrushchev's additional unilateral steps to reduce Soviet offensive forces radically, and were well aware that the US was far ahead by any meaningful measure. Nevertheless, they chose to reject Khrushchev's call for reciprocity, preferring to carry out a massive conventional and nuclear buildup, thus driving the last nail into the coffin of "Khrushchev's agenda of restraining the Soviet military," Matthew Evangelista concludes, reviewing the archival records.[18]

Kenneth Waltz observes that the US "in the early 1960s undertook the largest strategic and conventional peace-time military build-up the world has yet seen . . . even as Khrushchev was trying at once to carry through a major reduction in conventional forces and to follow a strategy of minimum deterrence, and we did so even though the balance of strategic weapons greatly favored the United States," predictably eliciting a Soviet reaction. Similar conclusions were drawn by the prominent strategic analysts Raymond Garthoff and William Kaufmann, who observed these processes from inside US intelligence and the Pentagon.[19]

The reaction of the Soviet military to the US buildup, influenced also by the demonstration of Soviet weakness in the Cuban Missile Crisis, effectively terminated Khrushchev's reformist project. Had it proceeded, it might have averted the social and economic stagnation in Russia from the 1960s on, and expedited the desperately needed internal changes that Gorbachev tried to implement, though too late. It might also have prevented the human catastrophe of the 1990s, as well as the destruction of Afghanistan and many other atrocities, not to speak of the serious danger of nuclear disaster as the arms race reached even more threatening dimensions.

Throughout history, aggressive and provocative measures have been justified in terms of defense against merciless foes; in Kennedy's case, defense against what he termed "the monolithic and ruthless conspiracy" dedicated to world conquest. That is another claim that carries little or no information, because it is so predictable, whatever the circumstances, whoever may be the source. To comprehend the underlying logic, it is well to recall a doctrinal truism: it is conventional for controversial initiatives, particularly when hazardous, to be called "defense." Current programs are no exception.

Missile defense is only a small component of much more ambitious programs for militarization of space, with the intent to achieve a monopoly on the use of space for offensive military purposes. The plans have been available in public documents of the US Space Command and other government agencies for some years.[20] The projects outlined have been under development with varying intensity since the Reagan administration proposed the "Star Wars" (Strategic Defense Initiative) programs. SDI appears to have been largely an effort to "disarm BMD opponents"—by then a huge international antinuclear popular movement—by "stealing their language and cause," invoking the terms *peace* and *disarmament,* while proceeding to construct a more advanced offensive military system.[21] The SDI program was in clear violation of the Anti-Ballistic Missile (ABM) Treaty signed in 1972, according to Raymond Garthoff and others. The Reagan administration sought to suppress their objections. State Department legal adviser Judge Abraham Sofaer even threatened legal action to block Garthoff from publishing his book on the topic, a book that, in Garthoff's words, refutes the flagrant efforts by Paul Nitze and other Reaganite enthusiasts for SDI "to distort the historical record and undercut U.S. legal commitment." They were later to claim that SDI was instrumental in ending the Cold War by forcing the USSR into heavy defense spending—a claim that has little merit, according to Garthoff's well-informed account.[22] A case can be made, however, that the Kennedy administration's rejection of opportunities for mutual reduction of armaments, and its general aggressiveness and arms buildup, may have had such an effect, at great cost and with the threat of far worse.

Missile defense and related initiatives were expanded in the first months of the Bush administration. By 9-11, US military expenditures already surpassed those of the next fifteen nations combined, but the opportunity to exploit the fear and horror engendered by the terrorist crimes was too tempting to ignore, and military programs were sharply increased across the board, with little if any relation to terror.

BMD is widely recognized to be a " 'Trojan horse for the real issue: the coming weaponization of space," with highly destructive offensive weapons placed in or guided from space.[23] BMD itself is an offensive weapon. That is understood by close allies, and also by potential adversaries. Canadian military planners advised their government that the goal of BMD is "arguably more in order to preserve U.S./NATO freedom of action than because U.S. really fears [a] North Korean or Iranian threat."[24] China's top arms control official was revealing nothing new when he observed that "once the United States believes it has both a strong spear and a strong shield, it could lead them to conclude that nobody can harm the United States and they can harm anyone they like anywhere in the world." China is well aware that it is a target of the radical nationalists designing policy in Washington, and presumably the prime intended recipient of the message in the National Security Strategy that no potential challenge to US hegemony will be tolerated. Chinese authorities are also surely aware that the US maintains the right of first use of nuclear weapons. And they know as well as US military analysts that "flights by U.S. EP-3 planes near China," such as the one shot down in early 2001, engendering a mini-crisis, "are not just for passive surveillance; the aircraft also collect information used to develop nuclear war plans."[25]

China's interpretation of BMD is shared by US strategic analysts, in virtually the same words: BMD "is not simply a *shield* but an *enabler* of U.S. action," a Rand Corporation study observed. Others agree. BMD "will facilitate the more effective application of U.S. military power abroad," Andrew Bacevich writes in the conservative *National Interest:* "by insulating the homeland from reprisal—albeit in a limited way—missile defense will underwrite the capacity and willingness of the United States to 'shape' the environment else-where." He cites approvingly the conclusion of Lawrence Kaplan in the liberal *New Republic* that "missile defense isn't really meant to protect America. It's a tool for global dominance." In Kaplan's own words, missile defense is "not about defense. It's about offense. And that's exactly why we need it."[26] BMD will provide the US with "absolute freedom in using or threatening to use force in interna-tional relations" (China's complaint, which Kaplan quotes approv-ingly). It will "cement U.S. hegemony and make Americans 'masters of the world.' "

The background assumption is the contemporary version of Wil-sonian idealism, a doctrine taken to be "so authoritative as to be virtually immune from challenge": America is the "historical van-guard" and must therefore maintain its global dominance and mil-itary supremacy forever and without challenge, for the benefit of all.[27] It also follows that "the absolute freedom in using or threatening to use force" to be conferred on the US by BMD is a precious gift we offer to mankind. Who can fail to perceive the impeccable logic?

It is well understood that BMD, even if technically feasible, must rely on satellite communication, and destroying satellites is far easier than shooting down missiles. Antisatellite weapons, banned by treaties that the Bush administration is dismantling, are readily available even to lesser powers. This paradox of the BMD program has been prominently discussed. But there is a possible solution, at least in some imagined world. Advocates of BMD place their faith in "full spectrum dominance," such overwhelming control of space (and the world in general) that even the poor man's weapons will be of no use to an adversary. That requires offensive space-based capacities, including immensely destructive weapons, "death stars" as they are sometimes called, possibly nuclear-powered, ready for launch with computer-controlled reaction. Such weapons systems greatly increase the risk of vast slaughter and devastation, if only because of what are called in the trade "normal accidents"—the unpredictable accidents to which complex systems are subject.[28]

Plans dated a few weeks after the National Security Strategy was announced take space systems to be "key to our nation's military effectiveness." The US must proceed from "control" of space to "ownership," which is to be permanent, in accord with the National Security Strategy. Ownership of space is to permit "instant engagement anywhere in the world" so that "attacks from space" can be integrated into combat plans. "A viable prompt global strike capability, whether nuclear or non-nuclear, will allow the US to rapidly strike high-payoff, difficult-to-defeat targets from stand-off ranges" and "to provide warfighting commanders the ability to rapidly deny, delay, deceive, disrupt, destroy, exploit and neutralize targets in hours/minutes rather than weeks/days even when US and allied forces have a limited forward presence."[29]

These plans had already been outlined in a May 2002 classified Pentagon planning document, partially leaked, which called for a strategy of "forward deterrence" in which hypersonic missiles launched from space platforms would be able to carry out almost instant "unwarned attacks." Military analyst William Arkin comments that "no target on the planet or in space would be immune to American attack. The United States could strike without warning whenever and wherever a threat was perceived, and it would be protected by missile defenses" as well as internal security measures. Hypersonic drones would monitor and disrupt targets. The new weapons systems would permit the US to bomb selected enemies instantly from US bases, assisted by a host of advanced intelligence systems, including surveillance systems with the ability "to track, record and analyze the movement of every vehicle in a foreign city," leaving the world at the mercy of US attack at will, without warning or credible pretext—the operational significance of the term *perceived threat*.[30] The plans have no remote historical parallel.

Even more fanciful ideas are being explored by the Pentagon's advanced research agency, DARPA, including technologies to interface brain and machine, leading eventually, it is hoped, to brain-to-brain communication. That may be "the future of warfare," researchers argue, but meanwhile it follows DARPA's traditional commitment to advance R&D at the boundaries of understanding so as to create the basis for the economy of the future, under the cover of defense.[31]

The goals of militarization of space are far-reaching. The Space Command's Clinton-era brochure *Vision for 2020* announced the primary goal prominently on the front cover: "dominating the space dimension of military operations to protect U.S. interests and investment." This is presented as the next phase of the historic task of military forces. Armies were needed "during the westward expansion of the continental United States"—in self-defense. Nations also built navies, the Space Command continues, "to protect and enhance their commercial interests." The next logical step is space forces to protect "U.S. national interests [military and commercial] and investments," including missile defense, as well as "space-based strike weapons" enabling "the application of precision force from, to, and through space."

US space forces, however, will be unlike navies in earlier eras. This time there will be a sole hegemon. The British Navy could be countered by Germany, with consequences we need not discuss. But the US will remain immune—except to the development of WMD by rogue elements, and the narrowly circumscribed category of "terrorism" that is permitted to enter the canon: *their* terrorism against *us* and our clients.

The need for full-spectrum dominance will increase as a result of the "globalization of the world economy," the Space Command explains. The reason is that "globalization" is expected to bring about "a widening between 'haves' and 'have-nots.' " Like the National Intelligence Council,[32] military planners recognize that the "widening economic divide" that they too anticipate, with its "deepening economic stagnation, political instability, and cultural alienation," will lead to unrest and violence among the "have-nots," much of it directed against the US. That provides a further rationale for expanding offensive military capacities into space. Monopolizing this domain of warfare, the US must be ready to control disorder by "using space systems and planning for precision strike from space [as a] counter to the worldwide proliferation of WMD" by unruly elements, a likely consequence of the recommended programs, just as the "widening divide" is an anticipated consequence of the preferred form of "globalization."

The Space Command could have usefully extended its analogy to the military forces of earlier years. These have played a prominent role in technological and industrial development throughout the modern era. That includes major advances in metallurgy, electronics, machine tools, and manufacturing processes, including the American system of mass production that astounded nineteenth-century competitors and set the stage for the automotive industry and other manufacturing achievements, based on many years of investment, R&D, and experience in weapons production within US Army arsenals. There was a qualitative leap forward after World War II, this time primarily in the US, as the military provided a cover for creation of the core of the modern high-tech economy: computers and electronics generally, telecommunications and the Internet, automation, lasers, the commercial aviation industry, and much else, now extending to nanotechnology, biotechnology, neuroengineering, and other new frontiers. Economic historians have pointed out that the technical problems of naval armament a century ago were roughly comparable to manufacture of space vehicles, and the enormous impact on the civilian economy might be duplicated as well, enhanced by the space militarization projects.

One effect of incorporating national security exemptions in the mislabeled "free trade agreements" is that the leading industrial societies, primarily the US, can maintain the state sector on which the economy substantially relies to socialize cost and risk while privatizing profit.

Others understand this as well. Retreating from his earlier critical stance regarding BMD, German chancellor Gerhard Schroeder observed that Germany has a "vital economic interest" in developing missile defense technology, and must be sure it is "not excluded" from technological and scientific work in the field. Participation in BMD programs is expected to strengthen the domestic industrial base generally in Europe. Similarly, the US BMD Organization advised Japanese officials in 1995 that Theater Missile Defense is "the last military business opportunity for this century." Japan is being drawn in not only to exploit its manufacturing expertise but also to deepen the commitment of the industrial world to the militarization of space, "locking the programs in," to borrow a standard phrase of policy-makers and analysts.[33]

Throughout history it has been recognized that such steps are dangerous. By now the danger has reached the level of a threat to human survival. But as observed earlier, it is rational to proceed nonetheless on the assumptions of the prevailing value system, which are deeply rooted in existing institutions. The basic principle is that hegemony is more important than survival. Hardly novel, the principle has been amply illustrated in the past half-century.

For such reasons, the US has refused to join the rest of the world in reaffirming and strengthening the Outer Space Treaty of 1967 to reserve space for peaceful purposes. The concern for such action, articulated in UN resolutions calling for "Prevention of an Arms Race in Outer Space," is motivated by widespread recognition that Washington intends to breach this barrier, so far maintained. The US was joined in its abstention in 1999 by Israel, in 2000 by Micronesia as well. As noted earlier, immediately after it was learned that the world had barely been saved from a war that might have "destroyed the Northern Hemisphere," the Bush administration effectively vetoed yet another international effort to prevent the militarization of space. For the same reasons, Washington blocked negotiations at the UN Conference on Disarmament during the sessions that opened in January 2001, rejecting the call of Secretary-General Kofi Annan that member states overcome their lack of "political will" and work toward a comprehensive accord to bar militarization of space. "The U.S. remains the only one of the 66 member states to oppose launching formal negotiations on outer space," Reuters reported in February. In June, China again called for banning of weapons in outer space, but the US again blocked negotiations.[34]

Again, that makes good sense if hegemony, with its short-term benefits to elite interests, is ranked above survival in the scale of operative values, in accord with the historical standard for dominant states and other systems of concentrated power.

Much the same can be said about the breakdown of efforts to ban chemical and biological weapons. That they pose significant threats is not seriously in doubt, but higher priorities stand in the way of banning them. In April 2001, arms control experts reported that international verification of the ban on chemical weapons would have to be sharply curtailed "because the United States and other key parties to the treaty [mentioning Russia] have not paid their way." A specialist at the Henry Stimson Center in Washington commented that the Clinton administration had "made a mockery" of the treaty by establishing "a separate set of rules for the United States," with unilateral exemptions. The US was the only country to insist on exemption from certain inspections and tests when the Senate ratified the Chemical

Weapons Convention in 1997. The Bush administration decided to withdraw from negotiations to institute verification measures for the 1972 Biological and Toxic Weapons Convention, effectively terminating them. The US had previously "worked to limit the scope of the visits by foreign inspectors in order to protect American pharmaceutical and biotechnology companies, which dominate the worldwide industry and are concerned with protecting their trade secrets."

The Bush administration proceeded to reject any form of verification on the grounds that mechanisms would be ineffective and "would simply raise the risk to legitimate United States activities," a position condemned as "completely unacceptable" by a senior European diplomat. Shortly after, other likely motives surfaced beyond protecting US corporate interests, when it was revealed that the US "has three clandestine defensive projects that mimic a complete bioweapons program," violating the spirit and perhaps the letter of the verification protocols that the US later officially rejected. Even before, Washington had argued that "access to American biodefense installations" might reveal military secrets—which is the purpose of enforcement mechanisms.[35]

Bioweapons specialists express concerns that the US "may have rejected the bioweapons protocol because it is committed to continuing and expanding its secret programs," in violation of treaties, pointing out that "Washington appears to have had no interest in developing a protocol acceptable to the pharmaceutical industry." Among the suspected plans is genetic engineering of vaccine-resistant anthrax, which the Russians may already have developed. The US "appears to have embarked on a largely classified study, across several agencies, of biotech applications for the development of new bioweapons," apparently ignoring treaties. Therefore "the rest of the world will be obliged to follow suit," perhaps sparking "a global bioweapons arms race." Proliferation of these technologies would also "dramatically increase the chances that terrorists would become capable of mass-casualty attacks using chemical or bioweapons," a threat also discussed in the 2002 Hart-Rudman report on terrorist threats to the United States.[36]

The Bush administration also announced that it "no longer support[s] some of the Article VI conclusions" of the 1970 Nuclear Non-Proliferation Treaty (NPT), the major international agreement on control of nuclear weapons, which has had some success, though far from complete: in particular, the five major nuclear powers have not abided by their commitments. Article VI is the primary element of the NPT applying to the nuclear powers: it commits them to "negotiations in good faith on effective measures relating to cessation of the nuclear arms race at an early date and to nuclear disarmament." The Bush administration went on to declare its opposition to the ABM Treaty (since revoked) and the Comprehensive Test Ban Treaty. It also undermined the first UN conference attempting to control the lethal international black market in small arms, while Bush's point man John Bolton informed the conference that the US opposed "the promotion of international advocacy activity by international or non-governmental organizations."[37] It is not difficult to detect the underlying logic or to perceive the likely consequences.

As it announced its imperial grand strategy in September 2002, the Bush administration moved to undermine continuing efforts to add enforcement mechanisms to the Biological Weapons Convention against germ warfare, preventing any further discussions for four years, and shortly after effectively barred reaffirmation of the 1925 Geneva Protocol prohibiting the use of poisonous gases and bacteriological methods of warfare.[38]

To move to another domain, the Bush administration has been widely criticized for undermining the Kyoto Protocol on grounds that to conform would harm the US economy. The criticisms are in a sense odd, because the decision is not irrational within the framework of existing ideology. We are instructed daily to be firm believers in neoclassical markets, in which isolated individuals are rational wealth maximizers. If distortions are eliminated, the market should respond perfectly to their "votes," expressed in dollars or some counterpart. The value of a person's interests is measured the same way. In particular, the interests of those with no votes are valued at zero: future generations, for example. It is therefore rational to destroy the possibility for decent survival for our grandchildren, if by so doing we can maximize our own "wealth"—which means a particular perception of self-interest constructed by vast industries devoted to implanting and reinforcing it. The threats to survival are currently being enhanced by dedicated efforts not only to weaken the institutional structures that have been developed to mitigate the harsh consequences of market fundamentalism, but also to undermine the culture of sympathy and solidarity that sustains these institutions.

All of this is another prescription for disaster, perhaps in the not very distant future. But again, it has a certain rationality within prevailing structures of doctrine and institutions.

It would be a great error to conclude that the prospects are uniformly bleak. Far from it. One very promising development is the slow evolution of a human rights culture among the general population, a tendency that accelerated in the 1960s, when popular activism had a notable civilizing effect in many domains, extending significantly in the years that followed. One encouraging feature has been a greatly heightened concern for civil and human rights, including rights of minorities, women, and future generations, the latter the driving concern of the environmental movement, which has become a powerful force. For the first time in American history, there was some willingness to look honestly at the conquest of the national territory and the fate of its inhabitants. The solidarity movements that developed in mainstream America in the 1980s, concerning Central America in particular, broke new ground in the history of imperialism; never before had substantial numbers of people from the imperial society gone to live with the victims of vicious attack to help them and offer some measure of protection. The international solidarity organizations that evolved from these roots now function very effectively in many parts of the world, arousing fear and anger in repressive states and sometimes exposing participants to serious danger, even death.[39] The global justice movements that have since taken shape, meeting at the World Social Forum annually, are an entirely new and unprecedented phenomenon in character and scale. The planet's "second superpower," which could no longer be ignored in early 2003, has deep roots in these developments, and considerable promise.

Over the course of modern history, there have been significant gains in human rights and democratic control of some sectors of life. These have rarely been the gift of enlightened leaders. They have typically been imposed on states and other power centers by popular struggle. An optimist might hold, perhaps realistically, that history reveals a deepening appreciation for human rights, as well as a broadening of their range—not without sharp reversals, but the general tendency seems real. The issues are very much alive today. The harmful effects of the corporate globalization project have led to mass popular protest and activism in the South, later joined by major sectors of the rich industrial societies, hence becoming harder to ignore. For the first time, concrete alliances have been taking shape at the grassroots level. These are impressive developments, rich in opportunity. And they have had effects, in rhetorical and sometimes policy changes. There has been at least a restraining influence on state violence, though nothing like the "human rights revolution" in state practice that has been proclaimed by intellectual opinion in the West.

These various developments could prove very important if momentum can be sustained in ways that deepen the emerging global bonds of sympathy and solidarity. It is fair to say, I think, that the future of our endangered species may be determined in no small measure by how these popular forces evolve.

One can discern two trajectories in current history: one aiming toward hegemony, acting rationally within a lunatic doctrinal framework as it threatens survival; the other dedicated to the belief that "another world is possible," in the words that animate the World Social Forum, challenging the reigning ideological system and seeking to create constructive alternatives of thought, action, and institutions. Which trajectory will dominate, no one can foretell. The pattern is familiar throughout history; a crucial difference today is that the stakes are far higher.

Bertrand Russell once expressed some somber thoughts about world peace:

After ages during which the earth produced harmless trilobites and butterflies, evolution progressed to the point at which it has generated Neros, Genghis Khans, and Hitlers. This, however, I believe is a passing nightmare; in time the earth will become again incapable of supporting life, and peace will return.[40]

No doubt the projection is accurate on some dimension beyond our realistic contemplation. What matters is whether we can awaken ourselves from the nightmare before it becomes all-consuming, and bring a measure of peace and justice and hope to the world that is, right now, within the reach of our opportunity and our will.

Afterword

The National Security Strategy (NSS) of September 2002, and its implementation in Iraq, are widely regarded as a watershed in international affairs. "The new approach is revolutionary," Henry Kissinger wrote, approving of the doctrine but with tactical reservations and a crucial qualification: it cannot be "a universal principle available to every nation."[1] The right of aggression is to be reserved for the US and perhaps its chosen clients. We must reject the most elementary of moral truisms, the principle of universality—a stand usually concealed in professions of virtuous intent and tortured legalisms.

Arthur Schlesinger agreed that the doctrine and implementation were "revolutionary," but from a quite different standpoint. As the first bombs fell on Baghdad, he recalled FDR's words following the bombing of Pearl Harbor, "a date which will live in infamy." Now it is Americans who live in infamy, he wrote, as their government adopts the policies of imperial Japan. He added that George Bush had converted a "global wave of sympathy" for the US into a "global wave of hatred of American arrogance and militarism." A year later, "discontent with America and its policies ha[d] intensified rather than diminished."[2] Even in Britain support for the war had declined by a third.

As predicted, the war increased the threat of terror. Middle East expert Fawaz Gerges found it "simply unbelievable how the war has revived the appeal of a global jihadi Islam that was in real decline after 9-11." Recruitment for the Al Qaeda networks increased, while Iraq itself became a "terrorist haven" for the first time. Suicide attacks for the year 2003 reached the highest level in modern times; Iraq suffered its first since the thirteenth century.[3] Substantial specialist opinion concluded that the war also led to the proliferation of weapons of mass destruction.[4]

As the anniversary of the invasion approached, New York's Grand Central Station was patrolled by police with submachine guns, a reaction to the March 11 Madrid train bombings that killed 200 people in Europe's worst terrorist crime. A few days later, the Spanish electorate voted out the government that had gone to war despite overwhelming popular opposition. Spaniards were condemned for appeasing terrorism by voting for withdrawing troops from Iraq in the absence of UN authorization—that is, for taking a stand rather like that of 70 percent of Americans, who called for the UN to take the leading role in Iraq.[5]

Bush assured Americans that "The world is safer today because, in Iraq, our coalition ended a regime that cultivated ties to terror while it built weapons of mass destruction."[6] The president's handlers know that every word is false, but they also know that lies can become Truth, if repeated insistently enough.

There is broad agreement among specialists on how to reduce the threat of terror—keeping here to the subcategory that is doctrinally acceptable, *their* terror against *us*—and also on how to incite terrorist atrocities, which may become truly horrendous. The consensus is well articulated by Jason Burke in his study of the Al Qaeda phenomenon,[7] the most detailed and informed investigation of this loose array of radical Islamists for whom bin Laden is hardly more than a symbol (a more dangerous one after he is killed, perhaps, becoming a martyr who inspires others to join his cause). The role of Washington's current incumbents, in their Reaganite phase, in creating the radical Islamist networks is well known. Less familiar is their tolerance of Pakistan's slide toward radical Islamist extremism and its development of nuclear weapons.[8]

As Burke reviews, Clinton's 1998 bombings of Sudan and Afghanistan created bin Laden as a symbol, forged close relations between him and the Taliban, and led to a sharp increase in support, recruitment, and financing for Al Qaeda, which until then was virtually unknown. The next major contribution to the growth of Al Qaeda and the prominence of bin Laden was Bush's bombing of Afghanistan following September 11, undertaken without credible pretext as later quietly conceded. As a result, bin Laden's message "spread among tens of millions of people, particularly the young and angry, around the world," Burke writes, reviewing the increase in global terror and the creation of "a whole new cadre of terrorists" enlisted in what they see as a "cosmic struggle between good and evil," a vision shared by bin Laden and Bush. As noted, the invasion of Iraq had the same effect.

Citing many examples, Burke concludes that "Every use of force is another small victory for bin Laden," who "is winning," whether he lives or dies. Burke's assessment is widely shared by many analysts, including former heads of Israeli military intelligence and the General Security Services.[9]

There is also a broad consensus on what the proper reaction to terrorism should be. It is two-pronged: directed at the terrorists themselves and at the reservoir of potential support. The appropriate response to terrorist crimes is police work, which has been successful worldwide. More important is the broad constituency the terrorists—who see themselves as a vanguard—seek to mobilize, including many who hate and fear them but nevertheless see them as fighting for a just cause. We can help the vanguard mobilize this reservoir of support by violence, or can address the "myriad grievances," many legitimate, that are "the root causes of modern Islamic militancy."[10] That can significantly reduce the threat of terror, and should be undertaken independently of this goal.

Violence can succeed, as Americans know well from the conquest of the national territory. But at terrible cost. It can also provoke violence in response, and often does. Inciting terror is not the only illustration. Others are even more hazardous.

In February 2004, Russia carried out its largest military exercises in two decades, prominently exhibiting advanced WMD. Russian generals and Defense Minister Sergei Ivanov announced that they were responding to Washington's plans "to make nuclear weapons an instrument of solving military tasks," including its development of new low-yield nuclear weapons, "an extremely dangerous tendency that is undermining global and regional stability, . . . lowering the threshold for actual use." Strategic analyst Bruce Blair writes that Russia is well aware that the new "bunker busters" are designed to target the "high-level nuclear command bunkers" that control its nuclear arsenal. Ivanov and Russian generals report that in response to US escalation they are deploying "the most advanced state-of-the-art missile in the world," perhaps next to impossible to destroy, something that "would be very alarming to the Pentagon," says former Assistant Defense Secretary Phil Coyle. US analysts suspect that Russia may also be duplicating US development of a hypersonic cruise vehicle that can re-enter the atmosphere from space and launch devastating attacks without warning, part of US plans to reduce reliance on overseas bases or negotiated access to air routes.[11]

US analysts estimate that Russian military expenditures have tripled during the Bush-Putin years, in large measure a predicted reaction to the Bush administration's militancy and aggressiveness. Putin and Ivanov cited the Bush doctrine of "preemptive strike"—the "revolutionary" new doctrine of the National Security Strategy—but also "added a key detail, saying that military force can be used if there is an attempt to limit Russia's access to regions that are essential to its survival," thus adapting for Russia the Clinton doctrine that the US is entitled to resort to "unilateral use of military power" to ensure "uninhibited access to key markets, energy supplies, and strategic resources."[12] The world "is a much more insecure place" now that Russia has decided to follow the US lead, said Fiona Hill of the Brookings Institution, adding that other countries presumably "will follow suit."[13]

In the past, Russian automated response systems have come within a few minutes of launching a nuclear strike, barely aborted by human intervention. By now the systems have deteriorated. US systems, which are much more reliable, are nevertheless extremely hazardous. They allow three minutes for human judgment after computers warn of a missile attack, as they frequently do. The Pentagon has also found serious flaws in its computer security systems that might allow terrorist hackers to seize control and simulate a launch—"an accident waiting to happen," Bruce Blair writes.[14] The dangers are being consciously escalated by the threat and use of violence.

Concern is not eased by the recent discovery that US presidents have been "systematically misinformed" about the effects of nuclear war. The level of destruction has been "severely underestimated" because of lack of systematic oversight of the "insulated bureaucracies" that provide analyses of "limited and 'winnable' nuclear war"; the resulting "institutional myopia can be catastrophic,"[15] far more so than the manipulation of intelligence on Iraq.

The Bush administration slated the initial deployment of a missile defense system for summer 2004, a move criticized as "completely political," employing untested technology at great expense.[16] A more appropriate criticism is that the system might seem workable; in the logic of nuclear war, what counts is perception. Both US planners and potential targets regard missile defense as a first-strike weapon, intended to provide more freedom for aggression, including nuclear attack. And they know how the US responded to Russia's deployment of a very limited ABM system in 1968: by targeting the system with nuclear weapons to ensure that it would be instantly overwhelmed. Analysts warn that current US plans will also provoke a Chinese reaction. History and the logic of deterrence "remind us that missile defense systems are potent drivers of offensive nuclear planning," and the Bush initiative will again raise the threat to Americans and to the world.[17]

China's reaction may set off a ripple effect through India, Pakistan, and beyond. In West Asia, Washington is increasing the threat posed by Israel's nuclear weapons and other WMD by providing

Israel with more than one hundred of its most advanced jet bombers, accompanied by prominent announcements that the bombers can reach Iran and return and are an advanced version of the US planes Israel used to destroy an Iraqi reactor in 1981. The Israeli press adds that the US is providing the Israeli air force with " 'special' weaponry." There can be little doubt that Iranian and other intelligence services are watching closely and perhaps giving a worst-case analysis: that these may be nuclear weapons. The leaks and dispatch of the aircraft may be intended to rattle the Iranian leadership, perhaps to provoke some action that can be used as a pretext for an attack.[18]

Immediately after the National Security Strategy was announced in September 2002, the US moved to terminate negotiations on an enforceable bioweapons treaty and to block international efforts to ban biowarfare and the militarization of space. A year later, at the UN General Assembly, the US voted alone against implementation of the Comprehensive Test Ban Treaty and alone with its new ally India against steps toward the elimination of nuclear weapons. The US voted alone against "observance of environmental norms" in disarmament and arms control agreements and alone with Israel and Micronesia against steps to prevent nuclear proliferation in the Middle East—the pretext for invading Iraq. A resolution to prevent militarization of space passed 174 to 0, with four abstentions: US, Israel, Micronesia, and the Marshall Islands.[19] As discussed earlier, a negative US vote or abstention amounts to a double veto: the resolution is blocked and is eliminated from reporting and history.

Bush planners know as well as others that the resort to force increases the threat of terror, and that their militaristic and aggressive posture and actions provoke reactions that increase the risk of catastrophe. They do not desire these outcomes, but assign them low priority in comparison to the international and domestic agendas they make little attempt to conceal.

As Colin Powell explained the National Security Strategy to a hostile audience at the World Economic Forum, Washington has a "sovereign right to use force to defend ourselves" from nations that possess WMD and cooperate with terrorists, the official pretexts for invading Iraq. The collapse of the pretexts is well known, but there has been insufficient attention to its most important consequence: the NSS was effectively revised to lower the bars to aggression. The need to establish ties to terror was quietly dropped. More significant, Bush and colleagues declared the right to resort to force even if a country does not have WMD or even programs to develop them. It is sufficient that it have the "intent and ability" to do so. Just about every country has the ability, and intent is in the eye of the beholder. The official doctrine, then, is that anyone is subject to overwhelming attack. Colin Powell carried the revision even a step further. The president was right to attack Iraq because Saddam not only had "intent and capability" but had "actually used such horrible weapons against [his] enemies in Iran and against [his] own people"— with continuing support from Powell and his associates, he failed to add, following the usual convention. Condoleezza Rice gave a similar version.[20] With such reasoning as this, who is exempt from attack? Small wonder that "if Iraqis ever see Saddam Hussein in the dock, they want his former American allies shackled beside him."[21]

In the desperate flailing to contrive justifications as one pretext after another collapsed, the obvious reason for the invasion was conspicuously evaded by the administration and commentators: to establish the first secure military bases in a client state right at the heart of the world's major energy resources, understood since World War II to be a "stupendous source of strategic power" and expected to become even more important in the future. There should have been little surprise at revelations that the administration intended to attack Iraq before 9-11, and downgraded the "war on terror" in favor of this objective. In internal discussion, evasion is unnecessary. Long before they took office, the private club of reactionary statists had recognized that "the need for a substantial American force presence in the Gulf transcends the issue of the regime of Saddam Hussein."[22] With all the vacillations of policy since the current incumbents first took office in 1981, one guiding principle remains stable: the Iraqi people must not rule Iraq.

The NSS was only one component of the Bush doctrine. A second was that those "who harbor terrorists are as guilty as the terrorists themselves" and must be attacked and destroyed.[23] The prominent strategic analyst Graham Allison regards this as the most important component of the Bush doctrine. In announcing it along with the invasion of Afghanistan (because of its refusal to hand over bin Laden without evidence), Bush "unilaterally revoked the sovereignty of states that provide sanctuary to terrorists." This component of the doctrine has "already become a de facto rule of international relations."[24] Allison and others do not add that they are calling for the bombing of the United States. By the narrowest definition of the term, the US clearly "harbors terrorists."[25] But such cases are irrelevant. The logical conclusion presupposes the principle of universality, and it is a central doctrine of the political culture that moral truisms must be forcefully rejected, much as Kissinger emphasized.

Presidents commonly have "doctrines," but Bush II is the first to have "visions" as well, possibly because his handlers recall the criticism of his father as lacking "the vision thing." The most exalted of these, conjured up after all pretexts for invasion of Iraq had to be abandoned, was the vision of bringing democracy to Iraq and the Middle East. By November 2003, this vision was taken to be the real motive for the war. Veteran correspondent and editor David Ignatius wrote that "this may be the most idealistic war fought in modern times—a war whose only coherent rationale, for all the misleading hype about weapons of mass destruction and al Qaeda terrorists, is that it toppled a tyrant and created the possibility of a democratic future." The president affirmed the vision in a widely lauded address a few days later.[26]

Reactions ranged from rapturous awe to criticism praising the nobility of the vision but warning that it may be beyond our means: the beneficiaries may be too backward, it might prove too costly. That this was the guiding vision, however, was presupposed as self-evident. News stories reported that "the American project to build a stable democracy in Iraq has encountered many obstacles." Commentators wondered whether "today's pseudo-Wilsonian campaign to make the Middle East safe for democracy" could really succeed. The harshest critics of the "neocons" conceded that their "decision to wage preemptive war in order to depose Saddam Hussein and trigger a democratic revolution across the Arab world has shaken the international system to its core."[27] With considerable search, I have yet to find an exception.

The evidence for faith in the vision consists of little more than declarations of virtuous intent. But it is the merest truism that such declarations carry no information, because they are predictable. In the present case, the reasons for dismissing them are unusually strong. To take them seriously, we would have to assume that our leaders are accomplished liars, for while mobilizing their countries for war, they were declaring that the reasons were entirely different: the "single question," as Bush-Blair and associates stressed, was Iraq's disarmament, not the new "vision." Mere sanity dictates skepticism about what they produce to replace pretexts that have collapsed.

There is no shortage of real evidence to assess the declarations. Consistent past practice provides compelling enough evidence of contempt for democracy, even without the dramatic reaffirmation during the build-up to the war, as countries were assigned to the categories Old and New Europe, the former condemned for adopting the positions of the overwhelming majority of their populations, the latter hailed because they overrode even larger majorities and followed Washington's orders. The most extreme stand was taken by Paul Wolfowitz, who berated the Turkish military for permitting the government to abide by the wishes of 95 percent of the population, and demanded that they apologize and recognize that the duty of a democratic state is to help America.

Wolfowitz's performance is particularly enlightening because he is cast as the visionary leading the crusade for democracy. Ignatius's acclaim for our nobility was inspired by "a classic Paul Wolfowitz moment" in Hilla, Iraq, where Wolfowitz quoted "de Tocqueville's theories about democracy" and called on Iraqis to "build democracy"—which doubtless impressed the audience at the site of the first well-substantiated massacre of civilians by US forces.[28] Wolfowitz is "the paradigmatic figure of the war,"

Ignatius explained, "and the Bush administration's idealist in chief."
He was concerned that Wolfowitz might be "too idealistic—that his
passion for the noble goals of the Iraq war might overwhelm the
prudence and pragmatism that normally guide war planners." But
he was reassured by the "genuine intellectual" who studies the Arab
world deeply, "bleeds for its oppression and dreams of liberating
it." Still, "the idealism of a Wolfowitz must be tempered by some
very hard-headed judgments about how to protect U.S. interests,"
Ignatius advises.

There is ample evidence of Wolfowitz's passion for democracy
and his concern for suffering people, as he lent strong support to
some of the most corrupt and appalling murderers, torturers, and
aggressors of the late twentieth century.[29] His dedication to democracy was revealed again after the invasion of Iraq, when he issued
his "Determination and Findings" (December 5, 2003) on contracts
for reconstruction. "It is necessary for the protection of the essential
security interests of the United States," he determined, that competition for prime contracts for reconstruction exclude all countries
that did not follow US orders. The phrase "security" has its usual
meaning. Halliburton, Bechtel, J. P. Morgan, and other supplicants
are therefore protected from competition from France, Germany,
and Russia, with any costs incurred by these market-friendly procedures borne by the US taxpayer.

There is one particle of (apparent) evidence in support of the new
vision: the invasion did depose Saddam Hussein, an outcome that
can be welcomed without hypocrisy by those who strenuously
opposed US-UK support for him through his worst crimes, including
the crushing of the Shi'ite rebellion that might have overthrown him
in 1991, for reasons that were frankly explained but are now kept
from the public eye. The end of Saddam's rule was one of two welcome "regime changes." The other was the formal end of the sanctions regime, which killed hundreds of thousands of people,
devastated Iraq's civilian society, strengthened the tyrant, and compelled the population to rely on him for survival. It is for these
reasons that the respected international diplomats who administered

the programs, Denis Halliday and Hans von Sponeck, resigned in protest at what Halliday called the "genocidal" sanctions regime. They are the Westerners who knew Iraq best, having access to regular information from investigators throughout the country. Though sanctions were administered by the UN, their cruel and savage character was dictated by the US and its British subordinate. The topic is therefore virtually excluded from discussion. Ending this regime is a very positive aspect of the invasion. But that could have been done without an invasion.

There is reason to believe—as Halliday and von Sponeck had argued—that if sanctions had been directed at preventing weapons programs rather than administered in the manner the US and UK demanded, the population of Iraq would have been able to send Saddam Hussein to the same fate as others supported by the current incumbents and their British allies: Ceaușescu, Suharto, Marcos, Duvalier, Chun Doo-Hwan, Mobutu . . . an impressive list of murderous gangsters, some of them comparable to Saddam, to which new names are being added daily by the same Western leaders. If so, both murderous regimes could have been ended without invasion. Postwar inquiries, such as those of Washington's Iraq Survey Group headed by David Kay, add weight to these beliefs by revealing how shaky Saddam's control of the country was in the last few years. We may have our own subjective judgments about the matter but they are irrelevant. Unless the population is given the opportunity to overthrow a brutal tyrant, as they did with other members of the rogue's gallery supported by the US and UK, there is no justification for resort to outside force to do so.[30] These considerations alone suffice to eliminate the particle of truth that might support the new doctrine contrived after the collapse of the official pretexts. But there are many others as well, some already discussed.

As noted, the professions of virtuous intent appear to be universally accepted. Almost. I did find one exception, a few days after the president's proclamation of his vision to bring democracy to Iraq and beyond: a report of a Gallup poll in Baghdad, asking about motives for the US invasion. Some agreed with articulate opinion among the invaders that the goal was to establish democracy: one percent. Five percent felt that the goal was "to assist the Iraqi people." Most assumed that the goal was to take control of Iraq's resources and to reorganize the Middle East in US and Israeli interests[31]—the possibility excluded in US commentary.

The results were in fact more nuanced. Though only 1 percent of Baghdadis thought the US invaded to bring democracy, 50 percent felt that the US wants democracy in Iraq. A contradiction? Not really. The full response is that the US wants to establish a democratic government but "would not allow Iraqis to do that without U.S. pressure and influence." In brief, democracy is fine, but only if you do what we say. Iraqis understand us better than we choose to understand ourselves: *choose,* because we have overwhelming evidence, if we are willing to look at it.

The consistent pattern was illustrated right on the front pages as the war's anniversary approached: the coup in Haiti in March 2004. Attention was focused on the final days, keeping to distribution of blame among Haitians in their "failed state." Omitted was the immediately relevant background. In brief, in 1990 Haiti had its first free election. A vibrant civil society had been organized in the slums and the hills, enabling the vast majority of the population to elect their own candidate, the populist priest Jean-Bertrand Aristide. Washington moved at once to undermine the democratic government. When it was overthrown by a military coup a few months later, Bush I and Clinton supported the military junta and its wealthy patrons, even authorizing illegal shipments of oil. After three years of state violence, Clinton allowed President Aristide to return, but on a crucial condition: that he adopt the economic program of the defeated US-backed candidate in the 1990 election, who won 14 percent of the vote—what we call "restoring democracy." As predicted, this harsh neoliberal program undermined what was left of Haiti's economic sovereignty and drove the country into chaos and violence, a process accelerated by Bush's banning of international aid on cynical grounds.[32]

The program that Clinton imposed on Aristide is approximately the same as the one dictated by Paul Bremer for Iraq, allowing effective takeover of the economy by foreign banks and businesses. It is a sound conclusion of economic history that such measures, undermining economic sovereignty, also restrict development and reduce political democracy to a shadow. In fact, these are the kinds of programs that helped create the "third world," where they were imposed by force while the imperial powers resorted to state intervention to protect the rich from market discipline, as they still do, the US prominently among them.

In the same days in late March, the standard pattern was also illustrated in an election in El Salvador. To ensure that the democratic vote would come out the "right" way, the Bush administration warned that if it did not, the country's lifeline—remittances from the US, a crucial pillar of the "economic miracle"—might be cut, among other consequences.[33]

Iraqis do not have to know US history to draw conclusions about Bush's noble vision. Their own suffices. Iraq was created by the British, its boundaries drawn to ensure that Britain, not Turkey, would gain the oil reserves of the north and that Iraq would be effectively barred from the sea by the British colony of Kuwait. Iraq was "independent," with a constitution and parliamentary government. Iraqis did not have to read classified British foreign office documents to understand that Britain intended to impose an "Arab façade" while continuing to rule behind various "constitutional fictions."

Furthermore, they can see what is happening before their eyes. Iraqis understand full well that "even after the transfer of power, US officials said they plan a huge military and diplomatic presence in the independent Iraq. 'The coalition authority will become the world's largest embassy America has,' Bremer said." It will include more than three thousand personnel, "the largest diplomatic staff anywhere in the world"—surely not with the mission of supervising transfer of meaningful sovereignty. And Iraqis would hardly be surprised to learn that US officials intend "to postpone some [Iraqi reconstruction] work until after the June 30 transfer of sovereignty, in part to maintain leverage over the next Iraqi government."[34]

In addition to restricting Iraqi sovereignty, Washington faces another "major challenge": "sorting out the terms of the U.S. military presence, which is expected to exceed 100,000 troops even after the occupation ends, U.S. officials say." They "do not expect the transfer of political power to lead to a short-term reduction in US military might there," and the US has "rejected the notion that handing over political power is the first step toward an immediate withdrawal of forces, citing ongoing security needs."[35]

The last phrase is for the US audience. To lend it credibility, some facts have to be avoided: crucially, that Iraqis want Iraqis to take responsibility for "security needs," so we learn from the most extensive recent Western-run poll[36]—reported, but keeping to useful trivialities (for example, that people are happy to be rid of the tyrant). The poll also found that although "people overwhelmingly worry about their security and the spectre of drifting into chaos . . . less than 1% worry about occupation forces actually leaving" and 60 percent want Iraqis to be in charge of security (7 percent prefer US forces, 5 percent other "coalition" forces, and 5 percent the US-appointed Governing Council). In general, "people have no confidence in US/UK forces (79%) and the Coalition Provisional Authority—CPA (73%)." Pentagon favorite Ahmed Chalabi had no support. In another poll, 57 percent said they would support "Arab forces" providing security.[37] When asked what Iraq needs right now, more than 70 percent "strongly agree" with the choice "democracy," while 10 percent choose the CPA, and 15 percent the Governing Council.[38] And by "democracy" they mean democracy, not the nominal sovereignty that the "idealist in chief" and his colleagues are designing.

The US-Iraqi conflict over sovereignty was highly visible on the first anniversary of the invasion. Wolfowitz and his Pentagon staff signalled that "they favor a sizable, prolonged US troop presence there and a relatively weak Iraqi army as the best way to nurture democracy"; the phrase "nurture democracy" is to be understood in the sense of Wolfowitz's reprimand to the Turkish military. Popular resistance was so strong, however, that even the US-appointed "interim leaders," bowing to public demands, said "they could not negotiate a formal agreement with the American military on maintaining troops in Iraq." Their refusal poses a problem for Wolfowitz-style democracy: "The delay could put the Americans in the position of negotiating an agreement with leaders they did not appoint on such sensitive issues as when the use of force would be allowed."[39]

From the outset, the US had been "planning a long-term military relationship with the emerging government of Iraq, one that would grant the Pentagon access to military bases and project American influence into the heart of the unsettled region, senior Bush administration officials say." The plans have faced firm resistance from Iraqis, who have maintained a steadfast effort to gain authentic sovereignty. This resistance, rather than bombs and killings, has been the most serious problem facing Washington, as occasionally recognized.[40]

There would have been no point to the invasion in the first place if it did not lead to stable military bases in a dependent client state of the traditional sort. Washington is particularly concerned about Iraqi demands that "directly elected representatives" approve any military agreement that would "allow more than 100,000 American troops to remain in the country after power is handed over to the Iraqis" in July 2004. Washington planners hoped, somehow, to tweak the "caucus system [effectively under US control] to look more democratic without changing it in a fundamental way." The UN might be brought in, but Washington is asking it "to endorse a future Iraqi government of only nominal sovereignty and questionable legitimacy, by whose invitation the occupying powers would remain in place."[41]

US officials "believe they have found a legal basis for American troops to continue their military control over the security situation in Iraq"; that is, to maintain their military presence despite Iraqi popular opposition, so as to keep a firm hand on the "strategic power" that is a primary lever of world control. Claiming frivolous Security Council authorization, Bremer ordered that Iraqi forces be placed under US command.[42]

Iraqis can also see the measures designed to reduce their country's economic sovereignty, including a series of orders that would open industries and banks to effective US takeover and impose a flat tax of 15 percent. This "stunning plan would immediately make Iraq's economy one of the most open to trade and capital flows in the world, and put it among the lowest taxed in the world, rich or poor," virtually eliminating the hope for funding of desperately needed social benefits and infrastructure, economist Jeff Madrick writes. The plan is "supported neither by theory nor experience, only by the wishful ideological thinking of its advocates," with consequences that "could be widespread cruelty." Not surprisingly, the proposals "were immediately attacked by Iraqi business representatives," who charged that they would "destroy the role of the Iraqi industrialist."[43]

There are fewer problems with Iraqi workers. The occupying forces took actions to destroy the unions, breaking into offices and arresting leaders, blocking strikes, enforcing Saddam's antilabor laws, handing concessions to bitterly anti-union US businesses, and in general ensuring that there will be no interference with approved economic policies from the underlying population. Nevertheless, strong Iraqi resistance and the remarkable failures of the military occupation have caused Washington to backtrack somewhat from the more extreme proposals.[44]

The plans to open the economy to effective foreign takeover excluded oil. Presumably that would have been too brazen. However, Iraqis do not have to read the Western business press to discover that "getting to know Iraq's ravaged oil industry in detail"—thanks to lucrative contracts provided it by US taxpayers—"eventually could help Halliburton win mainstream energy business there," joined by other state-supported multinational corporations that will do so as well.[45]

It remains to be seen whether Iraqis can be coerced into accepting the "nominal sovereignty" that is offered them under the various "constitutional fictions" devised by the occupying power. Another question is far more important for privileged Westerners: will we permit our governments to "nurture democracy" in the interests of the narrow sectors of power they serve, despite strong Iraqi opposition? Such questions extend to matters far beyond Iraq: to terror and intervention, weapons development, and a host of other policies that threaten decent survival. And to domestic affairs as well. It is no secret that a major domestic problem is the explosion of health care costs in the mostly privatized US system, far higher than in comparable societies and with relatively poor outcomes, results traceable in large measure to the enormous inefficiencies of privatization and the power of the pharmaceutical industry. Large majorities favor national health insurance, regarding it as "more important than holding down taxes," and favor legal imports of prescription drugs. But such notions are held to be "politically impossible": the pharmaceutical industry, insurance companies, and other private powers will not allow it.[46]

These are among the many signs of the serious erosion of a democratic culture under dedicated multipronged assaults. Americans are hardly less able to confront such problems than landless workers in Brazil, Haitian peasants, and many others: today Iraqis. There is no need to linger on what is at stake as Americans confront the severe democratic deficit in the world's most powerful state.

Noam Chomsky
April 2004

Notes

Please see www.hegemonyorsurvival.net or www.americanempireproject.com for expanded endnotes and an e-book with additional background, discussion, and sources.

Chapter 1: PRIORITIES AND PROSPECTS

1. Mayr, *Bioastronomy News* 7, no. 3 (1995).
2. Donald Kennedy, *Science* 299, 21 March 2003.
3. Howard LaFranchi, *Christian Science Monitor,* 30 October 2002.
4. Patrick Tyler, *New York Times,* 17 February 2003.
5. For sources on Wilsonian idealism and the seventeenth century, see my *Deterring Democracy* (Verso, 1991; extended edition, Hill & Wang, 1992), chapter 12, and my *Profit over People* (Seven Stories, 1999), chapter 2. For a more extensive discussion and contemporary scholarly sources, see my "Consent without Consent," *Cleveland State Law Review* 44, no. 4 (1996). Minor changes (punctuation, etc.) are introduced here for ease of reading.
6. Cited by David Foglesong, *America's Secret War Against Bolshevism* (North Carolina, 1995), p. 28.
7. Andrew Bacevich, *American Empire* (Harvard, 2003), pp. 200ff.
8. M. J. Crozier, S. P. Huntington, and J. Watanuki, *The Crisis of Democracy* (New York University, 1975), report to the Trilateral Commission.

9. Randal Marlin, *Propaganda and the Ethics of Persuasion* (Broadview, 2002).

10. For a discussion of this vast disinformation campaign, see my *Culture of Terrorism* (South End, 1988) and *Necessary Illusions* (South End, 1989), which draw particularly on the important but mostly neglected exposés by Alfonso Chardy of the *Miami Herald* and later official sources.

11. On the narrow limits of permitted discussion, see my *Necessary Illusions*. For case studies over a wider range, see Edward Herman and Noam Chomsky, *Manufacturing Consent* (Pantheon, 1988; updated edition 2002).

12. Latin American Documentation (LADOC), *Torture in Latin America* (Lima, Peru), 1987. Julio Godoy, *Nation*, 5 March 1990.

13. Juan Hernández Pico, *Envío* (Managua, Nicaragua), March 1994.

Chapter 2: IMPERIAL GRAND STRATEGY

1. White House, *The National Security Strategy of the United States of America*, released 17 September 2002.

2. John Ikenberry, *Foreign Affairs*, September–October 2002.

3. On this crucial distinction, see Carl Kaysen, Steven Miller, Martin Malin, William Nordhaus, and John Steinbruner, *War with Iraq* (American Academy of Arts and Sciences, 2002).

4. Steven Weisman, *New York Times*, 23 March 2003.

5. Arthur Schlesinger, *Los Angeles Times*, 23 March 2003.

6. Richard Falk, *Frontline* (India) 20, no. 8 (12–25 April 2003).

7. Michael Glennon, *Foreign Affairs*, May–June 2003 and May–June 1999.

8. Dana Milbank, *Washington Post*, 1 June 2003. Guy Dinmore, James Harding, and Cathy Newman, *Financial Times*, 3–4 May 2003.

9. Dean Acheson, *Proceedings of the American Society of International Law*, no. 13/14 (1963). Abraham Sofaer, US Department of State, *Current Policy*, no. 769 (December 1985). Acheson was referring specifically to US economic war, but he surely knew about the international terrorism.

10. President Clinton, address to the UN, 27 September 1993; William Cohen, *Annual Report*, 1999.

11. Memorandum of the War and Peace Studies Project; Laurence Shoup and William Minter, *Imperial Brain Trust* (Monthly Review, 1977), p. 130ff.

12. See Bacevich, *American Empire,* for unusually strong claims in this regard.

13. George W. Bush, State of the Union address, transcribed in *New York Times,* 29 January 2003.

14. Condoleezza Rice, interview with Wolf Blitzer, CNN, 8 September 2002. Scott Peterson, *Christian Science Monitor,* 6 September 2002. John Mearsheimer and Stephen Walt, *Foreign Policy,* January–February 2003. The 1990 claims, based on alleged satellite images, were investigated by the *St. Petersburg Times.* Experts who analyzed photos from commercial satellites found nothing. Inquiries were rebuffed, and still are. See Peterson, *Christian Science Monitor,* for a review of how "some facts [are] less factual." For independent confirmation, see Peter Zimmerman, *Washington Post,* 14 August 2003.

15. *Christian Science Monitor*–TIPP poll, *Christian Science Monitor,* 14 January 2003. Linda Feldmann, *Christian Science Monitor,* 14 March 2003. Jim Rutenberg and Robin Toner, *New York Times,* 22 March 2003.

16. Edward Alden, *Financial Times,* 21 March 2003; Anatol Lieven, *London Review of Books,* 8 May 2003.

17. Elisabeth Bumiller, *New York Times,* 2 May 2003; transcript of George W. Bush's comments, *New York Times,* 2 May 2003.

18. Jason Burke, *Sunday Observer,* 18 May 2003. See p. 211.

19. Program on International Policy Attitudes (PIPA), news release, 4 June 2003.

20. Jeanne Cummings and Greg Hite, *Wall Street Journal,* 2 May 2003. Francis Clines, *New York Times,* 10 May 2003; Rove's emphasis.

21. David Sanger and Steven Weisman, *New York Times,* 10 April 2003. Roger Owen, *Al-Ahram Weekly,* 3 April 2003.

22. Comment and Analysis, *Financial Times,* 27 May 2003.

23. Corfu Channel, 1949.

24. See my *New Military Humanism* (Common Courage, 1999).

25. See my *A New Generation Draws the Line* (Verso, 2000), p. 4ff. Statement by Nonaligned Movement, Kuala Lumpur, 25 February 2003.

26. Aryeh Dayan, *Ha'aretz,* 21 May 2003.

27. Amir Oren, *Ha'aretz,* 29 November 2002.

28. Suzanne Nossel, *Fletcher Forum,* winter–spring 2003.

29. Richard Wilson, *Nature* 302, no. 31 (March 1983). Michael Jansen, *Middle East International,* 10 January 2003. Imad Khadduri, *Uncritical Mass,* memoirs (manuscript), 2003. Scott Sagan and Kenneth Waltz, *The Spread of Nuclear Weapons* (Norton, 1995), pp. 18–19.

30. Neely Tucker, *Washington Post,* 3 December 2002; Neil Lewis, *New York Times,* 9 January 2003.

31. Ed Vulliamy, *Sunday Observer,* 25 May 2003.

32. See p. 200.

33. Jack Balkin, *Los Angeles Times,* 13 February 2003, and *Newsday,* 17 February 2003. Nat Hentoff, *Progressive,* April 2003.

34. Winston Churchill cited by A. W. Brian Simpson, *Human Rights and the End of Empire* (Oxford, 2001), p. 55.

35. Kaysen et al., *War with Iraq.* Michael Krepon, *Bulletin of the Atomic Scientists,* January–February 2003.

36. John Steinbruner and Jeffrey Lewis, *Daedalus,* fall 2002.

37. See my *Year 501* (South End, 1993), chapter 1.

38. James Morgan, *Financial Times,* 25–26 April 1992, referring to G-7, the IMF, GATT, and other institutions of "the new imperial age." Guy de Jonquières, *Financial Times,* 24 January 2001. Fukuyama cited by Mark Curtis, *The Ambiguities of Power* (Zed, 1995), p. 183.

39. Bush and Baker cited by Sam Husseini, *Counterpunch,* 8 March 2003. Dilip Hiro, *Iraq: In the Eye of the Storm* (Thunder's Mouth/Nation, 2002), pp. 102f.

40. Edward Luck, *New York Times,* 22 March 2003.

41. Elisabeth Bumiller and Carl Hulse, *New York Times,* 12 October 2002. Colin Powell cited by Julia Preston, *New York Times,* 18 October 2002. David Sanger and Julia Preston, *New York Times,* 8 November 2002. Andrew Card cited by Doug Saunders, *Toronto Globe and Mail,* 11 November 2002.

42. Mark Turner and Roula Khalaf, *Financial Times,* 5 February 2003.

43. David Sanger and Warren Hoge, *New York Times,* 17 March 2003. Michael Gordon, *New York Times,* 18 March 2003.

44. Excerpts from George W. Bush's news conference, *New York Times,* 7 March 2003. Felicity Barringer and David Sanger, *New York Times,* 1 March 2003.

45. Alison Mitchell and David Sanger, *New York Times,* 4 September 2002. Ari Fleischer cited by Christopher Adams and Mark Huband, *Financial Times,* 12–13 April 2003. Jack Straw cited by David Sanger and Felicity Barringer, *New York Times,* 7 March 2003.

46. "In Powell's Words: Saddam Hussein Remains Guilty," *New York Times,* 6 March 2003. Weisman, *New York Times,* 23 March 2003.

47. Condoleezza Rice, *Foreign Affairs,* January–February 2000. Cited by John Mearsheimer and Stephen Walt, *Foreign Policy,* January–February 2003. Note that 9-11 had no effect on these risk assessments.

48. Dafna Linzer, AP, *Boston Globe,* 24 February 2003.

49. Guy Dinmore and Mark Turner, *Financial Times,* 12 February 2003. Jeanne Cummings and Robert Block, *Wall Street Journal,* 26 February 2003.

50. Geneive Abdo, *Boston Globe,* 13 February 2003. Eric Lichtblau, *New York Times,* 11 February 2003. See p. 208.

51. Richard Boudreaux and John Hendren, *Los Angeles Times,* 15 March 2003.

52. Neil King Jr. and Jess Bravin, *Wall Street Journal,* 5 May 2003. For US attitudes quoted here, see 18–22 April 2003 poll by the Program on International Policy Attitudes (PIPA). On Iraqi attitudes, see Susannah Sirkin, deputy director, Physicians for Human Rights, reporting PHR poll finding that over 85% wanted the UN to "play the lead role" (Letters, *New York Times,* 21 August 2003).

53. John Ikenberry, *Foreign Affairs,* September–October 2002. Anatol Lieven, *London Review of Books,* 3 October 2002.

54. Samuel Huntington, *Foreign Affairs,* March–April 1999. Robert Jervis, *Foreign Affairs,* July–August 2001.

55. Kenneth Waltz in Ken Booth and Tim Dunne, eds., *Worlds in Collision* (Palgrave, 2002). Steven Miller in Kaysen et al., *War with Iraq.* Jack Snyder, *National Interest,* spring 2003. Selig Harrison, *New York Times,* 7 June 2003.

56. Bernard Fall, *Last Reflections on a War* (Doubleday, 1967).

57. See my *For Reasons of State* (Pantheon, 1973; New Press, 2003), p. 25, for a review of the final material in the *Pentagon Papers,* which ends at this point.

58. Maureen Dowd, *New York Times,* 23 February 1991.

59. World Economic Forum press release, 14 January 2003. Guy de Jonquières, *Financial Times,* 15 January 2003.

60. Alan Cowell, *New York Times,* 23 January 2003; Mark Landler, *New York Times,* 24 January 2003. Marc Champion, David Cloud, and Carla Anne Robbins, *Wall Street Journal,* 27 January 2003.

61. Foreign Desk, "Powell on Iraq: 'We Reserve Our Sovereign Right to Take Military Action,' " *New York Times,* 27 January 2003.

62. Kaysen et al., *War with Iraq.*

63. Hans von Sponeck, *Guardian,* 22 July 2002.

64. Ken Warn, *Financial Times,* 21 January 2003. On international polls, see chapter 5.

65. Glenn Kessler and Mike Allen, *Washington Post Weekly,* 3 March 2003. Fareed Zakaria, *Newsweek,* 24 March 2003.

66. See chapter 1, note 6. *Atlantic Monthly,* 1901, cited by Ido Oren, *Our Enemies and US* (Cornell, 2002), p. 42.

67. Andrew Bacevich, *American Empire,* pp. 215ff. His emphasis.

68. John Stuart Mill. See pp. 44–45. Britain's attitude toward the nobility of its successor was a bit different; see p. 149.

69. Andrew Bacevich, *World Policy Journal,* fall 2002.

70. Michael Glennon, *Christian Science Monitor,* 20 March 1986.

71. Sebastian Mallaby, *New York Times Book Review,* 21 September 1997. Michael Mandelbaum, *The Ideas That Conquered the World* (Public Affairs, 2002), p. 195. Senior administration policymaker cited by Thomas Friedman, *New York Times,* 12 January 1992.

72. Boot, *New York Times,* 13 February 2003. Robert Kagan, *Washington Post Weekly,* 10 February 2003.

73. On Mill's essay and the circumstances in which it was written, see my *Peering into the Abyss of the Future* (New Delhi, 2002). Britain's crimes in India and China shocked many Englishmen, including classical liberals like Richard Cobden. See chapter 7, note 52.

74. Henri Alleg, *La Guerre d'Algérie,* cited in Y. Bedjauoi, A. Aroua, and M. Ait-Larbi, eds., *An Inquiry into the Algerian Massacres* (Hoggar, 1999).

75. Walter LaFeber, *Inevitable Revolutions* (Norton, 1983), pp. 50ff., 75ff.

76. Mohammad-Mahmoud Mohamedou, *Iraq and the Second Gulf War* (Austin & Winfield, 1998), p. 123.

77. David Schmitz, *Thank God They're on Our Side* (North Carolina, 1999). "Japan Envisions a 'New Order' in Asia, 1938," reprinted in Dennis Merrill and Thomas Paterson, eds., *Major Problems in American Foreign Relations, Volume II: Since 1914* (Houghton Mifflin, 2000).

78. Soviet lawyers, see Sean Murphy, *Humanitarian Intervention* (Pennsylvania, 1996). Kennedy administration, see my *Rethinking Camelot* (South End, 1993).

79. Ivan Maisky, January 1944, cited in Vladimir Pechatnov, *The Big Three After World War II* (Woodrow Wilson International Center, Working Paper no. 13, May 1995).

80. Cited by LaFeber, *Inevitable Revolutions.* Robert Tucker, *Commentary,* January 1975.

81. Cited by Mexican historian José Fuentes Mares in Cecil Robinson, ed., *The View from Chapultepec* (Arizona, 1989), p. 160.

82. Cited by William Stivers, *Supremacy and Oil* (Cornell, 1982).

83. Morgenthau, *New York Review of Books*, 24 September 1970.

84. See regular Human Rights Watch and Amnesty International reports and, among many publications, Javier Giraldo, *Colombia: The Genocidal Democracy* (Common Courage, 1996), and Garry Leech, *Killing Peace* (Information Network of the Americas, 2002).

Chapter 3: THE NEW ERA OF ENLIGHTENMENT

1. Michael Wines, *New York Times*, 13 June 1999; Václav Havel, *New York Review of Books*, 10 June 1999; David Fromkin, *Kosovo Crossing* (Free Press, 1999). For a sample of the rhetoric, see my *New Military Humanism*.

2. Charles Tilly, *Coercion, Capital, and European States* (Blackwell, 1993), p. 70.

3. C. H. Chivers, *New York Times*, 5 December 2002.

4. In early August, the bishop's office in East Timor estimated 3,000 to 5,000 deaths through 1999. Historian John Taylor estimates 5,000 to 6,000 dead before the August 30 referendum, which set off the final paroxysm. See Taylor's *East Timor: The Price of Freedom* (Zed, 1999).

5. On Clinton's sudden conversion between September 8 and 11, 1999, see Joseph Nevins, *Counterpunch*, 16 May 2002.

6. The Australian-led UN peacekeeping force entered as the Indonesian army was withdrawing. An even earlier dispatch of forces would have been an "intervention" only in the sense that US-British forces "intervened" in France on D-Day.

7. Fromkin, *Kosovo Crossing*.

8. Yaroslav Trofimov, *Wall Street Journal*, 3 January 2003.

9. Ronald Paris, *Political Science Quarterly* 117, no. 3 (fall 2002).

10. Michael Mandelbaum, *The Ideas That Conquered the World*, p. 193.

11. Timothy Garton Ash, *Guardian*, 19 September 2002.

12. For Robertson quotes and discussion, see my *New Generation Draws the Line*, pp. 106–7. Cook, House of Commons Session 1999–2000.

13. Nicholas Wheeler, *Saving Strangers* (Oxford, 2000), pp. 34, 265ff.

14. Wesley Clark, *Waging Modern War* (Public Affairs, 2001), p. 171. Michael Ignatieff, *New York Review of Books*, 19 July 2001.

15. Bacevich, *American Empire*, pp. 104ff., 196.

16. Isa Blumi, *Current History*, March 2003.

17. Anne-Marie Slaughter, *New York Times*, 18 March 2003.

18. Charles Bergquist, in Bergquist et al., eds., *Violence in Colombia 1990–2000* (Scholarly Resources, 2001).

19. Anthony Lewis, *Daedalus,* winter 2003. Timorese were regarded as "citizens of Indonesia" by the US.

20. Editorial, *Boston Globe,* 6 March 2003. Aryeh Neier, *Dissent,* spring 2000. Neier is reacting to the review of US-backed atrocities in my *New Military Humanism,* which leaves no doubt as to the locus of responsibility.

21. Robert Cooper, *Observer,* 7 April 2002.

22. Robert Jervis, *American Political Science Review* 96 (2002).

23. Dexter Perkins, *The Monroe Doctrine, 1823–1826* (Harvard, 1927), pp. 131, 167, 176ff. Bismarck cited by Nancy Mitchell, *Prologue* 24, no. 2 (summer 1992).

24. Robert Lansing and Woodrow Wilson cited in Gabriel Kolko, *Main Currents in Modern American History* (Pantheon, 1984), p. 47.

25. President Taft cited in Jenny Pearce, *Under the Eagle* (South End, 1982), p. 17. Wilson's minister of the interior cited in Gordon Connell-Smith, *The Inter-American System* (Oxford, 1966), p. 16. John Foster Dulles cited in Stephen G. Rabe, *Eisenhower and Latin America* (North Carolina, 1988), p. 33.

26. David Schmitz, *Thank God They're on Our Side*; Schmitz, *The United States and Fascist Italy, 1922–1940* (North Carolina, 1988). Cable from British Embassy in Washington to Foreign Office in London, 24 November 1959, reporting conversation with Dulles.

27. Editorial, *New York Times,* 6 August 1954.

28. David Green, *The Containment of Latin America* (Quadrangle, 1971).

29. William Yandell Elliot, ed., *The Political Economy of American Foreign Policy* (Holt, Rinehart & Winston, 1955), p. 42.

30. Schmitz, *The United States and Fascist Italy,* p. 214.

31. See Ido Oren, *Our Enemies and US* (Cornell, 2002).

32. Schmitz, *The United States and Fascist Italy.* Kennan cited in Christopher Simpson, *The Splendid Blond Beast* (Common Courage, 1995). Newton, *Diplomacy and Statecraft* 2, no. 3 (November 1991).

33. See my *Deterring Democracy,* chapter 11, and sources cited there. Later material reviewed in my *Year 501,* chapter 2, and *World Orders Old and New* (Columbia, 1994, extended edition, 1996), chapter 1.

34. Schmitz, *Thank God They're on Our Side,* p. 305.

35. Alan Tonelson, *New York Times Book Review,* 25 December 1988.

36. Lansing and Wilson cited in Lloyd Gardner, *Safe for Democracy*

(Oxford, 1987). Alex Carey, *Taking the Risk Out of Democracy* (University of Illinois, 1997).

37. Cited by Melvin Leffler, *A Preponderance of Power* (Stanford, 1992), p. 78.

38. John Lewis Gaddis, *The Long Peace* (Oxford, 1987), p. 10.

39. Mark Laffey, *Review of International Studies* 29 (2003), a critical account of the convention.

Chapter 4: DANGEROUS TIMES

1. Michael Krepon, strategic analyst at the Henry L. Stimson Center, cited by Faye Bowers and Howard LaFranchi, *Christian Science Monitor,* 31 December 2002. Gary Hart and Warren Rudman (cochairs), *America—Still Unprepared, Still in Danger* (Council on Foreign Relations, 2002).

2. Marion Lloyd, *Boston Globe,* 13 October 2002; Kevin Sullivan, *Washington Post,* 13 October 2002.

3. Eisenhower quoted in Matthew Evangelista, Working Paper 19, Cold War International History Project (Woodrow Wilson International Center for Scholars), December 1997.

4. Lloyd, *Boston Globe,* 13 October 2002.

5. Raymond Garthoff, *Reflections on the Cuban Missile Crisis* (Brookings Institution, 1987), pp. 83, 89, 86, 37. Emphasis his. Warheads of course remained under US control.

6. The leading US government scholar recognized that the only "mass-based political party" in South Vietnam was the National Liberation Front and that the US must resort to violence to destroy it. Douglas Pike, *Viet Cong* (MIT, 1966). In Indonesia, the main target of the huge US-backed slaughter in 1965 was the PKI, which developed a "mass base among the peasantry" through its "vigor in defending the interests of the . . . poor." Harold Crouch, *The Army and Politics in Indonesia* (Cornell, 1978), pp. 351, 155.

7. William Safire, *New York Times,* 6 February 2003. Adam Clymer, *New York Times,* 6 February 2003.

8. Adlai Stevenson III, *New York Times,* 7 February 2003.

9. See Thomas Paterson, "Cuba and the Missile Crisis," in Merrill and Paterson, eds., *Major Problems in American Foreign Relations.*

10. Ernest May and Philip Zelikow, eds., *The Kennedy Tapes* (Harvard, 1998), p. 263.

11. Frank Costigliola, *Political Science Quarterly,* spring 1995. Costigliola in Thomas Paterson, ed., *Kennedy's Quest for Victory* (Oxford, 1989). The senior adviser, not clearly identified, may be Dean Acheson or Mike Mansfield.

12. Paterson, "Cuba and the Missile Crisis."

13. Morris Morley, *Imperial State and Revolution* (Cambridge, 1987). See Daniele Ganser, *Reckless Gamble* (University Press of the South, 2000), and Stephen Streeter, *Managing the Counterrevolution* (Ohio, 2000), p. 216. On Cuba's appeal to the UN, see Ganser.

14. "A Program of Covert Action against the Castro Regime," 16 March 1960.

15. British Cable No. 2455, 24 November 1959. See chapter 3, note 26.

16. Arthur Schlesinger, Memorandum for the President, 11 February 1961.

17. Thomas Paterson in Paterson, ed., *Kennedy's Quest.* For the full texts, see Mark White, *The Kennedys and Cuba* (Ivan Dee, 2001), pp. 37ff.

18. May and Zelikow, eds., *The Kennedy Tapes,* p. 134; 18 October 1962, during an internal discussion on the use of force during the missile crisis.

19. May and Zelikow, eds., *The Kennedy Tapes,* p. ix. On the US takeover under the guise of liberation, see Louis Pérez, *The War of 1898* (North Carolina, 1998).

20. Piero Gleijeses, *Conflicting Missions* (North Carolina, 2002), p. 16. The quoted phrase is Arthur Schlesinger's, referring to the goals of Robert Kennedy, in Schlesinger, *Robert Kennedy and His Times* (Ballantine, 1978), pp. 477–80.

21. Jorge Domínguez, *Diplomatic History* 24, no. 2 (spring 2000). Gleijeses, *Conflicting Missions,* pp. 402–3.

22. White, *The Kennedys and Cuba,* pp. 71, 95f., 106, 115ff.

23. Tim Weiner, *New York Times,* 13 October 2002, citing a February 1962 memorandum; also cited by AP, *Boston Globe,* 30 January 1998.

24. Memorandum for the Secretary of Defense, "Justification for the US Military Intervention in Cuba (TS)," Operation Northwoods, 13 March 1962.

25. Paterson in *Kennedy's Quest for Victory.*

26. Garthoff, *Reflections,* pp. 16ff.

27. Garthoff, *Reflections,* pp. 78–79, 108–9.

28. Memorandum of 12 November 1962 cited by Gleijeses, *Conflicting Missions,* p. 25. Garthoff, *Reflections,* pp. 91, 98.

29. Domínguez, *Diplomatic History*. May and Zelikow, eds., *The Kennedy Tapes*, p. 66.
30. Editorial, *New York Times*, 2 January 1989.
31. Reuters, *Boston Globe*, 15 October 1992. Juan Tamayo, *Miami Herald*, 16 November 1997; Tamayo, *Miami Herald*, 28 September 1997. Andrew Cawthorne, *Boston Globe*, 12 March 1999. Ann Louise Bardach and Larry Rohter, *New York Times*, 12 July and 13 July 1998. Anya Landau and Wayne Smith, *International Policy Report* (Center for International Policy), November 2002.
32. Duncan Campbell, *Guardian*, 7 April 2003. For an analysis of the charges and background, see William Blum, *Counterpunch*, 1 September 2002.
33. Ruth Leacock, *Requiem for Revolution* (Kent State, 1990), p. 33.
34. May and Zelikow, eds., *The Kennedy Tapes*, p. 91.
35. Morris Morley and Chris McGillion, *Unfinished Business* (Cambridge, 2002), p. 223n.
36. Morley and McGillion, *Unfinished Business*, p. 153. See my *Necessary Illusions*, pp. 177, 101. Shirley Christian, *New York Times*, 4 September 1992.
37. David Sanger, *New York Times*, 21 February 1997.
38. Gleijeses, *Conflicting Missions*, p. 26.
39. Paterson, "Cuba and the Missile Crisis."
40. Letter to Robert Livingston, 18 April 1802, cited in *National Interest*, spring 2003.
41. Robert F. Kennedy cited in Michael McClintock, *Instruments of Statecraft* (Pantheon, 1992), p. 23.
42. Cited in Adam Isacson and Joy Olson, *Just the Facts* (Latin America Working Group and Center for International Policy, 1999), p. ix.
43. See my *Deterring Democracy*, chapter 10.
44. Lars Schoultz, *Human Rights and United States Policy toward Latin America* (Princeton, 1981), p. 7.
45. For discussion, context, and sources, see my *Year 501*, chapter 7.
46. Thomas Skidmore, *The Politics of Military Rule in Brazil, 1964–85* (Oxford, 1988). Also see my *Year 501*, chapter 7.
47. "Indonesian-American Relations," 1965. SNIE, 1 September 1965. Cited by Mark Curtis, *Web of Deceit* (Vintage, 2003), pp. 399ff.
48. Gleijeses, *Conflicting Missions*, pp. 332, 346.
49. Victoria Brittain, *Race and Class*, April–June 2003.
50. Gleijeses, *Conflicting Missions*, p. 359.

51. David Gonzalez, *New York Times,* 14 October 2002. Barry Gewen, *New York Times Book Review,* 15 September 2002.

52. Alexander George, ed., *Western State Terrorism* (Routledge, 1991). See also Chomsky and Herman, *The Political Economy of Human Rights,* (South End, 1979), vol. I, chapter 3, section 1, and Edward Herman, *The Real Terror Network* (South End, 1982).

53. Jean Bethke Elshtain, *Just War against Terror* (Basic Books, 2003), p. 18, her emphasis. For a review of these operations, based in part on notes provided to us by *Newsweek* Saigon bureau chief Kevin Buckley, see Chomsky and Herman, *Political Economy of Human Rights,* vol. I, pp. 313ff., and *Manufacturing Consent,* pp. 196ff. Some of the same material appears in Christopher Hitchens, *The Trial of Henry Kissinger* (Verso, 2001), pp. 30ff.

54. Congressional testimony, 1986, 1983. See essays by Jack Spence and Eldon Kenworthy in Thomas Walker, ed., *Reagan Versus the Sandinistas* (Westview, 1987).

55. Remarks at a White House Meeting for Supporters of United States Assistance for the Nicaraguan Democratic Resistance, 3 March 1986. Walter Robinson, *Boston Globe,* 22 March 1986.

56. Kenworthy in Walker, ed., *Reagan Versus the Sandinistas.* See also my *Culture of Terrorism,* pp. 219ff., *Necessary Illusions,* pp. 71ff., and *Deterring Democracy,* p. 259, on various phases as the useful farce proceeded. National Emergency, see *New York Times*, 2 May 1985, and my *Turning the Tide* (South End, 1986), p. 144, for more detail. Libya, see my *Pirates and Emperors, Old and New* (South End, 2002, update of 1985 version), p. 72, on Reagan's address to the American Bar Association, July 1985.

57. George Shultz, Department of State, *Current Policy,* no. 820. Libya, see my *Pirates and Emperors, Old and New*, chapter 3.

58. Thomas Walker, *Nicaragua* (Westview, 2003). Thomas Carothers in Abraham Lowenthal, ed., *Exporting Democracy* (Johns Hopkins, 1991), his emphasis. See also his *In the Name of Democracy* (California, 1991).

59. For World Bank, IADB, and other sources, see my *Deterring Democracy,* chapter 10. For information on health effects, see Nicaraguan Society of Doctors and International Physicians for the Prevention of Nuclear War (IPPNW), *The War in Nicaragua* (MEDIPAZ, Managua and Cambridge, 2003).

60. See Paul Reichler, *Harvard International Law Journal* 42, no. 1 (2001).

61. *Military and Paramilitary Activities in and against Nicaragua*, International Court of Justice, 27 June 1986. Security Council S/18221, 11 July 1986.
62. For these and many other samples from the press, see Herman and Chomsky, *Manufacturing Consent*, pp. 240ff., and my *Necessary Illusions*, pp. 33ff., and *Year 501*, pp. 251ff.
63. Charles Radin, *Boston Globe*, 17 November 2000.
64. Anthropologist Ira Lowenthal, his emphasis. Cited in Paul Farmer, *AIDS and Accusation* (California, 1992).
65. See Paul Farmer, *The Uses of Haiti*, 2nd ed. (Common Courage, 2003).
66. Max Mintz, *Seeds of Empire* (New York University, 1999), pp. 75–76, 180ff.
67. General John Galvin, commander of the US Southern Command (SOUTHCOM), explaining strategy to Congress; see Fred Kaplan, *Boston Globe*, 20 May 1987.
68. Michael Kinsley, *Wall Street Journal*, 26 March 1987.
69. *Envío* (Managua, Nicaragua), March 2003; September 2001.
70. *Envío*, October 2001.
71. On the 1984 elections, see Walker, *Nicaragua*, pp. 156ff. On the reports of a wide range of expert observers, all ignored, and adherence within media and commentary to the Reaganite agenda on elections in enemy Nicaragua and its terrorist client states, see Herman and Chomsky, *Manufacturing Consent*, chapter 3.
72. *Envío*, October 2001.
73. Kenneth Pollack, *New York Times Book Review*, 6 April 2003.
74. News services, *Washington Post*, 3 December 2002.
75. On Abrams, see Steven Weisman, *New York Times*, 7 December 2002. On Reich and Noriega, see James Dao, *New York Times*, 10 January 2003.
76. ACLU news release, 14 November 2002.
77. *Envío*, October 2001.
78. Ricardo Stevens, 19 October 2001; cited in North American Congress on Latin America (NACLA), *Report on the Americas*, November–December 2001.
79. Interview, Institute for Public Accuracy, 22 March 2002. On polls, see pp. 199ff.

Chapter 5: THE IRAQ CONNECTION

1. Reagan cited in *New York Times,* 18 October 1985. George Shultz, State Department, *Current Policy,* no. 589 (24 June 1984) and no. 629 (25 October 1984).

2. For discussion of some of these questions, see Chomsky and Herman, *Political Economy of Human Rights;* Herman, *Real Terror Network;* my *Pirates and Emperors;* and George, ed., *Western State Terrorism.*

3. UN Inter-Agency Task Force, cited in Merle Bowen, "Mozambique and the Politics of Economic Recovery," *Fletcher Forum of World Affairs* 15, no. 1 (winter 1991). Dereje Asrat et al., *Children on the Front Line,* 3rd. edition (UNICEF, 1989). On ANC, see Joseba Zulaika and William Douglass, *Terror and Taboo* (Routledge, 1996), p. 12.

4. Raymond Garthoff, *A Journey through the Cold War* (Brookings Institution, 2001), pp. 338, 387. John Cooley, *Unholy Wars* (Pluto, 1999), pp. 11, 54.

5. Cooley, *Unholy Wars,* pp. 230ff.

6. Miron Rezun, *Saddam Hussein's Gulf Wars* (Praeger, 1992), pp. 58f.

7. See my *Deterring Democracy,* pp. 50–51, 236ff., and 278ff. On Duvalier, see my *Year 501,* chapter 8, section 4.

8. Hannah Pakula, *Washington Post,* 27 December 1989. Howard La-Franchi, *Christian Science Monitor,* 25 November 2002.

9. AP, 22 December 1989. State Department to Senator Daniel Inouye, 26 February 1990. See my *Deterring Democracy,* p. 152, for details.

10. Peter Spiegel and Richard McGregor, *Financial Times,* 10 April 2003. Spiegel, *Financial Times,* 10 April 2003. On Marcos, who was a particular favorite of President Reagan and Vice President Bush, see my *Deterring Democracy,* chapters 7, 8.

11. See Bedjauoi et al., eds., *An Inquiry into the Algerian Massacres,* for extensive documentation. William Burns cited in Steven Weisman, *New York Times,* 10 December 2002. Robert Fisk, *Independent,* 4 January 2003. Lara Marlowe, *Irish Times,* 31 December 2002.

12. See Thomas Ferguson and Joel Rogers, *Right Turn* (Hill & Wang, 1986), Michael Meeropol, *Surrender* (Michigan, 2003). See also my *Turning the Tide,* chapter 5, and my *Year 501,* chapter 11. On economic consequences, see *State of Working America* studies by the Economic Policy Institute; and Edward Wolff, *Top Heavy* (New Press, 1996).

13. On Libya's role in Reaganite demonology, see my *Pirates and Emperors, Old and New*, chapter 3; Stephen Shalom, *Imperial Alibis* (South End, 1992), chapter 7.

14. See my *Necessary Illusions*, pp. 176–80.

15. See pp. 96–97.

16. Anthony Lewis, *New York Times*, 17 April 1986.

17. Hodding Carter, *Wall Street Journal*, 14 September 1989; Thomas Pickering quoted by AP, 19 December 1989. For a detailed review, see my *Deterring Democracy*, chapters 5 and 6, and Shalom, *Imperial Alibis*, chapter 8.

18. Cited in Irene Gendzier, *Notes from the Minefield* (Columbia, 1977), p. 256.

19. Ferguson and Rogers, *Right Turn*, p. 122. Jackie Calmes and John D. McKinnon, *Wall Street Journal*, 11 November 2002.

20. Peronet Despeignes, *Financial Times*, 29 May 2003. Kotlikoff and Sachs, *Boston Globe*, 19 May 2003. Fleischer, *Financial Times*, 30 May 2003.

21. Paul Krugman, *New York Times*, 27 May 2003.

22. Anatol Lieven, *London Review of Books*, 3 October 2002.

23. Martin Sieff, *American Conservative*, 4 November 2002.

24. Donald Green and Eric Schickler, *New York Times*, 12 November 2002.

25. Peter Slevin, *Washington Post*, 19 September 2002.

26. Greg Gordon, *Minneapolis Star-Tribune*, 18 October 2002; *Jane's Terrorism and Security Monitor*, 12 November 2002; Sebastian Rotella, *Los Angeles Times*, 4 November 2002; Jimmy Burns and Mark Huband, *Financial Times*, 24 January 2003; Eric Lichtblau, *New York Times*, 25 January 2003; Marlise Simons, *New York Times*, 29 January 2003; and Philip Shenon, *New York Times*, 4 March 2003.

27. Richard Betts, *Foreign Affairs*, January–February 2003.

28. Kenneth Waltz in Booth and Dunne, eds., *Worlds in Collision*. US intelligence, see chapter 7, note 10, below.

29. Study cited by Charles Glaser and Steve Fetter, *International Security* 26, no. 1 (summer 2001). Richard Falkenrath, Robert Newman, and Bradley Thayer, *America's Achilles' Heel* (MIT, 1998). Barton Gellman, *Washington Post*, 20 December 2001. Hart and Rudman, *America—Still Unprepared, Still in Danger*.

30. Kaysen et al., *War with Iraq*, citing Daniel Benjamin, *Washington Post*, 31 October 2002. Barton Gellman, *Washington Post*, 10 May 2003.

31. Youssef Ibrahim, *International Herald Tribune,* 1 November 2002.

32. See, for example, International Physicians for the Prevention of Nuclear War and Medact, *Collateral Damage: The Health and Environmental Costs of War on Iraq,* 12 November 2002; Physicians for Human Rights, *Health and Human Rights Consequences of War in Iraq,* briefing paper, 14 February 2003; Nicholas Pelham, *Financial Times,* 28 February 2003; Kenneth Bacon, *Bulletin of the Atomic Scientists,* January–February 2003; James Politi, Guy Dinmore, and Mark Turner, *Financial Times,* 27 February 2003; and Ed Vulliamy, Burhan Wazir, and Gaby Hinsliff, *Sunday Observer,* 22 December 2002.

33. Turi Munthe in Munthe, ed., *The Saddam Hussein Reader* (Thunder's Mouth, 2002), p. xxvii.

34. The sanctions were technically imposed by the UN, but it was always understood that they were enforced by the US-UK, under UN aegis, and with little support, particularly in the cruel form that targets civilians.

35. Frances Williams, *Financial Times,* 12 December 2002. John Mueller and Karl Mueller, *Foreign Affairs,* May–June 1999.

36. Rajiv Chandrasekaran, *Washington Post Weekly,* 10 February 2003, a notable exception to the general lack of coverage.

37. Denis Halliday and Hans von Sponeck, *Al-Ahram Weekly,* 26 December 2002.

38. Joy Gordon, *Harper's,* November 2002. For extensive detail and rebuttal to official justifications, see Eric Herring, *Review of International Studies* 28 (2002), pp. 39–56.

39. ICRC, *Iraq 1989–1999: A Decade of Sanctions,* 14 December 1999.

40. Other arguments presented were too bizarre to discuss: e.g., that we should bomb and occupy Iraq because then we could stop torturing its population with sanctions.

41. John Burns, *New York Times,* 16 September 2001; Samina Ahmed, *International Security* 26, no. 3 (winter 2001–02).

42. Thomas Friedman outlining Bush I administration thinking after it effectively authorized Saddam to crush the rebellions that might have overthrown him, *New York Times,* 7 June 1991.

43. Mark Thomas, *New Statesman,* 9 December 2002. See chapter 3, note 5.

44. Gallup Poll International, December 2002; Marc Champion, *Wall Street Journal,* 30 January 2003; Steven Weisman, *New York Times,* 10 February 2003.

45. Powell cited by Weisman, *New York Times*, 10 February 2003. Reference is to the original eight and former Russian satellites.

46. Andrew Higgins, *Wall Street Journal*, 18 March 2003.

47. Holbrooke cited in Lee Michael Katz, *National Journal*, 8 February 2003.

48. Editorial, *Wall Street Journal*, 3 February 2003.

49. Thomas Friedman, *New York Times*, 9 February 2003.

50. Todd Purdum, *New York Times*, 30 January 2003. Max Boot, *New York Times*, 13 February 2003. Robert Kagan, *Washington Post Weekly*, 10 February 2003. See p. 44.

51. Mark Landler, *New York Times*, 20 January 2003, quoting the spokesperson for the right-wing Christian Social Union Party.

52. Polls from *Economist*, 18 January 2003. Morton Abramowitz, *Wall Street Journal*, 16 January 2003.

53. Recep Tayyip Erdogan cited in Brian Groom, *Financial Times*, 25 January 2003.

54. Dexter Filkins, *New York Times*, 6 and 26 February 2003; Amberin Zaman, *Los Angeles Times*, 8 February 2003.

55. Steven Weisman, *New York Times*, 30 March 2003.

56. Paul Wolfowitz quoted in Marc Lacey, *New York Times*, 8 May 2003.

57. Thomas Carothers, *Foreign Affairs*, January–February 2003.

58. Carothers in *Exporting Democracy*, and Carothers, *In the Name of Democracy*. On the "yearning for democracy" in the Reagan years, see Neil Lewis, *New York Times*, 6 December 1987. For more details, see my *Necessary Illusions*, p. 49.

59. Atilio Borón, *State, Capitalism, and Democracy in Latin America* (Lynne Rienner, 1995), chapter 7.

60. James Mahon, *Mobile Capital and Latin American Development* (Penn State, 1996).

61. Timothy Canova, *American University International Law Review* 14, no. 6 (1999), and *Brooklyn Law Review* 60, no. 4 (1995). César Gaviria, OAS secretary-general, cited in Guy Dinmore, *Financial Times*, 11 June 2003.

62. Ha-Joon Chang and Ajit Singh, *UNCTAD Review* 4 (1993), pp. 45–81.

63. Thomas Patterson, *Boston Globe*, 15 December 2000, and *New York Times*, 8 November 2000. Also see his book *The Vanishing Voter* (Knopf, 2002). Gary Jacobson, *Political Science Quarterly* 116, no. 1 (spring 2001). See also my articles in the January and February 2001 issues of *Z Magazine*.

64. Stuart Ewen, *Captains of Consciousness* (McGraw-Hill, 1976), p. 85. See Michael Dawson, *The Consumer Trap* (Illinois, 2003), for an extensive review of the technique of "off-job control" developed from the 1920s as a counterpart to the "on-job control" of Taylorism, designed to turn people into controlled robots in life as well as work.

65. Von Sponeck, *Toronto Globe and Mail*, 2 July 2002. Halliday, *Al-Ahram Weekly*, 26 December 2002.

66. Thomas Friedman, *New York Times*, 7 June 1991. Alan Cowell, *New York Times*, 11 April 1991. Friedman, *New York Times*, 4 June 2003.

67. Brent Scowcroft cited in Bob Herbert, *New York Times*, 10 April 2003.

68. Chart shown in *New York Times*, 7 May 2003; Source: Department of Defense, Office of Reconstruction and Humanitarian Assistance.

69. David Sanger with John Tagliabue, *New York Times*, 5 April 2003.

70. Arthur Schlesinger, see p. 12.

Chapter 6: DILEMMAS OF DOMINANCE

1. David Ignatius, *International Herald Tribune*, 14–15 December 2002, from *Washington Post*.

2. For *Financial Times, Business Week, Wall Street Journal*, and other sources, see my *World Orders Old and New*, chapter 2.

3. Arie Farnam, *Christian Science Monitor*, 10 June 2003.

4. UN Development Program cited by Duncan Green and Matthew Griffith, *International Affairs* 78, no. 1 (2002). David Powell, *Current History*, October 2002. For polls, see Michael Wines, *New York Times*, 5 March 2003.

5. Bruce cited in Costigliola, *Political Science Quarterly*, spring 1995.

6. Henry Kissinger, *American Foreign Policy* (expanded edition, Norton, 1974).

7. See p. 15.

8. Christopher Thorne, *The Issue of War* (Oxford, 1985), pp. 225, 211. For sources and general context, see my *Deterring Democracy*.

9. Howard Wachtel, *The Money Mandarins* (M. E. Sharpe, 1990), pp. 44ff. *Business Week*, 7 April 1975.

10. Melvyn Leffler, *Preponderance of Power*, p. 339.

11. Britain, see Mark Curtis, *Web of Deceit*, pp. 15–16. For the others, see Aaron David Miller, *Search for Security* (North Carolina, 1980);

Irvine Anderson, *Aramco, the United States and Saudi Arabia* (Princeton, 1981); and Michael Stoff, *Oil, War and American Security* (Yale, 1980). Eisenhower cited in Steven Spiegel, *The Other Arab-Israeli Conflict* (Chicago, 1985), p. 51.

12. Task Force on US-Korea Policy (Center for International Policy, Washington, and Center for East Asian Studies, Chicago), "The Nuclear Crisis on the Korean Peninsula: Avoiding the Road to Perdition"; abridged version, *Current History*, April 2003.

13. Cited by Selig Harrison, *World Policy Journal*, winter 2002–03.

14. What follows concerning the San Francisco Peace Treaty is drawn from John Price, Working Paper No. 78, Japan Policy Research Institute, June 2001.

15. Human Rights Watch press release, 15 May 2003.

Chapter 7: CAULDRON OF ANIMOSITIES

1. Bowers and LaFranchi, *Christian Science Monitor*, 31 December 2002, citing Michael Krepon.

2. Butler cited in Hans Kristensen, *BASIC Research Report* (British-American Security Information Council) 98, no. 2 (March 1998), appendix I. Aluf Benn, *Ha'aretz*, 2 June 2003, reporting Russia's demand that Israel's nuclear program "be placed on the agenda of international organizations concerned with preventing nuclear proliferation."

3. Knut Royce, *Newsday*, 29 August 1990; 3 January 1991.

4. Ruth Sinai, *Ha'aretz*, 3 December 2002.

5. Yitzhak ben-Yisrael, *Ha'aretz*, 16 April 2002.

6. Galal Nassar, *Al-Ahram Weekly*, 7 March 2002.

7. Robert Olson, *Middle East Policy* 9, no. 2 (June 2002).

8. Praful Bidwai, *News International*, 22 May 2003, citing Brajesh Mishra.

9. Lloyd George cited by V. G. Kiernan, *European Empires from Conquest to Collapse* (Fontana, 1982).

10. National Intelligence Council (NIC), *Global Trends 2015* (December 2000).

11. NIC, *Global Trends 2015*.

12. Mark Curtis, *Web of Deceit*, chapter 22.

13. Thom Shanker and Eric Schmitt, *New York Times*, 20 April 2003.

14. Herbert, *New York Times*, 21 April 2003.

15. On the planning context, see chapter 6. The specific topics reviewed

here are discussed in much greater detail in my *World Orders Old and New*, the updated edition of *Fateful Triangle* (South End, 1983; updated 1999), *Pirates and Emperors, Old and New*, and *Middle East Illusions* (Rowman & Littlefield, 2003). See these for sources, where not cited, and for fuller quotations. On broader issues there is a rich literature. Particularly pertinent for background here is Norman Finkelstein, *Image and Reality of the Israel-Palestine Conflict* (Verso, 2003, updated from 1995 edition).

16. Abraham Ben-Zvi, *Decade of Transition* (Columbia, 1998), p. 76. See Irene Gendzier, *Notes from the Minefield*, and William Roger Louis and Roger Owen, eds., *A Revolutionary Year: The Middle East in 1958* (I.B. Tauris, 2002). On Indonesia, see Audrey Kahin and George Kahin, *Subversion as Foreign Policy* (New Press, 1995).

17. Ben-Zvi, *Decade of Transition*, pp. 80ff. Separately, he attributes the statement to Eisenhower. See also Gendzier, *Notes from the Minefield*, and Ilan Pappé, in Lewis and Owen, eds., *A Revolutionary Year*.

18. Efraim Inbar, *The Israeli-Turkish Entente* (King's College London Mediterranean Studies, no. 75, autumn 2002), p. 25, written from a perspective close to official Israeli attitudes.

19. On these matters, see particularly Finkelstein, *Image and Reality*. Also my *Middle East Illusions*, chapter 5.

20. On the intricacies of this affair, see Irwin Wall, *France, the United States, and the Algerian War* (California, 2001).

21. See my *Fateful Triangle* for an account of the events and the reaction to them by media and commentators.

22. On Israel's record in Lebanon in the 1980s and 1990s, see my *Pirates and Emperors, Old and New* and *Fateful Triangle* (1999 edition).

23. Michael Walzer, *New Republic*, 6 September 1982 (his emphasis).

24. James Bennet, *New York Times*, 24 January 2002.

25. Mark Sappenfield, *Christian Science Monitor*, 15 April 2002. Program on International Policy Attitudes (PIPA), *Americans on the Israel-Palestinian Conflict*, University of Maryland, 8 May 2002.

26. See 'Abd al-Shafi's interview with Rashid Khalidi, *Journal of Palestine Studies* 32, no. 1 (autumn 2002).

27. Shlomo Ben-Ami, *A Place for All* (Hakibbutz Hameuchad, 1998). See my introduction to Roane Carey, ed., *The New Intifada* (Verso, 2001), reprinted in my *Pirates and Emperors, Old and New*.

28. Avi Primor, *Ha'aretz*, 19 September 2002. On current Israeli strategies, see particularly Tanya Reinhart, *Israel/Palestine: How to End the War*

of 1948 (Seven Stories, 2002); Baruch Kimmerling, *Politicide* (Verso, 2003).

29. Akiva Eldar, *Ha'aretz,* 14 February 2002.

30. Hussein Agha and Robert Malley, *Foreign Affairs,* May–June 2002.

31. B'Tselem, *Land Grab: Israel's Settlement Policy in the West Bank,* May 2002.

32. Geoffrey Aronson, *Report on Israeli Settlement in the Occupied Territories,* March–April 2003.

33. Cited in Harvey Morris, Guy Dinmore, Christopher Adams, *Financial Times,* 1 May 2003.

34. "Proposal for 'Final and Comprehensive Settlement' to Middle East Conflict," *New York Times,* 1 May 2003.

35. Sharmila Devi, *Financial Times,* 1 May 2003, citing *Ha'aretz.*

36. Harvey Morris, *Financial Times,* 5 May 2002. Eva Balslev and Katrin Sommer, *News from Within* (Jerusalem), October 2002.

37. Sara Roy, *Daily Star* (Beirut), 2 June 2003. On Sharon's 1992 plan, and others across the spectrum at the same time, see the analysis by Peace Now, reviewed in *World Orders, Old and New,* p. 224.

38. Amira Hass, *Ha'aretz,* 28 May 2003.

39. Greg Myre, *New York Times,* 27 May 2003.

40. "Conference of High Contracting Parties," *Report on Israeli Settlement in the Occupied Territories,* January–February 2002.

41. Cited in John Donnelly and Charles Radin, *Boston Globe,* 9 April 2002.

42. *Ha'aretz* and *Jerusalem Post,* 4 December 2003. The votes were reported by AP and AFP on 3 December 2003.

43. James Bennet, *New York Times,* 17 March 2003.

44. Elisabeth Bumiller, *New York Times,* 27 February 2003.

45. John Donnelly, *Boston Globe,* 11 September 2002.

46. Douglas Hurd, *Financial Times,* 3 December 2002.

47. Ben Kaspit, "Two Years of the Intifada" (Hebrew), part one, *Ma'ariv,* 6 September 2002.

48. Reuven Pedatzur, *Ha'aretz,* 12 May 2003, reviewing Motti Golani, *Wars Don't Just Happen* (Hebrew, Modan, 2003).

49. Kaspit, *Ma'ariv,* 6 September 2002. Doron Rosenblum, *Ha'aretz,* 26 September 2002.

50. Patrick Sloyan, *Newsday,* 12 September 1991.

51. *Air Universities Quarterly Review* 6, no. 4 (winter 1953–54). For more extensive quotes and discussion, see my *Towards a New Cold War* (Pantheon, 1982; New Press, 2003), pp. 112–13.

52. Jawaharlal Nehru, *The Discovery of India* (Asia Publishing House, 1961). Stanley Wolpert, *A New History of India* (Oxford, 1993). C. A. Bayly, *The New Cambridge History of India* (Cambridge, 1988). Jack Beeching, *The Chinese Opium Wars* (Harcourt Brace Jovanovich, 1975). This was the immediate background of Mill's classic essay on humanitarian intervention. See chapter 2, note 73.

53. Mark Curtis, *Web of Deceit,* chapter 15.

54. Kaspit, *Ma'ariv,* 6 September 2002.

55. On the methods of the first Intifada, see Norman Finkelstein, *The Rise and Fall of Palestine* (Minnesota, 1996). See also my *Fateful Triangle* (chapter 8) for personal account and Israeli sources, the latter extended considerably in *Necessary Illusions,* appendix 4.2. More generally, see Zachary Lockman and Joel Beinin, eds., *Intifada* (South End, 1989).

56. Yoram Peri, *Davar,* 10 December 1982. *Araboushim* is Israeli slang that is roughly equivalent to *niggers* or *kikes*. Moshe Dayan, internal government discussion, cited in Yossi Beilin, *Mehiro shel Ihud* (Hebrew, Revivim, 1985).

57. Editorial, *Ha'aretz,* 16 March 2003. The conclusion will come as no surprise to those who have been reading the regular reports of its correspondents, notably Gideon Levy and Amira Hass.

Chapter 8: TERRORISM AND JUSTICE: SOME USEFUL TRUISMS

1. Strobe Talbott and Nayan Chanda, eds., *The Age of Terror* (Basic Books, 2001).

2. For US definitions, see my "International Terrorism: Image and Reality" in Alexander George, ed., *Western State Terrorism*. British definition cited by Curtis, *Web of Deceit,* p. 93.

3. On the reformulation of the official definitions, see Scott Atran, *Science* 299 (7 March 2003). He notes that the revised definitions still make "no principled distinction between 'terror' as defined by the U.S. Congress and 'counterinsurgency' as allowed in U.S. armed forces manuals," one of the perennial problems in defining *terror* in a doctrinally suitable way.

4. McClintock, *Instruments of Statecraft,* chapter 3.

5. UN Resolution 42/159, 7 December 1987. The State Department identifies 1987 as the peak year of terrorism.

6. For a remarkable illustration concerning Vietnam, see p. 193. On Iraq,

see ABC Middle East correspondent Charles Glass, *London Review of Books*, 17 April 2003.

7. Charles Maechling, *Los Angeles Times*, 18 March 1982.

8. *Colombia Update* 1, no. 4 (December 1989). See my *Deterring Democracy*, 130f. See pp. 92–93, above.

9. McClintock, *Instruments of Statecraft*, p. 222.

10. Raymond Bonner, *New York Times*, 28 October 2002.

11. Talbott and Chanda, *Age of Terror*.

12. Martha Crenshaw, Ivo Daalder and James Lindsay, and David Rapoport, respectively, *Current History*, December 2001.

13. For details, see my *Pirates and Emperors, Old and New*. On Clinton-backed Israeli invasions of Lebanon in the 1990s, beyond the illegally occupied southern region, see my *Fateful Triangle* (1999 edition).

14. Crenshaw, *Current History*, December 2001.

15. John Burns, *New York Times*, 8 November 2002.

16. Justin Huggler and Phil Reeves, *Independent*, 25 April 2002.

17. See my *Fateful Triangle*, p. 136.

18. "Darts and Laurels," *Columbia Journalism Review*, July–August 2002.

19. See p. 52.

20. Judith Miller, *New York Times*, 30 April 2000. Robert Pearson, *Fletcher Forum* 26, no. 1 (winter–spring 2002).

21. See pp. 61–62.

22. Jean Bethke Elshtain, *Boston Globe*, 6 October 2002; also see her essay in Booth and Dunne, eds., *Worlds in Collision*. Much of the world will be interested to learn that the US has never engaged in the practice of "unleashing terrorists" or otherwise threatening or harming civilians.

23. Bill Keller, *New York Times*, 24 August 2002.

24. A media review by Jeff Nygaard found one reference to the Gallup poll, a brief notice in the *Omaha World-Herald* that "completely misrepresented the findings." *Nygaard Notes*, 16 November 2001, reprinted in *Counterpoise* 5, nos. 3/4 (2002). *Envío* (Managua, Nicaragua), October 2001.

25. Walter Pincus, *Washington Post*, 6 June 2002. Emphases mine.

26. Abdullah Ahmed An-Na'im in Booth and Dunne, eds., *Worlds in Collision*.

27. Abdul Haq, interview with Anatol Lieven, *Guardian*, 2 November 2001. Peshawar gathering, Barry Bearak, *New York Times*, 25 October 2001; John Thornhill and Farhan Bokhari, *Financial Times*, 25

and 26 October 2001; John Burns, *New York Times,* 26 October 2001; Indira Lakshmanan, *Boston Globe,* 25 and 26 October 2001. RAWA, Web sites. The relevant information was available throughout in independent ("alternative") journals, published and electronic, including ZNet (www.zmag.org). For additional quotes, see my "The World After September 11," reprinted in my *Pirates and Emperors, Old and New,* chapter 6.

28. See pp. 128–29.

29. Larry Rohter, *New York Times,* 18 May 2003.

30. Daniel Grann, *Atlantic Monthly,* June 2001.

31. Talbott and Chanda, eds., *Age of Terror,* pp. xv ff. Their emphasis. They add that the problem and solution are "more complicated" but appear to accept the conclusion and regard the US-UK bombing as appropriate and properly "calibrated."

32. Christopher Greenwood, *International Affairs* 78, no. 2 (April 2002). Thomas Franck, *American Journal of International Law* 95, no. 4 (October 2001).

33. Michael Howard, *Foreign Affairs,* January–February 2002.

34. Frank Schuller and Thomas Grant, *Current History,* April 2002.

35. Werner Daum, German ambassador to the Sudan, *Harvard International Review,* summer 2001. The same estimate is given by Jonathan Belke, regional director of the Near East Foundation, who has field experience in the Sudan, *Boston Globe,* 22 August 1999. Kenneth Roth, executive director of HRW, warned at once that the bombing had disrupted assistance to 2.4 million people at risk of starvation and had forced the indefinite postponement of "crucial" relief efforts in places where dozens of people were dying daily; letter to President Clinton, 15 September 1998, published on HRW Web site. On these and other assessments and related material, see my *9-11* (Seven Stories, 2001), pp. 45ff.

36. Christopher Hitchens, *Nation,* 10 June 2002.

37. George W. Bush cited in Anthony Shadid, *Boston Globe,* 6 August 2002.

38. Richard Aldrich, *Guardian,* 22 April 2002.

39. National Intelligence Council, *Global Trends 2015.*

40. Kenneth Waltz in Booth and Dunne, eds., *Worlds in Collision.* See above, p. 123.

41. International lawyer for multinationals quoted by Neil MacFarquhar, *New York Times,* 5 October 2001.

42. Sumit Ganguly, *Current History,* December 2001. Philip Wilcox, US

ambassador at large for counterterrorism, 1994–97, *New York Review of Books,* 18 October 2001. Rohan Gunaratna, quoted by Thomas Powers, *New York Review of Books,* 10 October 2002. Wolfowitz quoted in *Vanity Fair,* May 2003; he is referring specifically to the US presence in Saudi Arabia.

43. Editorial, *Financial Times,* 14 May 2003. P. W. Singer, *Current History,* November 2002; Daniel Byman, *Financial Times,* 27 May 2003.

44. Anthony Shadid, *Washington Post,* 26 February 2003.

45. James Bill and Rebecca Bill Chavez, *Middle East Journal,* autumn 2002.

46. David Johnston and Don Van Natta, *New York Times,* 17 May 2003. Byman, *Financial Times,* 27 May 2003. Don Van Natta and Desmond Butler, *New York Times,* 16 March 2003. Scott Atran, *New York Times,* 5 May 2003.

47. Faye Bowers, *Christian Science Monitor,* 5 May 2003.

48. Jason Burke, *Sunday Observer,* 18 May 2003. Jessica Stern, *New York Times* op-ed, 20 August 2003.

49. For further quotes and background, see Gilbert Achcar, *The Clash of Barbarisms* (Monthly Review, 2002), pp. 58ff. That these are their goals is also assumed by Washington planners; see note 42.

50. Michael Kranish, *Boston Globe,* 15 May 2003. Joseph Treaster, *New York Times,* 14 May 2003.

51. Michael Ignatieff, *New York Times Magazine,* 5 January 2003.

52. Ami Ayalon interview in *Le Monde,* 22 December 2001, reprinted in Roane Carey and Jonathan Shanin, *The Other Israel* (New Press, 2002). Uri Sagie, *Lights within the Fog* (Hebrew, Yedioth Ahronoth-Chemed, 1998), pp. 300ff.

53. Yehoshaphat Harkabi cited by Amnon Kapeliouk, *Le Monde diplomatique,* February 1986.

54. For sources and background discussion, see my *World Orders, Old and New,* pp. 79, 201ff. Now also Salim Yaqub, *Diplomatic History* 26, no. 4 (fall 2002).

55. Peter Waldman et al., *Wall Street Journal,* 14 September 2001; see also Waldman and Hugh Pope, *Wall Street Journal,* 21 September 2001. See my *9-11* and, for more detail, *Middle East Illusions,* chapter 10.

56. Ahmed Rashid, *Far Eastern Economic Review,* 1 August 2002. Professor El Lozy, writer Azizuddin El-Kaissouni, and Warren Bass of the CFR quoted by Joyce Koh, *Straits Times* (Singapore), 14 August 2002.

57. Youssef Ibrahim, *Washington Post Weekly,* 31 March 2003.

58. Jonathan Steele, *Guardian,* 9 April 2003.
59. Susan Sachs, *New York Times,* 8 April 2003.

Chapter 9: A PASSING NIGHTMARE?

1. Headline, *New York Times,* 23 September 2001.
2. Paul Krugman, *New York Times,* 21 December 2001.
3. STRATCOM, *Essentials of Post–Cold War Deterrence,* 1995. For more extensive quotes, see my *New Military Humanism,* chapter 6. On subsequent presidential directives, see Center for Defense Information, *Defense Monitor* 29, no. 3 (2000). See Morton Mintz, *American Prospect,* 26 February 2001, on legislative bar to de-alerting. On the 1969 alert, intended to "signal" to Moscow US intentions in Vietnam, see Scott Sagan and Jeremi Suri, *International Security* 27, no. 4 (spring 2003). The most crucial events ignored were a serious Russia-China border conflict, which might have led to Russian misinterpretation of the "signal," with grim consequences.
4. See chapter 5, note 29.
5. Scott Peterson, *Christian Science Monitor,* 9 May 2001; Walter Pincus, *Washington Post,* 18 March 2001. A terse announcement suggested a possible reversal of the policy, in reaction to 9-11; Elisabeth Bumiller, *New York Times,* 28 December 2001. On successes of cooperative threat reduction initiated by Senators Sam Nunn and Richard Lugar, see Michael Krepon, *Bulletin of the Atomic Scientists,* January–February 2003.
6. Steven Lee Myers, *New York Times,* 10 August 2000; Bob Drogin and Tyler Marshall, *Los Angeles Times,* 19 May 2000; Michael Byers, *London Review of Books,* 22 June 2000. See also Michael Gordon and Steven Lee Myers, *New York Times,* 28 May 2000, and Glaser and Fetter, *International Security* 26, no. 1 (summer 2001).
7. David Sanger, *New York Times,* 2 September 2001. Sanger, *New York Times,* 5 September 2001. Jane Perlez, *New York Times,* 2 September 2001. Clinton, see William Broad, *New York Times,* 1 May 2000.
8. John Steinbruner and Jeffrey Lewis, *Daedalus,* fall 2002.
9. David Ruppe, *Global Security Newswire,* 22 May 2003. Rand Corporation, *Beyond the Nuclear Shadow,* May 2003. Paul Webster, *Bulletin of the Atomic Scientists,* July–August 2003.
10. Judith Miller, *New York Times,* 20 January 2003. Nunn-Lugar initiative, see note 5.
11. Krepon, *Bulletin of the Atomic Scientists,* January–February 2003.

12. Michael Gordon, Eric Schmitt, *New York Times,* 11 March 2002. William Arkin, *Los Angeles Times,* 26 January 2003.

13. Carl Hulse and James Dao, *New York Times,* 29 May 2003.

14. Scott Baldauf, *Christian Science Monitor,* 15 May 2003.

15. Peter Slevin, *Washington Post,* 22 September 2002.

16. McGeorge Bundy, *Danger and Survival* (Random House, 1988), p. 326. Bundy is skeptical about the prospects, but his subjective judgment does not bear on the point here.

17. Adam Ulam, *Journal of Cold War Studies* 1, no. 1 (winter 1999). Melvyn Leffler, *Foreign Affairs,* July–August 1996. James Warburg, *Germany: Key to Peace* (Harvard, 1953), pp. 189ff.

18. See chapter 4, note 3.

19. Kenneth Waltz, *PS: Political Science & Politics,* December 1991. Garthoff and Kaufmann cited in my *Deterring Democracy,* p. 26.

20. See particularly US Space Command, *Vision for 2020,* February 1997.

21. *High Frontier* (Heritage Foundation) cited by Gordon Mitchell, "National Missile Defense," presentation to the Royal Defence College (Brussels, Belgium), 30 January 2001. See Mitchell's *Strategic Deception* (Michigan State, 2000).

22. Garthoff, *A Journey through the Cold War,* pp. 357–58.

23. Jack Hitt, *New York Times Magazine,* 5 August 2001, quoting intelligence consultant George Friedman.

24. David Pugliese, *National Post* (Toronto), 24 May 2000.

25. Sha Zukang cited by Michael Gordon, *New York Times,* 29 April 2001. EP-3 quote from William Arkin, *Bulletin of the Atomic Scientists,* May–June 2001.

26. Andrew Bacevich, *National Interest,* summer 2001; Lawrence Kaplan, *New Republic,* 12 March 2001. Rand study cited by Kaplan.

27. See pp. 42–43.

28. Michael Krepon, *Foreign Affairs,* May–June 2001; see also his comments in Hitt, *New York Times Magazine,* 5 August 2001. Gordon Mitchell, *Fletcher Forum* 25, no. 1 (winter 2001), citing Charles Perrow. See also Karl Grossman, *Weapons in Space* (Seven Stories, 2001).

29. Air Force Space Command, Strategic Master Plan (SMP) FY04 and Beyond, 5 November 2002.

30. William Arkin, *Los Angeles Times,* 14 July 2002. Michael Sniffen, AP, 1 July 2003.

31. Hannah Hoag, *Nature* 423 (19 June 2003).

32. See chapter 7, note 10.

33. Tomas Valasek, *CDI Defense Monitor* 30, no. 3 (March 2001). Mitchell, *Fletcher Forum,* winter 2001.

34. See p. 121. Agence France-Presse, 23 January 2001. Reuters, 15 February 2001; reported in the *Deseret (Utah) News,* virtually the only coverage of the 2001 conference meetings in the US media. Frances Williams, *Financial Times,* 8 June 2001.

35. Judith Miller, *New York Times,* 27 April 2001; Marlise Simons, *New York Times,* 5 October 2001; Michael Gordon and Judith Miller, *New York Times,* 20 May 2001; Richard Waddington, Reuters, *Boston Globe,* 8 December 2001. Oliver Meier, *Bulletin of the Atomic Scientists,* November–December 2001. Michael Gordon, *New York Times,* 24 July 2001. See also William Broad and Judith Miller, *New York Times,* 13 December 2001.

36. Mark Wheelis, Malcolm Dando, and Catherine Auer, *Bulletin of the Atomic Scientists,* January–February 2003. On Soviet programs in gross violation of treaty obligations, see William Broad, Judith Miller, and Stephen Engelberg, *Germs: Biological Weapons and America's Secret War* (Simon & Schuster, 2001).

37. *Bulletin of the Atomic Scientists,* July–August 2002, reviewing these and similar administration initiatives; George Perkovich, *Foreign Affairs,* March–April 2003.

38. See p. 121.

39. Rachel Corrie was killed by Israeli forces in Gaza in March 2003 with a US-supplied bulldozer, one of Israel's most destructive weapons; see p. 181. *Murdered* might be the more appropriate term, to judge by eyewitness reports. The killing of an American citizen by US clients using US equipment was not considered worthy of inquiry, even more than the barest report.

40. Cited by Judy Toth, *Bertrand Russell Society Quarterly,* February 2003.

AFTERWORD

1. *Chicago Tribune,* 11 August 2002. Kissinger was commenting on Bush's West Point address in which the NSS was presented in outline. Sources are omitted below when they appear in the text. For more extensive sources and discussion, see electronic edition (www.hegemony orsurvival.net).

2. Pew Research Center, 16 March 2004.

3. Gerges quoted by Howard LaFranchi, *Christian Science Monitor,* 3 November 2003. Jessica Stern, *New York Times* op-ed, 20 August 2003; *Foreign Affairs,* July–August 2003. Scott Atran, *New York Times* op-ed, 16 March 2004. Among many others, see Mark Mathews, *Baltimore Sun,* 22 November 2003; Raymond Bonner and Don van Natta, Jr., *New York Times,* 8 February 2004.

4. Selig Harrison, *USA Today,* 7 January 2004; Graham Allison, *Foreign Affairs,* January–February 2004; Morton Halperin, *American Prospect,* November 2003, among others.

5. Program on International Policy Attitudes, 3 December 2003.

6. Ron Hutcheson, *Boston Globe,* 28 September 2003.

7. Jason Burke, *Al-Qaeda* (I. B. Tauris, 2003; expanded ed., 2004).

8. Pervez Hoodbhoy, *Washington Post,* 1 February 2004; Tim Weiner, *New York Times,* 1 June 1998.

9. Burke, *Al-Qaeda,* pp. 239, 249. See chapter 8.

10. Burke, *Al-Qaeda,* pp. 247ff.

11. Kim Murphy, *Los Angeles Times,* 17 February 2004; *Boston Globe,* 19 February 2004; David Holley, *Los Angeles Times,* 26 March 2004; Vladimir Isachenkov, *Boston Globe,* 23 December 2003; Bruce Blair, *Defense Monitor,* January–February 2004; Mark Odell, *Financial Times,* 30 March 2004.

12. Anna Dolgov, *Boston Globe,* 21 February 2004; Sergei Blagov, *Asia Times,* 19 February 2004. Clinton doctrine, see p. 15.

13. Bruce Finley, *Denver Post,* 10 October 2003.

14. Blair, *Defense Monitor.* See also Chalmers Johnson, *The Sorrows of Empire* (Metropolitan, 2004), p. 288.

15. Janne Nolan, *Science,* 19 March 2004, reviewing Lynn Eden, *Whole World on Fire* (Cornell, 2004).

16. James Glanz, *New York Times,* 12 March 2004.

17. Hans Kristensen, Matthew McKinzie, and Robert Norris, *Bulletin of the Atomic Scientists,* March–April 2004.

18. *Ha'aretz* and Reuters, 19 February 2004; Alon ben-David, *Jane's Defense Weekly,* 19 November 2003; *Ha'aretz* (Hebrew), 10 February 2004.

19. Lawyers' Committee on Nuclear Policy, 9 December 2003, www.reachingcriticalwill.org. M2 PRESSWIRE, 4 November 2003.

20. Dana Milbank, *Washington Post,* 1 June 2003; Guy Dinmore and James Harding, *Financial Times,* 3–4 May 2003; Dana Milbank, *Washington Post,* 8 February 2004; George Tenet, *New York Times,* 6 February 2004; Glenn Kessler, *Washington Post,* 3 February 2004; Richard Stevenson, *New York Times,* 30 January 2004.

21. Michael Georgy, Reuters, 20 January 2004.

22. Project for The New American Century, cited by Johnson, *Sorrows of Empire,* p. 230.

23. President Bush, "Denial and Deception," speech, Museum Center, Cincinnati, Ohio, 7 October 2002.

24. Allison, *Foreign Affairs.* Toppling the Taliban was an afterthought, added several weeks later. See chapter 8, electronic edition, and my *Pirates and Emperors* (South End, 2002, updated edition), chapter 6.

25. See chapters 4 and 8 for a few of many examples.

26. David Ignatius, *Washington Post,* 2 November 2003. "President Bush Discusses Freedom in Iraq and Middle East," National Endowment for Democracy, Washington, D.C., 6 November 2003.

27. Thom Shanker, *New York Times,* 23 March 2004. David Greenberg, *New York Times Book Review,* 14 March 2004. Michael Steinberger, *American Prospect,* April 2004.

28. Ed Harriman, *London Review of Books,* 1 April 2004.

29. See electronic edition version of this afterword for a sample.

30. For more on these crucial matters, see chapter 5. See also Kenneth Roth, introduction, *Human Rights Watch Report 2004.*

31. Walter Pincus, *Washington Post,* 12 November 2003.

32. See chapters 4 and 8, and for background, Paul Farmer, *The Uses of Haiti* (Common Courage, 2003). On the restoration of democracy in 1994, see my "Democracy Restored," *Z Magazine,* November 1994. On the predicted descent into chaos, see my *Profit over People* (Seven Stories, 1999), chapter 4, and *New Military Humanism* (Common Courage, 1999).

33. Tim Weiner, *New York Times,* 22 March 2004; Mary Beth Sheridan, *Washington Post,* 23 March 2004.

34. Vivienne Walt and Farah Stockman, *Boston Globe,* 20 February 2004; Robin Wright, *Washington Post,* 2 January 2004; Neil King, Jr., and Yochi Dreazen, *Wall Street Journal,* 31 December 2003.

35. Wright, *Washington Post,* Robert Schlesinger, *Boston Globe,* 18 November 2003.

36. Oxford Research International, December 2003.

37. Dilip Hiro, *New York Times* op-ed, 16 November 2003.

38. Oxford Research International, December 2003.

39. Stephen Glain, *Boston Globe,* 6 March 2004; Dexter Filkins, *New York Times,* 23 February 2004.

40. Thom Shanker and Eric Schmitt, *New York Times,* 20 April 2003; Douglas Jehl and David Sanger, *New York Times,* 17 September 2003.

41. Steven Weisman, *New York Times*, 13 January 2004; *Financial Times*, 19 January 2004.

42. John Burns and Thom Shanker, *New York Times*, 26 March 2004.

43. Jeff Madrick, *New York Times*, 2 October 2003; Alan Beattie and Charles Clover, *Financial Times*, 22 September 2003. For a review of Bremer's orders, see Antonia Juhasz, *Tikkun*, January–February 2004.

44. David Bacon, *Dollars and Sense*, January–February 2004; *Z Magazine*, March 2004; Rajiv Chandrasekaran, *Washington Post*, 28 December 2003.

45. George Anders and Susan Warren, *Wall Street Journal*, 19 January 2004.

46. Peter Steinfels, *New York Times*, 2 August 2003; Ceci Connolly and Claudia Deane, *Washington Post*, 20 October 2003; Adam Clymer, *New York Times*, 17 October 1993.

Index

About the Author

NOAM CHOMSKY is the author of numerous bestselling works, from *American Power and the New Mandarins* in the 1960s to the international bestselling *9-11*. A professor of linguistics and philosophy at MIT, he is widely credited with having revolutionized modern linguistics. He lives in Lexington, Massachusetts.

The American Empire Project

In an era of unprecedented military strength, leaders of the United States, the global hyperpower, have increasingly embraced imperial ambitions. How did this significant shift in purpose and policy come about? And what lies down the road?

The American Empire Project is a response to the changes that have occurred in American's strategic thinking as well as in its military and economic posture. Empire, long considered an offense against America's democratic heritage, now threatens to define the relationship between our country and the rest of the world. The American Empire Project publishes books that question this development, examine the origins of US imperial aspirations, analyze their ramifications at home and abroad, and discuss alternatives to this dangerous trend.

The project was conceived by Tom Engelhardt and Steve Fraser, editors who are themselves historians and writers. Published by Metropolitan Books, an imprint of Henry Holt and Company, its volumes so far include *The Sorrows of Empire* by Chalmers Johnson, *How to Succeed at Globalization* by El Fisgón, *Crusade* by James Carroll, and *Blood and Oil* by Michael Klare.

For more information about the American Empire Project and for a list of forthcoming titles, please visit www.americanempire project.com.